THE GIRL
I LEFT
BEHIND

Jane O'Reilly

THE GIRL
I LEFT
BEHIND

Macmillan Publishing Co., Inc.
NEW YORK

Macmillan Publishing Co., Inc.
866 Third Avenue, New York, N.Y. 10022
Collier Macmillan Canada, Ltd.

Library of Congress Cataloging in Publication Data
O'Reilly, Jane.
The girl I left behind.
1. Feminism—United States. 2. O'Reilly, Jane.
3. Feminists—United States—
Biography. I. Title.
HQ1426.094   305.4′2′0973   80-36686
ISBN 0-02-593710-3

Book design by Constance T. Doyle

10 9 8 7 6 5 4 3 2

Printed in the United States of America

Parts of this book have appeared in somewhat differ-
ent form in the following publications: *Ms., The
Nation, New York* magazine, *Parents* magazine,
Savvy, the *Washington Star, Woman's Day,* United
Feature Syndicate, and *Vogue.*

For my family,
especially for my son, Jan

Contents

Acknowledgments

The acknowledgments page is traditionally written last, but read first. It usually reflects a sense of gratitude and sober conclusion. I would, in my own case, add to those feelings an immense sense of surprise that I have reached the end. This surprise is no doubt shared by the many people I wish to thank, all of whom provided, at some critical moment of crisis, either encouragement, wisdom, information, housing, hot cups of tea, typed manuscripts, or a general sense of purpose. Sometimes all of those things. Without these people (as the saying goes, and, I now realize, it is uttered more fervently than I had imagined) this book would never have been written.

In Washington, D.C.: Carol Burris, Kathleen Currie, Jane McMichael, Martin F. Nolan, Bernice Sandler, Eileen Shanahan, the Overseas Development Council, the U.S. Census Bureau, and hundreds of women bureaucrats who—contrary to popular opinion—have all the information and many of the ideas.

In New York City: my editor Elisabeth Scharlatt, my agent Lois Wallace, Lorraine Beaulieu, Linda Brumfield, Janelle Buff, Susan Chace, James Chace, Vincent Crapanzano, Judith and Ronald Daniels, Barbara Dolan, Diana Drake, Linda Francke, Ed Koren, Jane Kramer, Lilla Lyon, Robert Roy Metz, Rosalind Moore, Iceal Morgan, Lisa Phillips, Lois Smith, Gloria Steinem, Amanda Urban, Lindsy Van Gelder, and Betsy Williams.

In Cambridge: Kenneth and Kitty Galbraith, and Edith Tucker.

In Brookfield, Vermont: Jacalin Wilder, Crystal Gromer, and Thelma Hill.

Jane O'Reilly

Introduction

This book is a collection of responses to an idea, to my own discovery that, as Elizabeth Hardwick best put it, "There are cultural, social and economic boundaries for women which are immoral and unnecessary and which should be resisted publicly and privately."

It seems to have taken me quite a while to realize that the idea applied to me. Ten years, at least. Perhaps forty-four. Probably the rest of my life. At any rate, longer than I imagined when, sometime in the late 1960s, my attention was drawn to the possibility that what I accepted as normal was in fact an arbitrary distinction. Gloria Steinem was the person who first insisted I pay attention. I used to call her at two or three in the morning, whenever I lost track of whatever I was trying to write, and as she patiently eased me into the next paragraph, she also eased me into feminism's first premise: women are not equal members of the human society, and we are not equal simply because we are women. I remember thinking Gloria was becoming too preoccupied with the subject of women.

After all, why was it necessary to go on and on about it? The principle, once noticed, seemed so obvious. Women were not equal. Women should be equal. There had been some strange oversight which, once explained— "Hey guys, something seems to be unfair here"—would be remedied. I began to explain, often at the top of my lungs, pointing out that the women's movement would require us to question all our most basic assumptions. In my enthusiasm I forgot that, historically, revision of those assumptions had not usually occurred through the application of a sense of fair play (a concept that itself evades consensus).

In 1970, I spent a green summer afternoon in Vermont interviewing John Kenneth Galbraith. After a long discussion of such matters as inflation, war, unemployment, and Richard Nixon, he said: "I think we should have talked more about women's liberation. This will have a more permanent, a more lasting effect than any of the things we have been talking about." I was not surprised that he thought so. His instincts for justice, compassion, and generosity are as complete as any man's living. But I think I also really expected that women would be liberated by the next summer— certainly by the summer after that.

Confidently, I awaited equality. (Did I think it would come by United Parcel, gift wrapped? Or that there would be a sign— perhaps a tongue of flame over our heads?) Then for the first issue of *Ms.* magazine I was asked to write a light piece on housework— the only subject in the movement inventory I felt qualified to address. Housework turned out to involve the most basic of basic assumptions. I began to grasp that *waiting* for equality might not be the most effective political tool. It took me three months to write "Click! The Housewife's Moment of Truth" and when I finished, I had become a wild-eyed radical libber—a woman people edged away from at social gatherings. Writing "Click!" was my own moment of truth, my consciousness raising, my astonished realization that Gloria's "preoccupation" might be only the most rational and disciplined of possible responses.

And yet, I cannot tell you how silly I felt raving on about something so unimportant as housework.

I felt even sillier when *Ms.* dispatched me to various cities on a promotional tour. "Of course women are afraid of speaking out in public. So was I," said Gloria. "The only thing I've learned in all these years is you don't actually die." She did not add that I would wish I could. It is one thing to write about one's newly articulated principles. It is quite another to make a spectacle of oneself. "Oh, yes, you are the housework lady," welcomed a talk-show host. Hearty laughter from the audience. A weak smile from me. A strong urge to bite him. Equality for women seemed to be a far more complicated issue than I had thought. I was, after all, only talking about housework. Why, then, was a man from Vandalia, Illinois, calling in to a late-night radio show in St. Louis to accuse me of contravening natural law? I had no prepared answer for that accusation, was in fact woefully innocent of the implications of what I was saying, prattling on about sweet reason to an audience that would have more enthusiastically welcomed inside information about the end of the world. This seemed to see me as a symptom of an onrushing day of judgment. What manic impulse, what misdirected perception, had brought me into this dark midnight studio overlooking the Mississippi River? I wished, very much, to be back home.

Another voice came over the sound system, a woman from the Ozarks. "Honey," she said, "I've lifted bales of hay and calves and children all my life, and all the time they fed us a lot of nonsense about being the weaker sex. You just keep right at it." The next caller was a woman named Marcy, who made a statement I have found useful ever since. "Natural law," she observed, "is only whatever happens in your lifetime within fifty miles of you."

Very late that night I called Gloria to announce that sisterhood was powerful. She was not surprised. Several evenings later I turned on the television set in my Atlanta hotel room. A woman on the evening news was talking about the women's movement. She seemed to make a good deal of sense. Several long seconds passed before I realized she was me.

If, on that trip, I began to learn that They were really We, I had still not quite connected me—not connected the personal and the political. Matters such as wage disparities, role expectations, family breakups, working mothers, systemic sexual discrimination, could—if discussed at arm's length—be reasonably described as issues. If described in personal terms they could—and were—dismissed as the selfish whining of spoiled crybabies who placed self-fulfillment above responsibility. Besides, my situation was different. I blamed the oddities of my life on my own choices: I chose to be divorced (had so chosen, in fact, twice), chose to live in New

York City, chose to support myself and my son by working as a freelance writer. I considered myself excluded, by reason of eccentricity, from the general experience.

I blamed myself and missed the point: mine *was* the general experience—including the blaming myself. (Nowadays I divide the blame more equitably: half for me and half for societal arrangements.) Marriage had been, for me, a brief, destructive clash of irreconcilable expectations, our mistaken choices as much the fault of role modeling as of our own delusions. Divorced, as a Single Female Head of Household, I lived below the poverty line. My situation had much to do with responsibility and very little to do with self-fulfillment, and I still earned less than men. I cannot say what determined my choice of profession: a rather specialized skill perhaps, a fairly severe inability to cooperate (despite a solid childhood grounding in team sports). It could have been simply an impulse to remove myself from hierarchies after being told in 1962 that the Washington bureau of a national newsmagazine did not hire women reporters, not even a woman with a Radcliffe degree, a small file of clippings, and a strong urge to be a foreign correspondent. I never questioned the policy, never sought out advice from women who were already reporters for other publications. I simply withdrew from the field, remarried, took jobs as a researcher, wrote freelance articles at home, got divorced, moved to New York, plodded on, until something clicked.

What happened to me then is not very different from the experiences of many women over the last several years. For this book, I tried to arrange the articles and newspaper columns I wrote about those experiences according to the expansion, from the private to the public, of my own—our own—responses to the women's movement. I have added many new thoughts, and some second thoughts, and decided to include the contradictions because I have not, in fact, yet discovered how to resolve them.

The arrangement has turned out to be more like a kaleidoscope or a seismograph than the chronology we had hoped and expected to be tidy. The private and the public do not (cannot) conveniently separate. Issues are not settled, but only enlarged. We are nearer to seeing a woman on the Supreme Court than we are to solving the problems of housework and love and families, but at least we know now that the questions asked apply to both. Our resolve veers and ebbs; we are in turn exhilarated, exhausted, reasonable, enraged, full of hope, freshly surprised, newly incredulous. Without the reality of daily life—of family, friends, responsibilities, the pleasures of a summer's day—we would go mad.

I go mad quite regularly. Particularly when I realize I am still only beginning to identify the problem. Recently a man, a relative by marriage, arrived in New York and insisted on staying in my apartment. It was not a convenient time: a sick child, no baby-sitter, an essential trip to take, a deadline to meet. He promised: "You won't even know I'm here." He practiced invisibility by complaining, with wit and charm, that there was nothing to eat in the house and no one to talk to. One evening he proudly brought home a steak. Instead of offering the thanks he expected, I calculated the time necessary to cook, eat, and clean up after the steak. I do not know and cannot explain why, after all these years, I asked him how he would like it cooked instead of directing him to the stove. He said: "With a little béarnaise sauce?"

No, I did not make the béarnaise sauce. But three hours later, after the cooking, eating, and cleaning up, I sat down and began to write words I had never used before: images, explanations, accusations I had dismissed when they were used by earlier, quicker feminist writers as too extreme, strident, bewildering. (Even they did not know, then, how far back those unheard voices echoed. I certainly did not know when I "discovered" housework that Charlotte Perkins Gilman had said in 1903, "The home is a human institution. All human institutions are open to improvement.") My anger is still in front of me, written in blue ink on a page from a yellow pad: "Blood, death, suffocation, ruined lives wasted by oppression. Only now do I understand what I have written." The truth is, I am only beginning to understand what I have written.

"Don't you write about anything but *women?*" asks a crest-fallen voice. Sure. This book is a kind of scrapbook, but it does not tell the whole story, not of my life, still less of the women's movement. I could offer, with some satisfaction, published records of trips to Scotland, Italy, New Orleans. Book reviews, restaurant reviews, observations on the meaning of romance. Events recorded at political conventions, complaints about America's transportation system. Advice—written to pay the rent—on getting through a bad year and how to fight with your mate. Thoughts on buying children's shoes, methods of choosing schools and country houses and avoiding suicide. A lot of words, a lot of work, a certain amount of gaiety and excitement and achievement—a thought that somehow reminds me that there is something I have forgotten to mention. The effort was not easy, and it became much, much harder after I began to write about women.

There was a time, from about the middle of 1972 to the end of 1975, when I stopped speaking to old friends, provoked scenes in editorial offices, became irrationally attached to inexplicable love affairs. I could barely write, and finally I could barely speak. Yet not once did it ever occur to me that my terror, my outraged sense of betrayal, my insistence on romance as a solution, had anything at all to do with the phrases I was reading, and even writing. "The courage to change," "fear of success," "the risk of autonomy," did not seem to describe my feelings, which were, roughly: scared as a wet cat stuck out on a limb with no fireman in sight; sulky as a princess whose frog-kissing skills have been declared obsolete due to a shortage of bewitched princes; mad as a child who insists "I'll do it myself" and can't. I described this amazing disarray as "being depressed," ascribed it to a variety of irrelevent causes, and (I see now, peering at the spectacle with the wisdom of hindsight) thrashed bitterly against the discovery that the only way out was forward. There was no going back.

As an alternative to going forward, I chose to go limp. I decided (secretly, to myself) that I was bored with women's issues. It was boring to take so seriously what others took so lightly, to feel foolish, to have developed a reflexive index finger that pointed, hectoring and admonishing, at the most inopportune moments. (And, after all, hadn't women, in the last hundred years, been equally sure that the vote, or purity, or temperance, or a ban on contraceptives, would change the world?)

Then someone asked me to review Susan Brownmiller's book on rape, *Against Our Will*, a powerful, brilliant, enlightening work that wiped away all doubt. I was no longer bored by women's issues. Scared, but not bored. Jim Bellows, then editor of the *Washington Star*, invited me to be a guest columnist and suggested as a topic women in Washington. As it happened, in the fall of 1975 there were many, many women in Washington who had already figured out that the question of who is presumed to be responsible for the housework has something to do with the presumptions of public policy, and they seemed to have no qualms at all about hectoring and admonishing. They gave me facts, examples, phone numbers, observations, determination, and hope. I had a wonderful time.

Two years later thousands of women representing millions of women from all over the United States traveled to Houston, Texas, for the National Women's Conference. They, too, had a wonderful time, exchanging facts, experiences, phone numbers, hope, and determination, discovering they were not alone and had not imagined a women's movement. Again, They were revealed to be We.

Being able to take a joke is, perhaps, the first sign that you are taking yourself seriously, a rather necessary preliminary toward making anyone else take you seriously. One day in Washington a genial male colleague greeted me in the city room by shouting: "Here she comes, hormones raging." I laughed.

Washington is (muted roll of drums, flutter of flags) a contradictory city. Organized by and for the established power, it is still the place (and one bows toward the notion of Democracy) where people without power go to march for their civil rights, for the end of poverty, to stop a war. And they do not march entirely in vain. In the years that I wrote stories on those marches and those movements, I do not remember my male colleagues making jokes. They were part of those movements, took them seriously. But they, like most men, failed to take seriously women as a part of those movements—as indeed they did not take seriously the changing realities of women's lives, our contributions to the economy, even our part in civilization—and that reflexive omission resulted in the rebirth of the women's movement. Women marched again to Washington, this time demanding our own equal rights.

The usual justifications were invoked against us, and great was the confusion when we refused to agree that God's will, or natural law, or human nature, or the wishes of constituents, consign certain races, some nations, and one sex to inferiority. Instead we insisted on affirmative action, an Equal Rights Amendment, the right to choose abortion—and the more we insisted (which was not enough, but still far more than we achieved), the clearer the true meaning of those justifications became: "I've got mine and you can't have any because I want more."

Men—bureaucrats, elected representatives, newspaper editors, husbands—determined whether women's causes would be understood, and even the most sympathetic professed themselves to be baffled. "My wife doesn't feel oppressed," they assured themselves. That a large number of such men now find themselves referring to "my former wife" suggests that they were misinformed. As an argument, "my wife doesn't feel oppressed" was irrelevant. But as a response, it was at least an honest expression of surprise at the idea that men and women no longer shared the same basic assumptions about the arrangements that governed their lives.

Maybe their wives felt oppressed, and maybe they didn't. But the assumption that their wives did not, and that therefore all women did not (except for a few radicals in New York City), explains why the women's movement, because of its particular necessity to transform both the personal and the political, is a revolution like no other, one that, as Adrienne Rich has said, will transform thinking itself. Women are not the first group to find that our analysis of our condition can be dismissed *because* of our condition. But we are the only group that loves, marries, and raises children with the people who must change—as we must change—if our condition is to improve. And that is why there will be no liberation by next summer, or even the summer after that.

Where are we now, in this reborn revolution? Not very far, if all the numbers are added up: the number of women holding public office, the number of women with influence, the number of women and children who still make up three quarters of the poor in the United States. ("The movement is really over, accomplished, for middle-class women, isn't it?" asserts a well-meaning, white, male corporate lawyer. And I, now resigned to the fact that I will always, for the rest of my life, be the person who shouts at dinner parties, shout: "No! Without a man and his income, a woman is not yet even in the middle class." He smiles, and his elegant, graceful, talented wife avoids my eyes.)

But we no longer feel foolish. We have learned to take ourselves seriously, and that is very far to have come. We rejoice that we are struggling together, but the question remains: how goes the struggle? It goes slowly. We mark our progress in grains of sand heaped against the tide: a senator here, an executive there, a center for displaced homemakers, a sympathetic newspaper editorial, a construction job. We can take courage (whistling in the backlash darkness) from the opposition, because they have taken us more seriously than we have ourselves. They knew before we did that such apparently simple ideas as equal pay, equal rights, and equal parenting mean in fact redistribution of wealth, reallocation of power, and redefinition of roles.

Every woman who believes that becoming an executive is enough, every daughter who thinks she was accepted to medical school simply because she was smart (and forgets the women who fought a hundred years for her admission), every woman who accepts her own opportunity within the system and does not open a way for other women (and thus, inevitably, change the system), stands with the tide. The point of feminism is not that the world should be the same, but that it should be different.

We must remember the past, define the future, and challenge the present—wherever and however we can. It will take the rest of our lives even to begin.

But then, what else have we to do?

New York City and
Brookfield, Vermont
July 1979

THE GIRL
I LEFT
BEHIND

I.

Expectations

The women's movement, they said, was really just a bunch of radical women. Or intellectual women. Or lesbians. And then, apparently believing they had discovered the ultimate disqualification, they said the movement involved only middle-class women.

Ah! That one hit us where it hurt, an inspired accusation, one that made the women who were not middle class turn suspiciously on those who were, and flustered those who were into apologizing—always our first instinct: "So sorry, how selfish of me. I was just trying to make something of my life. My self-denial must have slipped." A female virtue, self-denial. We recovered, of course, because one of the first things we noticed—after a Click!—was that we were being dismissed not because we were or were not middle class but because we were women.

It was curious, that dismissal. The middle class, after all, is the guardian of the given, the upholder of tradition, the bedrock of perceived values, order, and predictability. The middle class is The Market; its women the unpaid Ladies' Auxiliary to our consumer economy (a role at least as important to the status quo as our "natural" role as the weaker sex). If middle-class women were dissatisfied, then surely the movement could not be dismissed?

As someone who perceived my teen-age years as seriously limited by the absence of a recreation room in my family's house, I feel competent to speak as a middle-class woman. Almost absurdly middle-class. I grew up in St. Louis, on a quiet street of middle-class houses, with a mother, a father, a sister, a brother, and a dog. Grandparents, cousins, aunts, and uncles were within walking distance. We went to Mass, raised the flag, did our best, and I enjoyed happy times, music lessons, orthodontia, dancing classes, allergy shots, and a bicycle. Jews, blacks, and, to a lesser extent, Protestants were different and did not play a large part in my consciousness, but "what people might think" did.

The Depression, the War, and the Ancestors were understood to have had an influence. There were also the usual variables: shadows, secrets, denials, disappointments—the mysteries that make, not history, but life. Every member of that household would have a different explanation of what went on there, and part of my particular situation is explained by the fact that I have no idea what those explanations might be. We did not, still do not, talk about such things to each other, of how we felt and why. Messages were oblique and seldom less than double. I grew up bewildered, slamming doors and trying to figure out what was expected of me.

It was easier to figure out what was expected of women and of me as a woman. The full weight of popular culture was devoted to providing direction. Since every woman I knew seemed to conform to specifications, it is not surprising that I failed to wonder enough if there might be a difference between me and the accepted model of "woman." Wondering about things was especially discouraged at the Convent of the Sacred Heart—an institution at that time and in that city so extreme in its dedication to the notion of genteel womanhood that it produced two extremes of reaction: Phyllis Schlafly, the antifeminist crusader, and me. I was taught and I have no doubt that Phyllis Schlafly was taught that women were incompetent and dependent and their only recourse was marriage.

Our children ask us how we could have believed that sex was sinful, that the object of a girl's life was a wedding ring, that only boys could play baseball, just as we might have asked our great grandmothers: "Why does a lady never mention pregnancy?" I believed such things (I would in fact have denied believing them if they had been put in quite that way, but they were never put quite that way—simply shown, demonstrated, assumed in every book, advertisement, and social arrangement around me) because those were what most people believed, just as they had once believed in Progress, and still believed that hard work inevitably was rewarded. To believe, to insist, that woman's place was in the home, was to ward off for a little while longer the painful adjustments of the twentieth century, which began and seems destined to end with magazine articles warning that the "new" woman will mean the end of the family. Even in Cambridge, Massachusetts, beyond the middle-class Middle West, people chose to believe those things.

I admit to a certain lack of imagination. But few of us are geniuses, able to imagine the unimaginable. (Where did Elizabeth Cady Stanton *come from?* And why was I never told about her? But that is part of the same explanation for my expectations.)

I was, in the most literal sense, unable to imagine that I was not raised to be equal.

When I graduated from college, I did not expect to receive, twenty years later, a questionnaire that would ask, among other things: "Have you met, or surpassed, the expectations you held for yourself in college?"

I responded to that question with low dread and the odd feeling that they were talking about someone else. The truth is, I could not immediately remember having any expectations at all while I was in college.

I knew we arrived as freshmen with vague notions of becoming huge successes: concert pianists, prize-winning journalists, ambassadors, poets. I remember a girl who wanted to be an archeologist until she found out it involved a knowledge of Greek, Latin, and desert survival skills. That girl was me, but I remember her less clearly than I remember my roommate, who expected to win a Nobel Prize but dropped out to get married in her sophomore year. By the time we graduated, we all expected only to get married. And we did.

I have never really understood how it happened, that narrowing-down of expectations to the point that we believed that marriage would take care of the whole rest of our lives. It has been the great riddle and regret of our generation of women. We made a mistake, and in trying to correct it, we restarted the feminist movement. I understood it in theory, but I did not understand how it happened to me.

Last week memory came to call. A man I had not seen for years was passing through New York and came to dinner. When I opened the door to him, my life from age fifteen to eighteen passed before my eyes. During those years the arrival of that man—then boy—meant that life had arrived.

Life included movies, hamburgers, swimming parties, picnics, dances, corsages, identification bracelets, and popularity. None of those things counted (or, in the case of popularity, was acknowledged) if they came without a boyfriend.

We were in love, and after a few months we allowed ourselves a good-night kiss, which was all we ever allowed ourselves. In return for his courtesies and investment he got a princess (me) whom he would some day marry and turn into a slave or a dependent (depending on which way you now look at it) for life.

It seems a literally incredible arrangement now, but I can see that girl sitting on the porch, waiting. I can see, and feel, and hear her, riding in the front seat of a Studebaker as it turns off Lindell into Skinker. The boy asks: "Why do you want to go to Radcliffe?" And the girl, who was me, answers: "Because it will make me a better wife and mother."

But wait. There are two girls sitting in that seat, two memories in one person. I knew even then that that was not the reason I was going to Radcliffe. I simply had not thought out any other expectations. Besides, how could I tell him I wanted to be an archeologist, when he was going to be a doctor? How could I admit to him or to me that the girl who waited on the porch was like a steel spring, coiled, waiting to be sprung, to get out of town, away from those dances and off toward her vague notions.

If there is one thing my classmates have learned, it is that there is always time for questions. After we fulfilled one set of expectations, we returned to the vague notions. My roommate had three babies, and then went to medical school. She, again, hopes for a Nobel Prize. We became doctors, journalists, and professors—but not yet ambassadors.

We first met "their" expectations (whoever "they" were), and then we surpassed our own. Perhaps it would have been better if we had been able to merge the two sooner. But I am surprised to conclude that expectations may matter less than flexibility.

———

The letter arrives every year. Mimeographed, with hand-drawn holly leaves around the edge, sent by someone I went to school with, it begins "Dear Friends," which presumably includes me. The letter reaches me correctly addressed and mailed early with the proper postage, despite my twenty years of wandering and two name changes. This year's letter reads:

Dear Friends,

It's hard to believe another year has passed! Time seems to grow shorter as we grow older—although not all that old, whatever the kids may think!

Speaking of the kids, they are all wonderful as ever. Timmy is 14(!) now, and doing extremely well at the new school. He's interested in track, tapes and girls . . . in that order. Bobby (11) fell off a horse this summer and spent two months in a cast. He's fine now, but the whole family feels the cast should be kept in our permanent trophy case. Sally (9) is growing up, really becoming a lady, and she seems to have all the brains in the family. Her I.Q. tests are really amazing. Linda (5) is the family devil, but we love her. And, this year's surprise is that number five will be coming along in March! Big surprise! No, seriously, the kids are our pride and joy, and watching them grow makes us feel we are growing more ourselves every day.

Other news: Roy and I spent a well-earned week in the Florida sun last March, and then came home to spend the whole summer adding a wing on the house. The kids were at camp and I sorely missed Lake Michigan, but Roy said it was better to build than buy this year, and I guess he was proved right by the grim business picture.

Roy's Dad, I'm sorry to say, died last April, very peacefully and easily. We all miss him terribly and I know many of you do, too. My mother is just fine, really amazing for "an old widder lady," as she says. She spent July traveling through the Smokies with my Aunt Martha.

This year Roy has been working too hard, but he loves it (he doesn't, he complains from across the room). I worked hard in the election last fall, and although I felt I had chosen the best man, the rest of the voters did not. Anyway, in these times, we feel everyone has to do what they can, whatever their "lights."

Every year we seem to be wishing you, our dear friends, peace and joy, and every year it seems further away. But we all, here at 6322 Pershing Avenue, wish all of you the very best for the new year, and hope to hear of your doings soon.

The Fishers

The last sentence is underlined by hand, and the same hand— of a woman I haven't seen since 1955—has written in a few details of deaths, disasters, and divorces among our classmates.

I look forward to these letters, enjoy them as messages from a more confident, complacent scheme of things, although I can read the uneasiness between the lines:

. . . Yes, we are all growing older and we never thought we would, and is this what being grown-up means? Having a teen-ager who has trouble in school, and four other kids who will be just as bewildering? We all said we would have five kids, but does anyone else wonder

if we were right? Roy and I almost got divorced last spring, but we went to Florida, and a new baby and a new wing will make it all right, if his business doesn't fail. Why is the world so confusing when we did everything they taught us to do back in the convent? Please, everyone, write and tell me your life is the same! ...

I never answer her. What would I say? I was raised for that world: babies and new houses, horses and faith in the middle class. I was supposed to be one of those women and it turned out differently. Not better, but different, and I can't explain it in a Christmas card.

If Christmas letters remind me that I was raised for a world I didn't choose to live in, they also remind me that that world had its points—especially during the holidays. Christmas was my grandmother's, and it was a peak experience. It began in November, when wrapping paper started to rustle behind locked library doors. Trees were erected, wreaths hung in every window, narcissus bloomed in Chinese pots. Seventy-five people came to sing carols on Christmas Eve, and to eat ham and turkey and baked beans and drink cocoa out of Dresden cups. Midnight Mass, jingle bells, and back to Grandmother's in the morning for ... well, presents stacked from the mantelpiece out to the middle of the room, tangerines and silver dollars in every stocking. Buckwheat pancakes and sausage, and more presents, and then goose and three kinds of pie.

And then there was New Year's Eve. My parents said it was better when they were young, when fifty people came every year for charades and champagne. But I was allowed to stay up in my bunny slippers and red bathrobe with jingle-bell buttons and wait by the green eye of the family Philco for midnight in New York. We heard the crowd go wild in Times Square and I knew—from the cartoons in the *Saturday Evening Post*—exactly what it was like. Men wore top hats and women drank champagne from martini glasses and the whole city was a swirling, looping confetti ribbon.

There was an hour to wait until the new year swept across the time zone and midnight came to St. Louis. In my memory the years are compressed into one perfect, significant hour between eleven and twelve. My sister and brother were too small to stay up. My parents were going out, my mother extraordinarily beautiful in purple satin dancing shoes and my father wearing his black-pearl studs, but they were also home with me drinking cocoa. At midnight I opened the front door to shout Happy New Year into the middle western air.

I thought it was all real life. I also thought the world would end in 1965 because, we were told at school, the pope had been so warned by three Portuguese children who had in turn gotten the word from Our Lady of Fatima.

In 1955 my Christmas vacation was a planned peak experience. I made my debut. We were not rich, only comfortable, but I took part in the lavish charade because my grandmother was dying and the sight of me as a debutante was thought to please her, even more than the sight of me as a Radcliffe student had been known to please her. I hope it did, because it was a difficult vision to accommodate. For two weeks I went to a brunch, a lunch, a tea, a tea dance, a dinner, a dinner dance, and a ball—*every* day, except Christmas Eve, when there was no ball. I went to the St. Louis Country Club night after night and listened to Polka Bands, Gypsy Violins, Waltz Bands, Steel-Drum Bands, and Jazz Bands. I slopped through puddles of champagne left on the floor by the St. Louis youth I was coming out to meet. I wore borrowed evening gowns, glowered intellectually, and no one ever asked me to dance. A Budweiser heiress gave a ball at which a baby elephant carried trays of drinks and other people danced in the Clydesdale horses' stalls. Women from my grandmother's mysterious social past came to my own tea bringing satin petticoats and monogrammed nightgowns, initialed silver earrings and complicated evening bags. In my shame I never thanked any of them.

Because I knew, or was beginning to guess, that it would not be my real life, and that there was no need for me to come out in St. Louis because I would never go back there again.

In 1963, in Washington, I had a baby. We carried him downstairs at four o'clock Christmas morning to see the tree, and he liked it.

In 1967, I was divorced and living in New York. A man I scarcely knew called me at six o'clock on New Year's Eve to see if by any chance I was free. I was. I borrowed a dress and some very long and real pearls from a friend, and I was picked up in a limousine and taken to the annual New Year's Eve party of a Famous Broadway Producer. He lived in a house in the east sixties, with glacéed paisley walls and strobe lights in the library, and going up the stairs I tripped on Leonard Bernstein.

I stopped borrowing dresses after that party, because it was clear that Angela Lansbury, Dustin Hoffman, Burt Bacharach, Adolph Green, Lauren Bacall, and others too numerous to mention did not care what I wore. There were one or two very thin girls, in open-work crochet, who leaned against space and focused on the middle distance, and no one seemed to care what they wore either. At midnight one of them kissed me, and so did a couple of people I happened to be next to, on their way to kiss the famous people.

In 1975 I finally realized that it is impossible to pose prettily in a red velvet robe under the tree and at the same time baste a goose in the kitchen. I could not remember a single Christmas from the time it became my job to provide traditional joyousness to whoever was gathered under whatever roof when I did not at some point lie beneath the tree—usually after it had fallen over or been pushed on top of me—and sob. The very words "stocking stuffers" made me sick to my stomach. My grandmother's goose, I suddenly recalled, was basted by a cook. My grandmother also had a large family and I did not. I felt inappropriately trapped in a cultural imperative. So I sent my son to his grandmother's and went to the office on Christmas morn. There was nothing around the house unwrapped, undecorated, and unmailed to remind me of my failure to be Woman: the Organized Provider. I wasn't even around the house. It was wonderful. Everyone felt sorry for me. "Alone at Christmas? How dreadful! You must come to our house." Perhaps only other mothers will understand the absolute liberation I felt when one of the children threw up on the lace tablecloth. It was not my child, or my tablecloth, or my responsibility. I decided never to celebrate Christmas at home again.

But here I am again, whistling the "Hallelujah Chorus." Non-tradition has become tradition. My friends are my family, and we will provide for each other. Gathered about the tree will be the intact family from upstairs, the broken family from across the park, an extended family from out of town, my own reconstituted family, and the various inexplicable attachments we have all acquired along the way. It is family tradition now for all the adults to fight over who will get to baste the goose.

The day will become a link in the chain of memories of where I was, and with whom, and how I felt on all the holidays that marked the change from "was" to "is." I am not, and yet I am, the person Mrs. Fisher remembers, but who she is and was is part of me and I am glad she reminds me every year. Her letter is my private rite of passage, annually raising old ghosts to be mourned a little, and sent away with relief.

My coffee table has a new book. It is *Life Goes to War*, a collection of pictures taken of World War II by *Life* magazine photographers. When my son and his friends look at the book, at the pictures of Guadalcanal, of people trampled to death on the steps of Chungking, of ships sinking and Hiroshima, and the bodies stacked up in concentration camps, they become silent and thoughtful. World War II was not, it seems, anything like "McHale's Navy."

I realize when I look at the book that I never expected to live long enough to have a coffee table, or a nearly grown son who would sit at it looking at pictures of the fires around St. Paul's Cathedral. I expected to be dead by now, killed by an atomic bomb. During my teens the word "motherhood" immediately made me imagine myself carrying a wounded child along the side of a road, part of a long line of refugees, while an enemy plane flew overhead shooting at us.

I don't think that was a particularly peculiar connection for someone of my generation to have made. What I do think is peculiar is that I seem never to have wondered about it before, and no one else seems to have brought it up.

Why, for example, did none of the expensive professionals I consulted during periods of acute depression in my life ever seem to think it worthwhile to examine the fact that I grew up during the war? I remember once trying to discover why I felt a sense of annihilating loss whenever I had to say good-bye to someone I liked. The wisdom directed toward my couch centered around an effort to learn if my mother had left me abruptly to go to the hospital to have another baby.

Perhaps she did, and perhaps she should be made to feel guilty forever because of her inconsiderate timing of labor pains. But if she did, she was no more to blame for that than she was responsible for sending her brothers off to war, or her husband off to direct local defense efforts, or for the planes passing over our house during a blackout, or for the determination that our baby-sitter was a German spy who should be deported.

My particular first memory is of the bombing of Pearl Harbor, a possibility Freud—himself overwhelmed by an evil he never imagined—did not take into account. I learned the size and shape of the world from maps covered by arrows indicating advancing and retreating troops. When I look at *Life Goes to War*, I remember my childhood as a series of days spent sitting on the floor studying pictures in *Life* magazine.

I have spent much of my life wondering what happened to the babies photographed crying in the rubble beside the bodies of their mothers. And imagining my child as one of them. What, then, explains the fact that the people my age have gone on? How was our ambition, our capacity to love, our understanding of power, affected? I don't know, and I would like to hear from anyone who thinks they know.

We are, as the saying goes, heavily into self-fulfillment now. But war is the ultimate self-fulfillment. The demagoguery, the medals, the descriptions of murder as "tactical brilliance," the closeness of working together for a common cause. Even fear is a peak experience. War can be fun.

A coffee table is the wrong place for this book. Church would be better. Some place where we can consider the fact that we are still too close to the cave.

———————

She sat at the head of the table, a handsome woman, charming, self-absorbed, the guest of honor in her daughter's house. Her conversation ranged from the peculiar way her daughter peeled potatoes to the peculiar pictures her daughter chose to put on the walls. Her remarks were most amusingly phrased, even those—spoken within hearing of the child—about the peculiar way her granddaughter was growing up.

We were guests, and we continued to pour fresh drinks and to speak only of the cultivation of begonias. We had been specifically asked not to argue, because this was the first visit she had ever made to her daughter's house. For ten years she had not spoken at all, because she disapproved of her daughter's marriage. When the grandchild was born, she spoke, but most often to point out what a pity it hadn't been a boy.

If we had pointed out that the marriage was extraordinarily successful, the child a delight, and the daughter a loving, successful, competent person, it would have been considered an argument.

If we had asked why she hated her daughter, she would have been shocked. Of course she loves her daughter, all mothers love their children. No matter how disappointing children may be. She would even believe it to be true. But she gave us an answer despite herself. The talk had slipped precariously away from her, to work, and she glared at us all and said firmly: "Don't ever forget all mothers were once daughters."

As a maxim the sentence has a fine hollow ring to it. A certain biological truth, perhaps, but scarcely a reliable signpost for life. But as a lament, and an accusation, it may explain why so many mothers of her generation are so angry with their daughters of my generation.

We, the daughters who have not become our mothers—not yet—comfort ourselves with generalization. We explain that mothers feel a natural ambivalence, wanting their daughters to succeed and also to fail. (I do not know why we think this is natural.) We know that too many mothers gave up their own visions, as their mothers had before them, and then expected us to fulfill all their lost hopes and dreams. Vicarious living is always disappointing.

We know that the society they grew up in was itself ambivalent, claiming to value motherhood, but at the same time shutting women out, refusing to admit them as serious contenders for jobs and power and participation, simply because they might become pregnant. No wonder our mothers complained when we did not have children, and retired to bed in depression when we did.

Perhaps the impulse to cast blame is inevitable in women who were so thoroughly blamed themselves: wrong if they took men's jobs during the Depression, wrong if they didn't during the war; wrong if they were not virtuous before marriage, wrong if they were not sexy afterward; wrong if they coddled their babies in the twenties, wrong if they did not provide the precisely calibrated, expert-approved "right kind of love" in the thirties and forties, wrong ever after if their children took to the psychoanalytic couch "because of my mother." ("Indeed?" one wants to ask. "And where was your father?")

But generalizations are no comfort to a woman whose mother refuses to learn to spell her daughter's married name correctly. Or to another whose mother attacks her for not keeping a special drawer in which to store old wrapping paper and ribbons, in the same tone she uses to attack another daughter who drinks.

There seems to be no rational explanation (except perhaps that they never really knew us) for mothers who are not satisfied if we are intelligent, kind, and independent, but want us also to be sexy, fashionable, and more devoted. We could understand that our mothers might feel we have repudiated their lives by our efforts to change our own, but that is not the whole explanation either, because those of us who are old-fashioned are criticized for not making something of ourselves.

"We only want you to be happy," they say, and when we protest that we are happy, they quickly point out reasons we should not be. They mean: "Be happy my way." Worse, they mean: "Make me happy." And there seems no way to do that, to ever repay them for the fact that they were daughters who grew up to be mothers, to release them from the awful self-hate that came from being raised to despise and resent other women—a release we have sought for ourselves and our daughters.

They write us dunning letters, reminding us that they are our mothers. We know that. We are often enough glad of it. We would be glad to share more of our lives with them, if only we could figure out some way it would be an acceptable offering. They complain that we are holding back. And when we try to share, they say we are taking. We cannot please.

They seem to want it all back, every diaper changed, every temperature taken, every dream forestalled. But motherhood is not an investment. It is no longer a hedge against old age. We have ourselves been astonished to discover it is not even necessarily a major sacrifice. It is a reward in itself, even the diapers. Interest is not compounded with every peanut butter sandwich made.

Of course, our daughters are only beginning to grow up. It has yet to be seen if what is freely given will be given freely in return. But I hope we will remember that a little acceptance might fill up the mailboxes of our old age.

———

I once spent a morning trying to force a man to read a newspaper, and in the process I rediscovered some of the reasons the woman's movement causes so much confusion and anxiety.

It was a Sunday morning, and I was at another woman's house. I was sitting all alone in the living room reading the paper when another guest, a man, came downstairs and began to make himself breakfast.

The fact that he could make a cup of coffee for himself without either of us thinking that I should do it might have caused me to reflect on the great advances men and women have made in the last few years. But I didn't have time for reflection. I was too busy folding up the newspaper so the man could receive it in a pristine, unrumpled condition.

"Here is the paper," I said, carrying it into the kitchen.

"But you were reading it," he said.

"Oh, that's all right, you can have it," I said, with just the slightest trace of a sigh.

"But I don't want it, I'm going sailing," he said, adding, "Anyway, why should you stop reading it?"

I thought that was a good question. I stood in the kitchen, holding the carefully folded newspaper, and tried to figure out what I was doing there. I felt like someone coming out of a hypnotic trance.

I was there because men get the paper first. Morning papers are divided at the breakfast table: news for father, fashion for mother, and comics for children. Evening papers are refolded and placed next to father's chair. Mother and children get to read the paper when father is finished. If there is no father in the house, any available man gets priority. Even if he is going sailing and has no connection at all with the woman who really wants to read the paper. That is the way I was raised, and that is the way I respond to the problem of a newspaper and a man in the house—just like Pavlov's dog.

I was raised to defer and submit to the man in the house, which must explain why I am terrified of my friends' husbands. Whenever I visit a friend, I regress about thirty years. The friend and I may be sitting in the kitchen, drinking coffee and solving the world problems at the top of our lungs, but if The Husband should wander in, I scamper out the door feeling like an intruder.

If the friend suggests we watch a television program, and The Husband is in the room with the television set in it, I creep back out whispering that we had better not disturb him. At the dinner table I chew each mouthful twenty times and try not to spill, terrified that The Husband will start pounding the table and behaving like a scene out of *Life with Father.*

In fact, none of The Husbands I actually know would dream of pounding on the table (nor would my own father have dreamt of it). Usually they have helped cook dinner, and their wives help pay the mortgage. Probably they think I am an extremely odd person, lapsing into meek and uncharacteristic silence whenever they enter the room. They could not guess that I expect to be thrown out of the house, by virtue of the authority that I assign to them, simply because they are "the man of the house."

Most of the husbands I know deny that they feel any sense of authority. They are bewildered when their wives start stamping around the house talking about equality. It is odd, the way men suddenly discover they were raised to expect authority (and in fact do expect it) the minute their wives discover they were raised to defer and submit (and in fact defer but resent it).

The trouble is, we were not raised to be equal.

One evening I came quite late into a room on the Upper West Side of Manhattan. Within were academic people holding plastic glasses of champagne and discussing topics such as early Greek society and Marxist feminism. A few were exchanging footnotes, an activity that indicated the party had reached fever pitch.

A man on his way out of the room muttered a warning: "A woman in there," he whispered, "has just told me in all seriousness that Homer was a sexist." I grasped wildly for a remnant of my liberal education. Homer. *Odyssey.* Dido, Cassandra, Penelope, Helen. Sexist? Probably. But, frankly, just a trifle too arcane for me that evening. My life's ambition, as a matter of fact, has always been to grow up arcane, but on that particular night what I had in mind was pointless cocktail party drivel. I had exhausted my ability to find sexism lurking everywhere the night before, when I sat through the current Broadway revival of *Guys and Dolls*.

A musical inspired by the Broadway tales of Damon Runyon, *Guys and Dolls* opened in November 1950 and played 1,194 times. The revival, with an all-black cast, was very enjoyable. It was more enjoyable if you didn't go to the theater with me. I insisted on seeing it as a metaphor for the sexist society of the fifties.

"Cover your ears, close your eyes," I admonished the youths in our party as Adelaide and Sarah rendered "Marry the man today, and change his ways tomorrow." During the intermission I explained that the formative years of my generation had been spent whistling "I'll Know," the lesson of which is when your love comes along you'll know and everything will be all right forever. "Now children," I said, "you see an example of how your mothers got to be so foolish before the women's movement came along and the scales dropped from our eyes."

The children, unimpressed, slunk off for some overpriced orange drink. But I trapped them in the bus on the way home. Speaking in a style more appropriate to a Modern Language Association convention, I analyzed the lyrics of "Take Back Your Mink." A parody, rooted nonetheless in truth, of the relationship between men and women, I asserted.

Even the mothers, who until that point had been warning me against hypersensitivity, had to agree that "Adelaide's Lament" is a gruesome song, with its repeated theme that a woman can get a bad, bad cold if she fails to legally acquire a ring for the third finger, left hand.

A couple of nights later I went to see a revival of *My Fair Lady*, which originally opened in March 1956 and ran for 2,717 performances. I remembered it as charming, and wished it to remain so. But this time my companion sank into a depression. He began lecturing his children on the human relationships displayed. "Hateful, masochistic, sadistic," he muttered, as the children again crept off for an orange drink.

"Why would Eliza go back to Henry Higgins?" he demanded.

"She is a strong, intelligent woman; why would she ever go back to a man who sings, 'Why can't a woman be more like a man?'" Why indeed? I have always objected to the scene where Eliza comes creeping in and picks up Professor Higgins's slippers. Even in the old English movie version of George Bernard Shaw's *Pygmalion*, from which *My Fair Lady* was drawn almost verbatim, Eliza reappears in the lamplight and we are meant to be consoled by a romantic ending, hoping that she found a soft heart where we could not.

Shaw wrote an epilogue for *Pygmalion*, and, on reading it, I discovered that what we have been seeing all these years isn't what he had in mind at all. Someone else, no doubt someone with an eye on "what the audience would stand for," assumed that a really romantic ending had to have Eliza in love with Higgins. That she would also be dominated and insulted and despised was immaterial.

Shaw himself says that Eliza knew Higgins was not a marrying man, but she also knew they would always play a strong part in each other's lives. But "Eliza has no use for the foolish romantic tradition that all women love to be mastered, if not actually bullied and beaten," Shaw wrote. His Eliza married Freddy; they opened a flower shop, and she continued to arrange everyone's lives.

Shaw's version is much more satisfactory.

I found a photograph in the back of a closet. It is a bridal portrait, large and artfully airbrushed. The girl is wearing a veil, and under it an expression of belligerent innocence. I do not remember her very well, but she is me.

I made the silk dress. It is still around somewhere in the back of another closet, and I must check sometime to see if I really finished off the hem with Scotch tape, as I remember. I did not, at the time, admit to innocence, and I did not—in time—recognize the belligerence.

I found the picture on the twentieth anniversary of that wedding. The marriage lasted only three years but, because there were no children from that one, we were spared the lifelong semiwarfare that people who share children, but not a life, suffer. After twenty years I can enjoy this anniversary when I remember it. The memory of the end has disappeared and I recall only the hope and affection of the beginning. We meant the vows at the time, and if we did not know what the vows themselves meant, or that we were a very unlikely pair to be exchanging them, well, we were not alone.

The marriage lasted such a short while that we never pasted the snapshots into books. They are still heaped up in a box. We all appear in them as buds of hope, looking younger than people have ever looked. How could we have been so young? Because we were—as our parents warned us at the time. We were not unsophisticated, but we were innocent, in the sense of being woefully ignorant. We married, all of us in those pictures, because that was what people did after they graduated from college. It had not, at that time, occurred to many people to warn us that marriage was a tricky business. It wasn't because our parents did not know; it was because no one had yet realized that there might be other choices to consider.

We are standing on the lawn looking wistful and pleased (and, yes, belligerent). There is an atmosphere of crystal patterns picked out and going-away dresses pressed. It was a ceremony of completion, social expectations met. Odd that we did not think of it as a beginning.

The bridesmaids are still my best friends. Two have been divorced and remarried and both became doctors during the divorced interim. Another one is my sister. She has been happily married for twenty years. I wonder how she achieved that? The fourth has been a perfect wife for sixteen years. Only recently did she decide to become liberated, but she did so in the most enviable way—by bringing her husband along.

The ushers are now journalists, except one who is a psychoanalyst. As I remember, they variously expected to be H. L. Mencken, president of the United States, and to die young. The groom is now eminent—as I expected. What is significant is that the women did not expect much for themselves, except to marry. The cravings came later, and it is not too much to say that we made a revolution of them.

There has been quite a long period for us when the feelings about weddings and old wedding pictures were not bittersweet, but bitter. We stood in the back of churches at first marriages, and second, and sometimes third, and muttered together cynically about "till death do us part." The young heard us, and now they are more serious about marriage, not less. They agonize about commitment and wonder if living together isn't better.

Maybe. Maybe not. There are other commitments and other ties in life that might satisfy more. In my pictures there are three old ladies. They were my grandmother's bridesmaids, and for them their marriages were—at the end of their lives—an interval in the long tie of their friendship.

The most astonishing thing about my pictures is that so many of the people, the then young, are dead now. Life has turned out to be very short. The women have spent part of our short lives in the revolutionary struggle for independence. Maybe the greatest challenge now is to find a way to keep independence while also committing ourselves to the ties that bind people, families, and ultimately societies together.

II.

Click!
The Housewife's
Moment
of Truth

The gentleman in the back row asks, what do I mean by equal? Is this a point which needs clarification? Very well. I was, being a woman, not raised to be equal: that is, I was raised without the same status, privileges, and rights as men. I am, by custom and law, considered unequal: less than whole. No, sir, I do not think that the fact that I cannot lift heavy weights has anything to do with it. Yes, sir, I recognize that you too have suffered some disadvantages in your life, but they were not because you were born a woman. (Probably it was because you are too stupid to know what equal means.) Nothing, just a private remark. No, sir, this women's lib stuff does not mean that you may no longer open doors for ladies, although I would prefer that the doors opened were doors to equal opportunity. Excuse me? Yes. Yes, I do really believe what I am saying.

It was heady stuff, recognizing ourselves as an oppressed class, but the level of discussion was poor. We explained systemic discrimination, and men looked prettily confused and said: "But, I *like* women." Even that assertion was open to doubt. Men did not really like women very much. They thought of us, after all, as inferior beings (although they would not have put it quite that way, preferring the more subtle indicators of custom and law).

It is hard to live with someone who does not like us, but hard, too, to live alone. Divorce is only less painful than the need for divorce. I believe in duty, honor, and responsibility, but I incline also toward love, autonomy, and choice. Commitment seems as important to structuring life as anything, but it must be able to stop short of martyrdom. The luster of the wedding ring is dimmed by the fact that a woman who wears one signifies she has entered into a legal arrangement in which she is still, in most states, only half a person.

All this ambivalence is very confusing, and although we hesitate to call it a power struggle, that is what it is—he to keep his, she to get hers. No amount of arbitration or eloquent explication by the powerless will ever persuade the powerful that "equality" does not mean "loss." Much domestic turmoil results.

It was the summer of 1971. We closed our eyes and cleared our minds, forty people lying on a floor in Aspen, Colorado, floating free and uneasy on the indoor/outdoor carpet, being led through the first phase of a "Workshop in Approaching Unisexuality." It would turn out later that the aim of the exercise was not to solve the problem of who does what and to whom, but to reveal to the participants that adjectives such as warm, violent, soft, timid, peaceful, and aggressive are not necessarily definitions for male or female.

We began to evolve into the animal that most expressed our own ideas of ourselves—of our sensual selves. Minutes passed and we became aware of the other animals around us. At last we opened our eyes and those animals that felt like it did whatever seemed natural. Most of the women twittered or purred. Most of the men growled or attempted to wag tails. I was a cat, black, with a lovely long tail, sitting under a red geranium in a sunny window. We formed groups in our part of the conference-room forest, and told each other what we had become.

"I was a snake," said a beautiful young woman, a professional designer. "As I was moving through the grass, enjoying my slithering, curving progress, I realized I had no fangs. No bite. I couldn't even hiss. My only protection was that I could change color in reaction to the people that passed by. I started to go through my garden and I saw that there were panthers draped over all the lawn furniture. I went into my house, and there were panthers everywhere, filling every chair, curled up in groups in all the rooms. They were eating, rather elegantly, and no one paid any attention to me, even when I asked if they wanted anything more to eat. I was interested, but I was different, and finally I withdrew."

The women in the group looked at her, looked at each other, and . . . click! A moment of truth. The shock of recognition. Instant sisterhood. "You became a *housewife*," we said, together, excited, turning to the men to see if they understood. "She is describing a housewife. Do you know that?"

"Hmm, yes, well, uh . . ." they said, sensitized for the morning but eager to recount their own stories of becoming spotted leopards in green forests, of turning to griffins with human heads who know and see all. The next time, or perhaps the time after that, they will recognize the click! of recognition, that parenthesis of truth around a little thing that completes the puzzle of reality in women's minds—the moment that brings a gleam to our eyes and means the revolution has begun.

One little click turns on a thousand others. I had been sitting in that Aspen room, feeling a very liberated cat—alone on my windowsill, self-sufficient and self-enclosed, able to purr or scratch as I chose. I was fooling myself. I had really followed the pattern of my socialization, becoming a nice, domestic cat, sitting under a healthy well-watered geranium, watching the sunlight fall through a clean window, over a dust-free windowsill, across a polished floor. The room was cozy, with a tea tray by the fire. In another five minutes of meditating evolution I would have jumped off the windowsill and started curling around the leg of a dog.

In fact, parables are unnecessary for recognizing the blatant absurdity of everyday life. Reality is lesson enough. In Houston, Texas, a friend of mine stood and watched her husband step over a pile of toys on the stairs, put there to be carried up. "Why can't you get this stuff put away?" he mumbled. Click! "You have two hands," she said, turning away.

On Fire Island my weekend hostess and I had just finished cooking breakfast, lunch, and washing dishes for both. A male guest came wandering into the kitchen just as the last dish was being put away and said, "How about something to eat?" He sat down expectantly and started to read the paper. Click! "You work all week," said the hostess, "and *I* work all week, and if you want something to eat, you can get it, and wash up after it yourself."

In New York last fall my neighbors—named Jones—had a couple named Smith over for dinner. Mr. Smith kept telling his wife to get up and help Mrs. Jones. Click! Click! Two women radicalized at once.

A woman I know in St. Louis, who had begun to enjoy a little success writing a grain company's newsletter, came home to tell her husband about lunch in the executive dining room. She had planned a funny little anecdote about the deeply humorous pomposity of executives, when she noticed her husband rocking with laughter. "Ho, ho, my little wife in an executive dining room." Click!

Last August I was on a boat leaving an island in Maine. Two families were with me, and the mothers were discussing the troubles of cleaning up after a rental summer. "Bob cleaned up the bathroom for me, didn't you, honey?" she confided, gratefully patting her husband's knee. "Well, what the hell, it's vacation," he said fondly. The two women looked at each other, and the queerest change came over their faces. "I got up at six this morning to make the sandwiches for the trip home from this 'vacation,'" the first one said. "So I wonder why I've thanked him at least six times for cleaning the bathroom?" Click! Click!

Attitudes are expressed in semantic equations that simply turn out to be two languages: one for men and another for women. One morning a friend of mine told her husband she would like to hire a baby-sitter so she could get back to her painting. "Maybe when you start to make money from your pictures, then we could think about it," said her husband. My friend didn't stop to argue the inherent fallacy in his point—how could she make money if no one was willing to free her to earn it? She suggested that instead of hiring someone, he could help with the housework a little more. "Well, I don't know, honey," he said. "I guess sharing the housework is all right if the wife is really contributing something, brings in a salary. . . ." For a terrible minute my friend thought she would kill her husband, right there at breakfast, in front of the children. For ten years she had been covering furniture, hanging wallpaper, making curtains, and refinishing floors so that they could afford the mortgage on their apartment. She had planned the money-saving menus so they could afford the little dinners for prospective clients. She had crossed town to save money on clothes so the family could have a new hi-fi. All the little advances in station—the vacations, the theater tickets, the new car—had been made possible by her crafty, endless, worried manipulation of the household expenses. "I was under the impression," she said, "that I *was* contributing something. Evidently my life's blood is simply a nondeductible expense."

In suburban Chicago the party consisted of three couples. The women were a writer, a doctor, and a teacher. The men were all lawyers. As the last couple arrived, the host said jovially, "With a roomful of lawyers, we ought to have a good evening." Silence. Click! "What are we?" asked the teacher. "Invisible?"

In an office a political columnist, male, was waiting to see the editor-in-chief. Leaning against a doorway, the columnist turned to the first woman he saw and said, "Listen, call Joe Brown and tell him I'll be late." Click! It wasn't because she happened to be an editor herself that she refused to make the call.

In the end we are all housewives, the natural people to turn to when there is something unpleasant, inconvenient, or inconclusive to be done. It will not do for women who have jobs to pretend that society's ills will be cured if all women are gainfully employed. In Russia 80 percent of the working-age women are employed outside the home, but none of them is at the top level of the government. They are, however, still in charge of all the housework.

It will not do for women who are mostly housewives to say that Women's Liberation is fine for women who work, but has no relevance for them. Equal pay for equal work is only part of the argument—usually described as "the part I'll go along with."

We are all housewives. We would prefer to be people. That is the part they don't go along with.

"That broad . . ." begins a male guest who hasn't thought.

"Woman," corrects the hostess, smiling meaningfully over her coffeepot.

"Oh, no," groans the guest. "Don't tell me you believe in this Women's Lib stuff!"

"Yes," says the hostess.

"Well, I'll go along with some of it, equal pay for equal work, that seems fair enough," he concedes. Uneasy now, he waits for the male hoots of laughter, for the flutter of wives rushing to sit by their husbands at the merest breath of the subject of Women's Liberation. But that was a decade ago. Too many moments have clicked in the minds of too many women since then. This time the women in the room have not moved to their husbands' sides; they have . . . solidified. A gelid quality settles over the room. The guest struggles on.

"You can't tell me Women's Lib means I have to wash the dishes, does it?"

"Yes."

They tell us we are being petty. The future improvement of civilization could not depend on who washes the dishes. Could it? Yes. The liberated society—with men, women, and children living as whole human beings, not halves divided by sex roles—depends on the steadfast search for new solutions to just such apparently trivial problems, on new answers to tired old questions. Such questions as:

Denise works as a waitress from 6:00 A.M. to 3:00 P.M. Her husband is a cabdriver who moonlights on weekends as a doorman. They have four children. When her husband comes home at night, he asks: "*What's for dinner?*"

Jonathan and Joanne are both doctors. They have identical office hours. They come home in the evening to a dinner cooked by a housekeeper. When they go to bed, he drops his clothes on the floor and she picks them up. In the morning he asks, *"Where is my striped shirt?"*

In moments of suburban strife Fred often asks his wife Alice, "Why haven't you mended my shirt and lubricated the car? *What else have you got to do but sit around the house all day?"*

How dare he ask such a question? What sort of bizarre social arrangement is post–industrial-revolution marriage? What kind of relationship involves two people sharing their lives without knowing, or apparently caring, what the other does all day?

Alice, being an average ideal suburban housewife with small children, works 99.6 hours a week—always feeling there is too much to be done and always guilty because it is never quite finished. At the minimum-wage level it would cost Fred $16,055.52 a year to replace Alice's services. At the management level it would cost him $35,000 a year—it depends how Fred values Alice, and if he could find any one person willing to do all Alice's jobs.

But her work doesn't seem important. After all, Fred is paid for doing whatever it is he does. Abstract statistics make no impact on Alice. "My situation is different," she says. Of course it is. All situations are different. But sooner or later she will experience—in a blinding click—a moment of truth. She will remember that she once had other interests, vague hopes, great plans. She will decide that the work in the house is less important than reordering that work so she can consider her own life.

The problem is, what does she do then?

The first thing we all do is argue. We present our case: it is unfair that we should bear the whole responsibility for the constant scheme of household management; that this burden should be as implanted, inescapable, in our minds, as planning *boeuf bourguignon* is in Mrs. Ramsay's in Virginia Woolf's *To The Lighthouse*.

Soon we find out that argument serves no practical purpose. We may get agreement, but we will never get cooperation or permission. Rebuttals may begin at the lowest level: "It is a woman's job to wash dishes." Men at a higher stage of enlightenment may argue, "Why do we need a washing machine? I wash my socks and we send everything out." They simply cannot understand that we are the ones who must gather and list and plan even for the laundry we send out. It is, quite simply, *on our minds*. And *not* on theirs. Evenings of explanation and understanding will still end with, "Honey, do I have any clean shorts for tomorrow?" Most women will decide that it is not worth making an issue out of shorts.

In fact, underwear is as good a place to begin as anywhere. Last summer I carried the underwear downstairs, put it in the hamper, sorted it, washed and dried it, folded it, carried it upstairs, and put it away. One day I decided that as an act of extreme courage I would not carry the laundry upstairs. I put it on the couch in the room with the television set. The family moved it to one side of the couch so they could sit down. I left it there. I put more on the couch. They piled it up. They began to dress off the couch. I began to avoid the television room. At last, guilty and angry, my nerve failed and I carried the laundry upstairs. No one noticed. Out of that experience I formulated a few rules, which I intend to follow as soon as I finish the painful process of thinking about the assumptions that make them necessary.

(1) *Decide what housework needs to be done. Then cut the list in half.* It is no longer necessary to prove ourselves by being in motion all day and all night. Beds must be made and food cooked, but it is unfair to demand that the family share the work if your standards include cooking like Julia Child and bouncing dimes on the bedspread. Beware of useless and self-defeating standards. It is preposterous and not unusual for a woman to feel her house must look as though no one lived there. Who's looking? Who cares?

(2) *Decide what you will and will not do.* Keep firmly in mind the notion of personal maintenance as an individual responsibility. If children cannot put away their clothes and therefore cannot find them and have to go to school looking like ragpickers— well, presumably they will learn from experience. Their appearance does not make *you* a bad person. (If you can acknowledge and act on that fact, you are becoming liberated.) If you spend four or five hours a day driving your children places, ask yourself why. Are they cripples? Are there no safe streets they can walk along?

Why? Seizing responsibility from children has been woman's way to compensate for their own lack of responsibility for themselves, and it has resulted in generations of non-adults.

(3) *Make a plan and present it as final.* There will of course be democratic argument, but it is only fair to state your purpose. Not that anyone will pay attention. They will laugh nervously and expect life to go on as usual. Do not be distracted by sophisticated arguments, such as "Well, let's take the relative value of our days." Yes. Let's. When your husband sits down at his desk after dinner, to use his brain, do you murmur, "Poor darling," as you wash up, tidy the living room, start the wash, and check the bathroom for clean towels? Why? A game of role reversal can be most enlightening. A wife who figures out that his important business meeting is no different from her PTA committee meeting may opt for equal hours—and quit her own work at five o'clock.

Another diversionary remark is: "But, honey, this isn't a business agreement. This is a home. It is a question of helping each other reach fulfillment." In my home when I am working against a deadline, I sit in front of a typewriter and shout, "More tea!" The whole family hustles in with more tea. I call out, "Go to bed," "Get some lamb chops." It is an emergency situation and they all spring to, helping me fulfill myself. But *I* am still in charge of remembering to get the lamb chops. It is a problem that may not be solved in my lifetime.

Almost equally difficult is deciding who does what. Men will always opt for things that get finished and stay that way—putting up screens, but not planning menus. Some find washing dishes a peaceful, meditative experience. It has to be worked out. The important thing is to get the argument away from philosophy and on to assigned chores.

(4) *Think revolutionary thoughts.* The nineteenth century ended eighty years ago, but we are still trying to arrange our households according to that "ideal" image of family life. Think of something new. I know a man and woman who decided to stop eating dinner. She had been rushing around putting children to bed, and then laying on a candlelit dinner with three kinds of food on the

plate for her husband. They liked chatting at dinner. He helped clean up. They never finished before ten. But one night they discovered that both were dreaming of long cozy evenings, reading by the fire. So they have skipped the ritual feast—and replaced it with sandwiches. They get up earlier and have family talks at breakfast. Who knows what daring innovations may follow? He may demand an end to success based on overtime. Both may demand less homework so the children can assume some responsibility.

This is, after all, part of the revolution we are talking about. The woman in Aspen who imagined herself a snake happened to be a nursing mother. One day a complaining note appeared on the conference bulletin board saying: "Why are there crying babies in the tent? Signed, Father of Five." The conference was discussing designs for the future, and Father of Five learned that, in the future, children and their mothers will no longer be quarantined.

(5) *Never give in.* Empty one dishwasher, and it leads to a lifetime of emptying dishwashers. Remember that nothing will ever get done by anyone else if you do it. If you are the only person who worries about it, perhaps it isn't worth worrying about. If it is very important to you that you not live in a sty, then you must persuade everyone else that what is important to you counts.

It is very hard not to give in. One evening recently two men came to our house for the weekend. "When shall we eat?" they asked, beaming. "Whenever you want," I said, bravely. "I'm not cooking. I'm working tonight." They cooked while I held myself in my chair by an incredible effort of will, the words blurring before my determined eyes. The next day I expiated my guilt by going the whole route, including homemade bread. "Ah!" they said. "How wonderful! You are a real woman. And working, too."

(6) *Do not feel guilty.* I have never met a woman who did not feel guilty. We can post signs in our hearts and on our walls saying: "It is not wrong to inconvenience my family—it is making us all responsible, ego-strong adults." But when a man we are attached to goes out with a button off his coat, we—not he—feel feckless. The only near-cure is to have something more interesting to think about. Even if "something to do" means going back to easy

courses in school—back to the point where we abdicated for marriage—it is a beginning, and we are older now and will learn rapidly, because at least we know we want things some other way.

(7) *Expect regression. And remember, the next step is human liberation.* The slightest mischance in my life makes me want to fling myself into the protection of someone else's bank account. And yet I still speak of "our money" as clearly separated from "my money." Occasionally men become liberated and it is a dreadful shock. "I'm not going to work this year; I need to think," announced a friend's husband. She had spent seven years in his care and keeping and then, as she put it, "Finally, I get my own business going and *he* wants to lie around all day." Why not? Women who say, "I like my freedom—I have my day organized and I can do what I like with my time," forget that men are entitled to some of that freedom. They are also prisoners of the rigid structure of their roles and jobs.

I cannot imagine anything more difficult than incurring the kind of domestic trauma I describe. It requires the conscious loss of the role we have been taught, and its replacement by a true identity. And what if we succeed? What if we become liberated women who recognize that our guilt is reinforced by the marketplace, which would have us attach our identity to furniture polish and confine our deepest anxieties to color-coordinating our toilet paper and our washing machines? What if we overcome our creeping sense of something unnatural when our husbands approach "our" stoves? What if we don't allow ourselves to be treated as people with nothing better to do than wait for repairmen and gynecologists? What if we finally learn that we are not defined by our children and our husbands, but by ourselves? Then we will be able to control our own lives, able to step out into a new tomorrow. But the sad and solemn truth is that we may have to step out alone.

The more we try and argue and change, the more we will realize that the male ego will be the last thing in this world to change. And the last place it will change is at home.

Some women pride themselves on the intransigence of their men. I have always taken pride in the liberated attitudes of mine. And yet, last weekend, when I buckled my seat belt in the car, he growled: "You don't have to do that with *me* driving." My God! We were back to Start; he was threatened by my safety measure. How do we argue with feelings like that? With the constant demands to bolster and boost egos grown fat and fragile, with the blocks and jealousies and petty meannesses that drain off our energies? Too often the only way to survive is to leave.

Men's resistance is more subtle than simply leaving the dishes unwashed for a month. A woman I know was married for seventeen years to a man who threatened to smash her sculpture whenever they fought. He complained continuously about the cost of her tools; he laughed at her work in public. When she finally left, she was dazed to discover that the critics found her work excellent.

I have a friend in Cleveland who left high school to marry. She raised two children and worked nights in her husband's office. When she went back to college, it happened mysteriously that they had an exhausting fight the night before every exam. When she still got high marks, he took credit for encouraging her.

I know a writer whose husband never once read her work. She visited an analyst who declared her role conflict a character defect. Her husband told the analyst he wouldn't mind his wife's inadequacies so much if she did something. "But she does write," said the doctor. "Oh. That," said the husband bitterly, dismissing the work he would eventually feel reflected credit on him, but only after their divorce.

No, the question of housework is not a trivial matter to be worked out the day before we go on to greater things. Men do not want equality at home. A strong woman is a threat, someone to be jealous of. Most of all, she is an inconvenience, and she can be replaced. Men like things as they are. It's pleasanter—for them.

The drive to the part of Vermont where I like to grow vegetables takes any normal person, driving as a normal person should, seven hours. We will skip lightly over the question of what kind of person would find it normal to drive seven hours just to spend a weekend in a preferred part of the country.

The simple fact is, it was Memorial Day weekend, and that is the time that vegetables are planted in Vermont. The person who usually drives the car in which I ride to my distant agricultural paradise likes to make the trip in five and a half hours. He usually succeeds, with a little help from his many road-friends with CB radios, and by totally disregarding either the law or the energy crisis.

I am not sure that I, if I were ever allowed to drive the car, would not approach the journey in the same spirit of reckless defiance. However I am not allowed to drive the car. Ever. For no very good reason as far as I can see except that if I were allowed to drive the car, he might have to make the sandwiches.

I want to share with other women, and with such men as may occasionally consent to sitting in the sandwich-making seat, how I feel about this task. I hate it, have probably always hated it, and have seized on it as the focal point for several, apparently long-standing, domestic grudges. I am told that my attitude is unreasonable, probably weird, and certainly unhelpful.

This is what happened. We were about two hours into the trip when a popcorn and hot-dog wagon appeared in the distant horizon. The children, at my prompting, set up a forceful howl, and we stopped. We didn't turn off the motor, but the vehicle did come to a complete halt.

I asked the driver if he thought it was a good idea to let those children ("those" because they were his children, not mine) exist from lunchtime to bedtime on popcorn and ice cream. I admit that my tone of voice may have been irritatingly reminiscent of his mother or my mother, both of those worthy women being the sort who predict malnutrition if it has been four hours since the last chicken soup.

I would have been quite happy myself to exist on popcorn and ice cream, and I was only speaking out of some residual reflex, an involuntary need to recognize that the children might need more substantial protein. I really wanted the driver to say: "No, they are fine living on popcorn."

Instead he handed me a repulsive paper bag and a Swiss knife and suggested that I make sandwiches. My life passed before my eyes: years and years and years of making sandwiches on my lap in the cramped front seat of a moving car, shoving the unappetizing results through the narrow passage between the headrests to the children mewling and growling in the back, moaning as we passed each McDonald's and every rest room.

I remarked that he, the driver, would probably prefer to make the trip with the children sedated and attached to catheters. He retorted that he was probably the only man in America who would remember to bring food. I asked if he called this food: a huge lump of an uncut health loaf and some mashed hard-boiled eggs. He suggested I order a picnic from Bloomingdale's next time. I said paper bags and milk-soaked plastic-wrapped salami and stone-hard cheese make me sick.

We both simultaneously suggested I hitchhike home. I didn't. But tell me, am I being too sensitive?

I have known husbands and wives who would rather be divorced than praise their spouses where it counts—to the spouse. Most of them are quite willing to say something nice about the other if the other cannot hear it. It is, however, tiring to be one of the friends who keeps the marriage together by carrying the good word back and forth.

Very often the words withheld are "I love you." The most that can be hoped for is, "Of course I love you." Sometimes I wonder what people are saving their feelings for. Are they under the impression that this life is just a practice session for the next?

I suppose they are simply suffering from the human condition, which includes a terrible fear that making someone else feel better will somehow be a loss that will make oneself feel worse.

The good news from the census bureau for Valentine's Day is that the divorce rate has more than doubled since 1963. The number of Americans living together out of wedlock has more than doubled since 1970, and people are marrying, when they marry, later. One thing seems certain. There is no crisis of confidence in romance. All that divorcing and withholding of commitment offers unlimited opportunity for romance freaks to experience the *sturm und drang* of falling in love.

I once wrote, in a list of things I was pleased about, that I was not in love with anyone. I got a great many letters in response to that statement, most of them from men, all of whom seemed more or less to agree that I was once more revealing myself as a lunatic feminist, willing to fly in the face of convention, virtue, and natural law. It was almost enough to make me believe that men are more romantic than women. I do not actually believe it; otherwise I would have received more bunches of white lilacs in my lifetime.

I am more romantic than anyone, which is why it was so relaxing not to be in love. Have you any idea how much energy can be expended waiting for the white lilacs to be delivered? How much time can be abandoned to waiting for the phone to ring? How absurd, as a human endeavor, is the effort to make meaningful that which is not?

Furthermore, falling in love is a risk. You might marry. There is a reason they use the term "wedlock," as in "bear trap." No one should seek to navigate the rocky shoals of matrimony these days without first consulting prayerfully with a lawyer, an accountant, and an analyst. The analyst will counsel maturity and mutual fulfillment of needs and will ultimately have not the slightest effect on how it works out, except perhaps to pick up the pieces later.

It is the consultations with lawyer and accountant that are important. Will the woman be able to continue to use her own name? Will the couples' taxes go up or down if they are married? Or not married? If married, will the woman's income be treated as incidental and taxed totally? If she works only in the home, is she prepared to stick it out for ten years before the divorce so that she has some claim on her husband's Social Security benefits?

The dewy-eyed couple would be wise to seek guidance on such matters as who will give up seniority privileges on the job by staying home to care for the children, and whose job will determine where the family lives.

The most useful way to begin such a discussion is to attempt to work out who will do the housework. That topic is almost always clarifying, although with the number of out-of-wedlock couples these days it would seem that the issue should have been resolved long before marriage. Alas, romance is romance, and one of the principal aspects of romance is the belief that it will all be better later.

I am, in fact, no longer the authority on romance that I once was. I have recently fallen quite peacefully in love, and my experience is now somewhat outside the mainstream. My friends can no longer count on me for sympathetic cynicism. I now say things like, "You threw leek soup in his face? Whatever for?" and, "So, he didn't come home for three nights. Obviously you weren't meant for each other. Why waste time on it?" There is no firmer division of understanding than that between the happily settled and the miserably mated.

I am not yet ready to report the triumph of hope over experience, but just in case this lasts for a while, I would like to pass on my major rule of modern romance before all memory fades. If you are thinking of marrying, be sure to marry a man you would want to be divorced from. Forget the white lilacs, the round-trip tickets to Acapulco, the nights spent wading in fountains.

Acapulco can come later. What you need first is a man who will help solve the problems of the broken home. Does he pay his bills? Does he send the checks out in time? Will he walk the dog and does he play Monopoly with other people's children? When he says he will be there at eight, is he there by at least eight thirty? Do you like the other women in his life? Especially his previous wife, whom you will eventually get to know much better than you know him.

Is he, in short, what Mother used to call a nice family man? Mother, it turns out, was right.

We tried to live the way we always heard it should be, and we discovered, are still discovering, that sooner or later we have to learn to be just ourselves, by ourselves. I hope there will not be many more women who will have to file late reports that they are trying to grow up, despite the accumulated complications of thirty-odd years.

Last month a friend of mine, a settled, long-married friend, was driving me to a supermarket in her station wagon. She was embarrassed by her car, called it her portable cage. We were like two women with our noses pressed against opposite sides of the same windowpane.

"But I want a station wagon with a baby seat in the back," I said, a self-pitying sob caught in my throat.

"But you are free," she said. "You can do anything you want."

"But I'm lonely," I said, the sob a little closer to the air. "Free for what?"

"We . . . ell," said my friend, "you can sleep with anyone you want."

How very groovy. Italian counts, English bankers, Idaho cowboys, rock stars—the whole smorgasbord, mine for the tasting, because I am free. Never mind that they are all theoretically as available to her as they are to me. Never mind, because that is not the way it works out. The smorgasbord has its own problems, and it does not find its way to anyone's front door automatically. Even if it did, I can think of better reasons for freedom than that. I have not spent the last fifteen years growing up just so I could screw around.

Fifteen years ago I had never earned my own living, never taken a trip alone, never taken total responsibility for a single decision. The only time I ever tried to give a speech, I fainted. I had been divorced once, and lasted four months before I remarried in a fit of terror. I had never gone to a party by myself, never even gone to the movies by myself. I wanted to run away from home, but I felt I had to ask permission.

Luckily, no one gave me permission. I had to learn all by myself and I had taken such a preposterously long time in starting that I probably overdid my efforts to stand alone without crutches. It was perhaps not necessary to reject the notion of alimony, to stop speaking to my parents, to gain thirty-five pounds, and to remain solely attached—although unmarried—to a kind man who lived 250 miles away.

The only thing I had ever done was write, so I moved myself and my son to New York and wrote. I learned to give parties and go to the movies, to pay my own bills and to give speeches. I could probably walk through brick walls now if I had to. I could say that I simply had to do it and so I did and, having done it, learned that I could. But that would be denying all the friends who helped me, and the fact that it was hard and brave.

And so, it comes as an annoying shock, after all that effort and struggle, to discover that the ability to walk through brick walls is not a helpful talent when it comes to resolving the still hopelessly entangled problems of love and sex. I have spent the last fifteen years learning I could be alone. But I also learned why I would rather not be. And then what?

It seems logical at this point to talk about my bed. Twelve years ago I bought a brass bed in London. The man who ran the shop on Kensington Church Street told me the bed was too large and too high to be of any use to anyone, so I paid him thirty dollars and shipped it home for fifty dollars. I was a bride then, and I imagined that I would conceive and bear children between the bed's plain but comforting ends, and grow old companionably and finally die peacefully upon the embroidered sheets the bed deserved and would eventually receive. It turned out that my imagination overstepped the limits of my experience with married life.

The bed has lost some parts here and there, and needs polishing more often than not, but it has by now acquired its own symbolic meaning, more appropriate to the life I live. My bed is my best friend. I live in it, and it accommodates itself agreeably to my unreasonable habits. It does not mind when I huddle in its center for a week's midwinter depression, or when I abandon it for the summer. I type in it, telephone in it, think in it, and stare at the wall from it. Some morning, a long time from now, I hope I will be found peacefully dead in it, lying in a narrow but cozy space between old manuscripts, lost books, empty teacups, misplaced nightgowns, and unsharpened pencils. In the meantime, my bed patiently accepts my occasional clearances of the debris of daily life, my festive efforts with flowered (not embroidered) sheets. It knows that a man is a better companion than a typewriter.

But I know, now, that one is not so good without the other. The typewriter, the work, is fundamental. Without it, I hate myself and destroy everything in my path. But without sex, I can't concentrate enough to type. And without love, I do not look forward to tomorrow.

And so it was that my bed was the first to get the blame when, one summer, I drove away from another house and another bed, leaving a front door that was no longer ours, but his. I came back, quite surprised, to my own bed, to cry for a month, and explain, and turn over again each limp illusion searching for the mistake, and finally I decided there had been no mistake, only change, and what had been very good was no longer possible.

It was sad. For the first time I wished I were twenty-five again, when men were like streetcars and new beginnings seemed logical and hopeful. Instead, being thirty-six, I could find no satisfying drama in an ending, which at best could lead only to a new beginning. Logic and hope fade somewhat by thirty-six, when endings seem more like clear warnings than useful experience. I was sick of endings and distrusted beginnings. I wanted it all *settled*. I had believed it was.

"Always be on with the new love before you are off with the old."

Failure to follow that rule—which, like most maxims, refers only to the ideal arrangement and not the random schedulings of real life—results in an interim period of profound psychic imbalance. How unsettling then, how boringly, inconveniently, demeaningly unsettling, to find myself—again—in an interim period, susceptible to all the absurdities of our culture and to my own vulnerabilities. Instead of feeling twenty-five or acting thirty-six, I was sixteen and seventy-five.

I thought of sending my bed away. A tatami mat and a typing table were all I would be needing in the flat, gray plane of life stretching ahead of me. I could not bear my bed's hopeful presence. It looked so much more hopeful than I, who could not imagine the possibility of new beginnings offering themselves. Sleeping, or typing, or thinking could be done anywhere. And as for the rest, well, what was the point of keeping up the pretense? The cud of experience could be chewed at leisure while sitting on the rug, without the sight of that brassy, tarty old bed reminding me that the part of my life that made a bed a necessity was over.

Over. Nothing good—that is, sexy, compelling, romantic— would ever happen again. We never look back when we are happy, but I was miserable, and a nostalgic tour through lost memories, courtesy of Madison Avenue, seemed better than a view of the flat, gray plane ahead. Magazine ads showing lithe young girls crossing the footbridge to the Ile St.-Louis . . . ah! I would never again be twenty-three and in love in Paris. (I considered taking satisfaction in the fact that at least I had once been twenty-three and in love, in Paris yet, but that seemed really grasping at the resigned contentment of old age.) Ads showing happy couples flinging themselves about in meadows—ah! *hélas!* The meadowlands are swampy bogs for me now. "Show her you care . . . give her diamonds, dinner, cars, a new vacuum cleaner." I bought myself a new vacuum cleaner, paid a hundred dollars of my own money for it, and in another context and another month that would seem a minor but pleasurable accomplishment. But not that month: I was one of the Vulnerables, on the outs with the entire American economy, exquisitely sensitive to its most relentlessly clever mechanism, the steady rhythmic programmed tweaking on the collective nerves of what we have been led to understand means *love.*

I began to spend all night in bed with the radio. The stations that played songs like "A Small Hotel" blended into 2:00 A.M. fantasies (I was waltzing in a red satin dress, the most admired woman in the world . . .) Stop! Turn the dial to Stravinsky. (Now I am playing the cello, and everyone is applauding.) I was past the age of blank obsession, but I was appalled that narcissistic Romance was still the first refuge of my lonely fantasies. I tried being culturally adolescent. I read Yeats. "When I am old and gray . . ."

Oops. Wrong poet. I thought of hard, angular subjects: the gross national product, atomic physics, Republican politics. My hand crept back to the dial, switching over to "Tonight you're mine . . . com-plete-ly." (I am softly, gently, passionately . . .)

Now really! This is absurd. Soon I will be one of those people who walk down the street being perfectly charming in conversations with themselves. What is the matter with me?

I think I have identified the problem. I need to get laid. No wonder I feel flat, gray, unused—like a wad of well-chewed gum. Maybe a brisk shower and a run around the park to get the blood flowing? Phooey. Perhaps a severe concentration on a serious subject? Damn it, I said I want to get laid. Who can work? The brain cells are degenerating. I can only focus on the . . . ummm . . . textures of things. Very odd ideas begin to float along. If there were icemen these days I would consider one of them. As it is, the doorman is beginning to seem quite an amiable seventy-two-year-old alcoholic. I enjoy going to the dentist—it is so tactile. Old address books, lost in back drawers, seem full of promise. I am definitely in need. Many of my sisters speak well of masturbation. Why not? But why bother? What I need is a warm body.

What is stopping me? This is, after all, the age of the sexual revolution. What is the big problem?

The big problem is, I don't know how to go about it. I am pretty sure that sitting listlessly on my bed is not, even in the age of sexual revolution, a reliable way to attract a sexual experience. But I was raised in the fifties, and the one absolutely unbreakable rule, guiding and controlling all contacts with the opposite sex, was *never call a man*. I still believe that if I pick up the phone and dial a man, my hand will grow warts and I may even go blind or insane.

Which brings me (just briefly) to sex—the great inequality, the great miscalculator, the great Irritator. But it's too large a subject. It's not till sex has died out between a man and a woman that they can really love. And now I mean affection. Now I mean to be *fond of* (as one is fond of oneself)—to hope, to be disappointed, to live

inside the other heart. When I look back on the paint of
sex, the love like a wild fox so ready to bite, the antag-
onism that sits like a twin beside love, and contrast it
with affection, so deeply unrepeatable, of two people
who have lived a life together (and of whom one must
die) it's the affection I find richer. It's that I would have
again. Not all those doubtful rainbow colors. (But then
she's old, one must say.)

Enid Bagnold's *Autobiography*
(Atlantic—Little, Brown)

I belong to a generation of women who are doomed to stagger
forever down the thin line between our upbringing and our now
allowable, indeed heavily overencouraged, inclinations. We were
raised not to do it, and now we are urged and exhorted to do it—
continuously, enthusiastically, and expertly. We know, and we are
too confused to admit, that if we don't do it, we lose the spring in
our step and the roses in our cheeks, but if we *do* do it, as pre-
scribed, we will suffer not only various psychic disabilities but regular cycles of the full range of vaginal disorders from fungi to cys-
titis and worse. On the whole, we would prefer the more occasional
ecstasies of monogamy.

We are the only generation who really understands that sex is
the great paradox: the most universally available way to transcend
our lumpen bodies and unpoetic lives, but also the surest way to
reveal our most embarrassing absurdities. What is more incandes-
cently splendid than the morning after an unexpectedly successful
one-nighter? But what is more absurd, more essentially vulgar,
than feeling horny?

Is it possible that other women, presumably not raised under
telephone interdiction, really behave like the (male, I presume)
screenwriters' versions of women? What would happen if *I* drove
into a gas station, gave the mechanic a big smile, and said, "Hiya,
good-lookin', wanta fuck?" Would it be any easier than saying,
"Hello there, would you like to go to the movies?" Eighteen-year-
old women can do it, and their tongues don't turn black. My tongue
would turn black. Maybe I could put an ad in some discreet literary

journal saying, "Ms. O'Reilly will be auditioning new lovers from two to four on Tuesdays."

Why, come to think of it, is Ms. O'Reilly's romantic calendar so remarkably empty? I am intelligent, self-supporting, a good mother, and I laugh enough. I can also cook, sew, bake, and put up preserves, if those talents should prove an additional incentive. But I live in New York City, which has—for some curious reasons of demographic fallout—fewer men one would consider even having lunch with, much less sleeping with, than any other city in the world. Those few are mostly married, and those that are coming back on the market are snapped up before they hit the ground.

Anyway, I am not looking for a husband. I am looking for immediate sensual gratification. What do men do? We imagine, less accurately than we think, that they keep dialing until they find someone—the point is, *anyone*—who also needs help making it through the night. A kind of sexual ablution, good for clearing out the system.

What did I do? I left my bed, flew three thousand miles, pretended to be primarily concerned with interviewing for a story, found—among the interviewees—a desirable sexual partner, and naturally, I fell in love. "Listen," I said, in a burst of mature insight, "I'm madly in love with you, but it's nothing personal and I'll get over it soon. It's simply a temporary fulfillment of a psycho-physiological need. Entirely temporary." I now think that was a peculiar thing to say, although not a bad thing to know. It turns out that more often than is absolutely necessary a piece of ass is a piece of self, and when we give it away, we want something in exchange.

At least, I want something in exchange. Flowers, passionate declarations, repeat performances, lifelong respect and admiration come immediately to mind, along with highly detailed visions of rose-covered cottages and twenty-fifth wedding anniversaries. When I am once more back in my own bed, alone with the gum wrappers and overflowing ashtrays, I manage to reduce my demands to more reasonable and modern expectations. I will settle for a postcoital postcard, the odd phone call, a jolly handshake, any message of reaffirmation of friendship. Why can't a man at least let us know he *noticed*? Probably because he is terrified we will start pushing mash notes through his mail slot. Probably some of us will, sometimes. Perhaps he, or we, should have thought of that possibility beforehand. Not that it would help.

I used to believe that nothing ruined a good friendship as thoroughly as taking it to bed. I had good reason to believe it. When I remember the humiliations, the confusions, the expenditure of misplaced energy that followed my compulsion to equate agreeable sex with love's inevitable blossoming, I realize that it had more to do with masochism and a displaced sense of myself than anything remotely like friendship. Now the cards and flowers and friendship can and do arrive, because I like myself. I can afford to choose. I can even consider someone who likes me without undue suspicion or gratitude. If I like someone who turns out not to like me, I can shrug my shoulders, mutter, "Oh, well, it's his loss," and go back to my work.

Eventually, under strong discipline, I can do that. At the immediate moment, there is no consolation at all in the wizardry of self-confidence. At the immediate moment, be it beginning or end, I spend the same number of long incapacitated hours staring hopefully at the telephone. For a while I thought there might be safety in numbers. I overbooked the bedroom, hoping for a placid dilution of emotion. Instead, I got hung up on everybody, spent long hours waiting for three phone calls instead of one. I couldn't even keep the cast of my fantasies straight. My rather mild version of a Molière comedy—doors opening and closing, overlapping romantic allusions—was exhilarating, but it quickly became confusing and it seemed not entirely to my point. Apparently it is not in my character to appreciate distraction.

> *"The healthy aging woman normally has sex drives that demand resolution."*
> William H. Masters and Virginia E. Johnson.
> *Human Sexual Response*, Little, Brown.

That is not exactly my idea of good news. Falling in love is a sure way to revive the vital functions, to keep life fresh and to feel sixteen again. But I can't afford to be sixteen again many more times. It takes up too much of life. Not the sex. The side activities. The tremulous quivering. The hours spent sitting on the bed with a nonringing phone. The hours spent replaying the conversation if the phone rings and then resolving the subsequent profound dilemmas, such as: should I put the wine in the icebox now, in case he drops in, or should I leave it out so I seem cool and unexpectant? How many more times can I go though the ritual of rearranging the books on my night table so they form a pleasing, possibly impressive panorama of my private intellectual life? Sweep away the mysteries, bring out *An Invitation to Phenomenology*. Hide the hole in the quilt, take down *The Life of Mozart*. Most women get new nightgowns for a serious new lover. I usually burn someone else's old love letters. Later, I always wish I hadn't.

I practiced and practiced taking the sexual initiative. Finally, I managed to utter the equivalent of "Hiya, good-lookin'" without choking. I learned to recognize and suppress my residual instincts for false drama and unreasonable demands, and I discovered that the phone always rings again if it was worth it, and if it doesn't ring soon enough, a little friendly prompting that fails is insufficient reason for character disintegration.

Unfortunately there are not ten easy steps to sexual security. The first giant step is to like yourself enough to pick someone who likes you too. The next step is to realize that all the useful, cool, and collected lessons will have to be learned again the next time. It's anarchy out there!

These days, there are some surprises along the way. All that emotional flux was absurd enough before we began to question ourselves, to wonder if we really needed men, and if so (yes, so) then what New Arrangements would have to be made? Now that our own consciousness has been raised, and that of the better men, the situation is, well, sometimes different. Once, wafting spontaneously toward my bed, liberated at last, I heard a slow shuffle and an ominous mumble behind me. "Well, gee, do you act like this all the time? I mean, uh, I don't usually . . . ummm. Let's just talk for a while. I'm really very shy, and you are a feminist after all, and. . . ." What was this? Some new and clever way to push the male ego up front again? Has this very nice man read too many reports of "liberationist sexual demands"? Is he, after all, a stickler for domination instead of mutuality? No. It turns out he is making a real effort to express hitherto forbidden hesitancies and feelings. How horrible and terrifying it must have been all those years to be a man, always forced to take the initiative, always vulnerable to rejection. But I was unprepared for this crossing on our different routes to consciousness.

It is very hard, adjusting ourselves to the New Assumptions, and not at all the way it seems to women who are not on the open market, but apparently think the open market might be a fun place to be. I explained to my friend who thought freedom meant sexual diversity that I did not really want a station wagon with a baby seat in the back. I had already had one at the appropriate time, and it is not a beginning I would welcome again if it meant I had to trade in anything else. But I wish that I could have had both— my life now and the life I planned when I bought my bed as a bride in London. I explained to her that what I really envied was that she seemed to be, from my side of the windowpane, one of the lucky ones whose early choices made it possible for her to start over, work it through, find herself, with what she had, without having to leave. It will take a long time for me to collect again what she already has, and I will need it. Sooner or later, life stops being a question of happiness depending on a straightened-out psyche, and it starts being real. Friends die, children get sick, desperate, and unaccountable—still less avoidable—tragedies occur, and when they do, a typewriter on the other half of the bed is proof that we can cope, but it is lonely comfort.

"Aha," said my friend, "but it's not sex you want. It is love."

Of course.

The men who were boys when I was a girl used to be able to dance. They never danced with me, and at the time I took it hard.

Now, looking through the merciful veil of time, I can explain my years as a wallflower by believing that the reason the boys never danced with me was because they were all lined up trying to dance with two girls named Frisky and Gigi.

Those girls' fairy godmothers had bestowed on them such bonuses as naturally curly hair, naturally rosy lips, and naturally tiny feet. They were perky. I had straight black hair and a straight dark scowl. I am willing to admit, now, that Frisky and Gigi were more fun.

They danced, while I sat in my best blue taffeta on a small gilt chair at the edge of the room. I scowled because it was not especially encouraging to watch a recalcitrant youth being propelled toward me by a determined chaperon's fist placed firmly between his shoulder blades. It would have been useful if someone had told me that a smile instead of a scowl might make the youth less reluctant. But, at that time, girls did not confide their secrets of success to each other.

Every evening of dancing class was a chapter of my life titled "The Agony of the Empty Dance Card." I filled in those cards by myself, ignominiously, after the dance. Perhaps I pretended they had been filled in before, gloriously, by eager suitors, because I have them all pasted into scrapbooks. I haven't fooled myself yet. I remained unpopular through the basic box step, through the tango, beyond the conga and the Charleston, into and including the grapevine step of the waltz.

Even now I cannot hear "Tea for Two" or "A Tree in the Meadow" without developing sweaty palms. At the same time, my feet—responding to different reflexes—break into a box step. I remember, whenever I hear "Just One of Those Things," why I was willing to face failure over and over again. It was because every so often someone who could really dance would be forced to ask me to dance. And dancing was worth it all.

As I remember (and my memory is flawless on these matters), I met my first love at a dance. The band was playing "La Vie en Rose," and I found myself dancing with a boy who had red hair, chestnut eyes, and a perfect sense of rhythm.

After some months of perfect compatibility, he went to college. I remained in high school and, more specifically, in the ladies' room with the rest of the wallflowers. We played bridge and adjusted our strapless bras and formed lasting friendships. I would trace my feminism to those early outcast evenings, except that we never seemed to have considered that sisterhood might be powerful enough to allow us to ask someone to dance ourselves.

The years passed. I grew, struggled, raised my consciousness and developed my potential, and at last became strong enough to ask men to dance. And almost none of them could. Some of them would, but that isn't the same thing.

Recently I met a man who could dance. We happened to be at a dance at the time, an event almost rarer than meeting a man who can dance. I am not talking about discos and other manifestations of the existential solitude of modern life. I am talking about *dancing:* arms around each other, leading and following, dipping and twirling. Well, this man I met really could dance. Instantly, we were Fred Astaire and Ginger Rogers.

By the time we had worked our way through a samba, I knew I had discovered the limits of my liberation. Racks and thumbscrews, ridicule and contempt, could never make me stop believing that women should be equal, independent, and assertive. But bring me a man who can dance, and sisterhood goes glimmering. In the first place, I cannot dance by myself. I never graduated to toe shoes in ballet class. In fact, I never really thoroughly mastered fifth position at the *barre.* I could not possibly lead even the box step. But I am a born follower. It is bliss to relax and be managed and become part of someone else's rhythmic imagination.

In the second place, I will do absolutely anything to keep a man who can dance dancing with me.

"He's my husband and I want to dance with him too," said the wife of the man who could dance. She plucked wistfully at his sleeve. I snatched him away. "Oh no, you can't be married to him and dance with him too," I said. Any specious logic will do in a crisis. For all I knew, she married him only because he could dance.

I managed to keep him dancing, with me, all evening by applying the oldest sexist trick—flattery. "Wonderful, marvelous, heavenly, best ever, never before," etc. We whirled around and around, and to every woman standing glowering and non-dancing around the floor, I threw a Significant Glance, the one that means "I've got a live one and you don't. Nyah, nyah." It had taken me thirty years, but at last I knew how Frisky and Gigi had really felt. They felt terrific.

The next day I reported the news to my friends. "I met a man who can dance," I said, and they gasped and exclaimed and each one offered her own memory of such an event.

"I met a man who could dance once," said Diana. "It was the year after I graduated from school and we went to the Rainbow Room. It was wonderful. We never saw each other again."

"I waltzed once in Boston with a man who was seventy-two," said Louisa, "but I never met another man who could dance, not even in Cairo during the war."

I remembered that I had met other men who can dance. Three other men, to be precise. One was named Peter and he danced with me in my living room, and although it was only fourteen feet square and I was married and nine months pregnant—perhaps because of that—I will never forget that he made me feel like the seventeen-year-old I never was.

One was named Miguel, and we were both at a dance so far out in the country that we could not gracefully leave, although the company was very dull. When he found that I could dance, he kept me for the evening. When the music finally ended, he bowed, kissed my hand, and disappeared with his wife.

The last was named—well, it's better not to say—but I met him on a ship. It is possible to dance all night, every night, on a ship, and we did. I count that cruise as the happiest two weeks of my life. Well . . . very close to the happiest.

That makes five men, all told, who could dance. My friends tell me that five is each woman's lifetime quota, the modern world being what it is. I am sure they cannot be right. If we start right now, making sure that our sons learn to dance, perhaps they will be willing to twirl us around in a waltz step once in a while. If we ask them.

It says right here on my Liberated Women's Appointment Calendar: "February 29: Leap Year Day. Propose to the person of your choice."

So I did. "No," he said.

Then I proposed to my second, third, fourth, and fifth choices. Then I moved onto column B and proceeded further to Random Selections.

They all said "No." They said: "I can't face commitment," and "I want to be alone," and "Sorry, I already have a wife." I would have settled for a good laugh and an alternative offer, something like a movie or lunch. What I got was No, and however they said it, they used the frozen, flat, final tone men use for rejection, just in case I wasn't joking.

As a matter of fact, I don't know if I was joking. But I know one thing now, you don't joke around about natural law. Even on leap year, when the law that women don't ask for what they want (what they want is always assumed to be a man) is traditionally suspended. Women have been trying to ask for what we want for about the last two hundred years. It will probably take men a couple of centuries longer to learn to say yes.

It is extraordinarily absurd to consider the fact that for centuries all men have been trained to ask, and all women have been trained to wait. If we don't wait, we spoil their fun, ruin their sense of role, nip the achievement of pursuit and conquering.

An example of the resulting dichotomy in interpersonal relations once occurred during the postgame locker-room interviews after a Super Bowl.

"Good luck in your quest," wished the crazed interviewer to a player who had just admitted to being a bachelor. And then, to the next hapless player he said, "No one's put her brand on you yet, right?" In this confusion of attitude women cannot win. The trouble is, neither can men.

During my leap year quest for rejection, I did get one unqualified "maybe." But the man lives in Alaska and the logistics seemed somewhat difficult. But if I seriously wanted to marry, wouldn't I be willing to move to Alaska? Do I really want to marry? That is probably the most often asked question in my peer group.

Married women are especially opposed to the idea that marriage might be a comfortable institution. Widows are particularly fierce in their determination never to be trapped again, perhaps because they do not have the failure of divorce to redress. We all shrug our shoulders and say, "Oh, no, I guess not actually marry, just live with, or feel close to, or have someone to love." And then we quote Flo Kennedy's line: "A woman without a man is like a fish without a bicycle."

But I notice we all marry as soon as someone we like wants us to. "Being in love" is still like an apple orchard in bloom. "We" is still a word that feels like butterscotch sauce on the tongue. Women are enthralled by the idea of commitment. Men are terrified of it.

I don't know why. I think commitment is kind of liberating, myself. It is very supportive and frees the energies for other things. I don't know why men see it as a bear trap, and I would like to know, but they never speak up in the conversations about marriage and relationships.

Maybe they are afraid if they offer an opinion, they will wake up the next morning to find themselves responsible for a family, a mortgage, and a half-baked feminist who says, "I demand to be treated as a person, and by the way, who am I?"

We are all, most of us, half-baked feminists, still depending on a man to provide fulfillment and self-definition and approval. As Elizabeth Friar Williams, author of *Notes of a Feminist Therapist*, says: "The moment she attaches herself in a committed way to a man, a woman in love often begins to see herself as society sees her—that is, as inferior to him." Theoretically, it will come as a great relief to men, too, when women see themselves as equals.

Perhaps a fourteen-year-old of my acquaintance is already

such a woman. She refuses to believe that there was ever such a bizarre and negative idea as leap year. She believes if God hadn't meant girls to call boys, the telephone would not have been invented. "Well, if someone doesn't like me the way I am, I don't want him," spoke this person-of-the-future.

I no longer remember why I believed that love was a necessary component, or cause, or effect, of equality. I now think love is somewhat beside the point.

Ease up, men told me. They said that I was too energetic, too eager. They said I had spoiled the joy of pursuit. They complained that I did all the heavy lifting in the affair (and I did; I thought love was giving, but now I see that taking, insisting on being given to, is just as important). And then they told me they felt trapped. They couldn't take yes for an answer.

O readers, spare me the cards and letters with helpful hints and wise explanations of where I went wrong. I can make those lists myself.

Where I went wrong: once men complained that I didn't do enough. They meant I did not do enough for them because I was not a full-time housewife. Now they complain that I do too much for them *and* I want too much. How many more years and generations will pass before the assigning of needs and wants finally stops resulting in the woman being the guilty one? Before we stop thinking of a relationship as a situation in which one person must be the winner and the other the loser?

So I want too much. Well, let's see, what do I want? I want to share my life. I want to eat English muffins together on Sunday mornings. Sometimes. I want to have a place in someone's life, and to have him have a place in mine. I want stability, cooperation, and commitment.

What I do not want: to be supported, to be given an identity, to have my dog walked. I don't need someone else to give me security.

"Well," men say, "if we can't be dominant, what can we be?" And women say: "Equal."

And some of the men try being equal for a while, because women have changed, despite men's amusement and consternation, and men have to respond. They feel awfully brave about it. For a while the balancing act works: her friends, his friends, her house, his house, her children, his children, their children, her work, his work. Her feelings, his feelings. He likes to discuss his feelings. It makes him think he has changed.

Men consider it very new to say to women: "Why don't you women ever talk about men's problems?" It is, in fact, the same old question. Men have always considered that the proper concern of women is men and their problems. That women and men no longer have this concern in common is one of the things men see as a problem.

The effort fails. "Feelings" turns out to be the new word for the old overinflated ego, a new weapon for passive-aggressive resistance to change. She begins to suspect a kind of malevolent insensitivity behind his endless willingness to talk about his confusion and damaged emotions, while remaining absolutely unwilling to change, to take responsibility for himself.

He begins to feel she wants too much, which means she wants something he hasn't been trained to expect or to give. If he can't dominate, he withdraws (sometimes he calls it jogging). He decides and then announces, "I don't know how to love," and she accuses him of finding a poetic metaphor for selfishness, lack of commitment, and fear of intimacy. Eventually he goes off to find another woman, who, if she has not learned to recognize the line as a clear warning, sets about trying to teach him how to love. Again. Sometimes he gives up, just as many women do, and decides it is easier to be alone.

The men who say they do not know how to love speak the simple truth. Love, for men, used to be handing over the paycheck and having the final word. They have not yet had time to realize that they have been released from a tremendous burden if they are no longer expected to spend their lives solely supporting women and children. Instead of learning to share responsibility, they are still grieving for their lost authority. Some of them have abandoned responsibility altogether. They feel crippled and resentful, selfish and inadequate, vulnerable to an adolescent notion of love that involves a more chaotic assault on their emotional equilibrium than the most romantic woman has ever dreamed of.

When they murmur, as explanation, "I'm not sure I know what love is," they mean they are afraid of what they think it is. Impossibly idealistic, men imagine love as something frightening and weakening, something that will devour them, that can never be lived up to. They fear love as something that interrupts life and somehow endangers and diminishes the lover. They withdraw; and women are supposed to coax them out. We are expected to try to understand and explain what love is. We are, in other words, supposed to do all the heavy lifting in the affair.

We have to stop. Women have to withdraw ourselves now—not only because men can gain the use of their atrophied emotions only by learning for themselves, but also because we have other important things to do.

"But wait," men say before we reach the door, wanting us to go over it one more time, "what do you women want?" (They seem to think it is a new question.) "What," they ask, "would you want your son to be like when he grows up?" Okay, all right, I have time for that question.

I don't want my son to grow up dismissing people because of their sex, or color, or class, or religion. I do not want him to expect that women have been placed on earth to serve him, nor do I want him to feel that women—because a woman raised him and introduced him to the world—are responsible for all the ills of the human condition. I want him to take responsibility for his own life and to be able to share it, not least because if he cannot he will drive away the woman who tries to share it with him. I hope he will be able to love and to know that love is something that involves faith, reciprocity, honor, and commitment: something that grows as it is used.

You say I haven't exactly given you any solid guidelines?

Well, I would also like my son to rise, without thinking too much about it, and to go into the kitchen and start making lunch if the other people in the house are hungry, even if some of them are women. I would hope he could approach the same degree of spontaneity about laundry and shopping. I hope he doesn't think children are interesting only after they are toilet trained. I hope he gets into the college he wants to attend, but if he doesn't, I hope he doesn't think a woman or a minority man took away his rightful place. I hope he will change the system, not simply accept it.

I am told that a few men are already like that. Men under thirty, say, can go out to dinner with a woman without feeling they have lost their manhood if they don't pay. Younger men have different ideas about success and ambition, I am told, and they know more women as people (although not yet as equals).

But most older men are cast in stone—and I fear they are raising a lot of sons who are like them. Sometimes I think women over thirty-five are like the survivors of world wars. There are no partners left for us. We will have to make the best of such bits of love as come our way, and get on with it. We will have our friends.

Some of my friends are men, and I suppose that is something new. We have let down our role barriers; we are not simply sex objects to each other. We take each other seriously. But then, these men were always tender and pleasant. And, it occurs to me, while they don't mind hanging around with a feminist, they still wouldn't want to marry one.

In short, I seem to have a cognitive dissonance problem. I keep reading about the New American Man, and I can't find one. I asked my men friends about signs of change. "No, I haven't seen any," they said complacently. "Most men still think in the same dreary categorical terms."

I surveyed the suburbs, seeking change. A friend thought she had noticed some. "Oh, I think men are more aware of the ways they behave toward women. They are beginning to do a few pans now and then; they are more patient about our troubles. They are even beginning to make sorrowful noises about what they want out of life."

The New American Man, I am assured, has stopped moving his family every ten months because the corporation demanded it. If he had kept moving at that rate, he would have been dead by now so I cannot really count his refusal to continue as a deep inner recognition of his human potential. He has started to use makeup. Nice for the economy, but scarcely an exchange of old values for newer, better values. He takes care of his kids, sometimes, and the other men don't kid him about it. He doesn't mind, sometimes, if the wife wants to work, as long as it doesn't interfere with his career or comforts, and he doesn't mind helping out around the house.

I cannot deny that these concessions are new, but the use of the word "helping" makes me wonder if they represent any basic change. "Helping" implies that the woman is still totally in charge of domestic arrangements. Five years ago a man who occasionally dealt with a pot or pan might have seemed to be taking a big leap forward toward equality. Not anymore.

Murmurs and whimpers and tiny first steps on the private level cannot obscure the obdurate stonewalling going on at the public level. Men, the so-called new men and the old men who never questioned their dominance, are still the people making public policies. And those policies—in case you have been too busy teaching men to love and children to cross the streets alone to notice—are presently directed toward obstructing our right to choose abortion, letting the Equal Rights Amendment die unpassed, maintaining women at half the wage level of men, and ignoring the fact that three-quarters of the poor in this country are women and children.

That is why I feel love is somewhat beside the point. Love is nice. It is better to feel it than not to feel it. But after all, even the achievement of the perfect orgasm won't do a damn bit of good for the women who follow after us.

III.

But Who Will Take Care of the Children?

THE POLITICAL

The prince—a resident prince, an elusive prince, even a prince who can dance—does not seem to be the promised key to living happily ever after.

So, we must figure out another way to live happily ever after.

It is not yet clear what that way might be (we live, after all, in a period described as "rapid change"), but the interim guidelines suggest that people—men and women—might more successfully pursue happiness if we are free, each of us, to define happiness for ourselves.

This is a very radical idea.

The princes had assumed that feminine happiness lay in the home. The particular model they had in mind was a suburban split-level in which Dick, Jane, Spot, and color-coordinated laundry facilities were tended unceasingly by a happy woman as though it was all her very own.

The picture was not unappealing (an ideal, in a consumer economy, had better be appealing). Those women who found themselves in such a situation felt neurotic if they were not content. The far, far greater number of women who lived differently felt, with varying frequency, pangs of deprivation.

Throughout the history of the United States, the ideal of "woman's place" has been evoked, thundered from pulpits both religious and secular. The reality, the way most women actually lived, has always been different, as it is now. More than half of us now have jobs (a change, all agree, which, even in a period of rapid change, amounts to a social revolution). Married, unmarried, mothers, old, young—we work. We also—and this is often unacknowledged—work at home, whether we have a paying job or not.

Millions of us are now displaced homemakers, women with no other job training who stayed at home and discovered—when we were widowed or divorced—that what we did at home was not considered "work" because it was not paid and that the property we had tended, because we had not "contributed" to its purchase, was not necessarily considered half ours.

Only 7 percent of all Americans live, at any given time, in an "ideal" family: working father, nonworking mother, two children at home. The other families group themselves differently: empty nests, single parents, working mothers, spinsters with cats, curmudgeons with canes, the Brady bunches, reconstituted households of halves, steps, formers, and presents.

Why, in our society of 218.5 million people, is it assumed that slightly more than half of this infinitely diverse population—the women—are *all* happiest at home, an assumption that denies both the necessities and inclinations of millions of women, and consigns us all to the status of casual labor in the work force?

Because women have the babies.

This achievement is always spectacular. But it is not something all women do, or a process that occupies a lifetime. It does, however, involve the continuing presence of a child who must be raised, a task that our society—despite its sentimental protestations—has always considered no fit occupation for a grown man. So deep is the repugnance to the notion of caring for children that it has extended into contempt for motherhood, and finally to potential mothers—women.

It is here that we cross the line from the personal to the political.

Suddenly, it seems reasonable to stop arguing with the prince and to start questioning the kingdom, the society that poses as insoluble the question: "But who will take care of the children if women work?"

The leaps of logic involved in this social conundrum lead to further riddles. I imagine a lot of frogs leaping aimlessly around an ostrich with its head hidden firmly beneath the stone of the unexamined first principle: someone must care for the children. The frogs peep insistently but unpersuasively: women have babies; therefore women care for children. Women care, therefore the fulfillment of the eight beatitudes is women's sacred duty. Sacred duty is not paid work, therefore men will do the paid work, which includes thinking, commerce, art, waging war, and other important aspects of civilization. Men are paid to do the important work, therefore men support women, who therefore do not need to be paid as much as men for comparable work. A woman too ill paid to support herself, and her children, should find a man. Because a woman can't work equally. Because she might have a baby.

An so on and so on. The solutions presently being offered to the problems of reality—women *are* working and children still need care—reflect all the perspicacity of the ostrich. Voices from the political right insist that all will be well if women go back home. This extremely convenient allocation of responsibilities became unwieldy the moment our society passed the subsistence level.

Day care, baby-sitters, Aid to Dependent Mothers, are inadequate solutions, not because they must be, but because of the assumptions behind the question. If women are the people in charge of caring, but caring is not seen as important, then no one will want to do it—*including women*. Those who need help are resented, those who provide help are despised, and the very existence of need becomes someone else's problem (the kind of problem that women should be solving). The connection between our immediate families and the human family is forgotten. The social contract breaks down.

It will not be renewed by the solutions women are presently attempting. College graduates wonder if they should choose a career or motherhood—a choice their grandmothers considered new and necessary. It is not a choice men are ever asked to make and therefore it does not change anything. This year's model of the ideal woman is Superwoman. She does it all: successful executive, wife, mother, feminist, gourmet cook, and public servant. In other words, a woman who has made no demand on institutions and men other than asking to be allowed to do more.

It is impossible to do it all.

Furthermore, the question is, in fact, insoluble if we continue to accept the definition of "work" as something arranged entirely for the convenience of the employer and not the worker, and if we continue to believe that some*one* must take care of the children.

Try it this way instead: some *two* must take care of the children. There now, look what we've got: a redefinition of work, a redefinition of male and female roles, a reallocation of responsibilities, a reordering of society's priorities.

See what I mean about the women's movement requiring us to question all our most basic assumptions?

Many sincere and concerned folks ask if we feminists have really considered the effects of the women's movement on the family, marriage, and society.

Well, yes, we have, and we feminists think family, marriage, and society are all going to be a good deal better off—in fact, darn near perfect—as soon as one or two little social upheavals we are working on have taken place. At the moment we are experiencing a slight delay because of the vast number of ways people define marriage, family, and society.

The particular kind of family we are arguing about here is the family with children. The only apparent point of agreement is that this family, keystone of society, is in trouble, and it is women's fault. Everything has always been women's fault, *toujours cherchez la femme*. But in the specific case of the women's movement, the fevered perception seems to be that we are dragging women out of their homes away from their children, luring them into lesbian liaisons, and undermining the self-respect of men. And more.

The fevered perception seems to be outrunning the facts. Several professionals, people who have spent years poring over census figures, tell me the family as we know it is not in as much trouble as everyone thinks. Mary Jo Bane, author of *Here to Stay*, a definitive study of the family today, says: "No evil movement is destroying the family. People still care for their children. If women are divorcing more because of the movement, it is not very significant. There is no evidence very many people are remaining childless. And there have always been a large number of children with one parent, due to a combination of death and divorce, but the difference now is that mothers and kids set up their own households instead of sending the kids off to Granny. It is striking to see how stable the family still is. People still see their relatives, and they keep married, at least to their second partner."

Dr. Paul C. Glick, senior demographer of the United States Census Bureau, says that most people who get divorced (about 38 percent of first marriages now end in divorce) remarry. "It is not the end of family life, it is a change," says Dr. Glick. "More people now accept divorce as a transition state to new family life."

Heather L. Ross and Isabel V. Sawhill reported in *Time of Transition: The Growth of Families Headed by Women*, published by the Urban Institute, that although the fastest growing type of family in America is mothers heading up their own households, single parenthood is typically a transition period in a woman's life, lasting perhaps three or four years before she remarries.

So. Marriage and the family are not disappearing. They are not even changing very much or very fast. This is not news to brighten a feminist's day. The family *must* change (I didn't say disappear, I said change) if anything else is to change.

There is something very wrong with an institution that so often disintegrates at the very point it is supposed to be the most useful. It is obviously absurd that we should marry, have children, get divorced, and then start the whole thing over in an even more difficult and complicated way. The "reconstituted" families of remarriage give statistical stability to the big picture. But the clue to what is wrong with the big picture lies in the "transition period to new family life," which is likely to be three or four years when a woman is caring for very small children. Nearly half the children born today will spend a significant part of their lives in a single-parent home. Raising a child or—worse—children, alone, is the wrong way to do it. It is too hard, not on the children—if recent studies mean anything—but on the mother. Of American women divorced and separated, only 4 percent receive alimony, and only 23 percent with children receive child support. Women earn, on the average, fifty-nine cents for every dollar men earn. And of all female-headed families, 41.8 percent live below the poverty level.

No wonder women remarry. Says Dr. Glick: "A woman with no resources wants to marry again." Togetherness is still the utilitarian answer to the problem of women's economic disadvantages. But why is it that the divorced people least likely to remarry are women in the upper income, upper education brackets? Because remarriage is still marriage. The new husband may be more agreeable, but the institutional arrangements, the emotional and economic dependency, which drive women to despair, or to drink, have not changed. The ones who take care of young children are, as a group, the ones who are the most depressed, most suicidal people in the United States.

Where can these people, the mothers of young children, turn for help? Keeping in touch with our relatives is not the same thing as being able to call on Aunt Sophie if the baby has a cold. Aunt Sophie now has a job and Granny lives in a mobile home in Oregon and she isn't very keen on child care. We depend on each other far more than the cruel adage "women don't help each other" insists. Without the help of other women I would not have survived as a single parent. But this is a mother's underground, which runs counter to the prevailing notion of the family as an isolated nucleus, free from interference, almost pioneer in its self-sufficiency. That notion of the family as an island not only withers the connections between families that form a community, it also makes women feel guilty about asking for help, which may partially explain why there are day-care places for only 20 percent of the children who need them in this country. Fifty-three percent of the mothers in this country work, five and a half million of them mothers of children under six. And women *still* do most of the housework.

Indeed, marriage and the family have not changed. Marriage is still an institution that depends on the oppression and exploitation of women in our service role. We are even poorer, more oppressed and exploited, outside of marriage, which is why many women are afraid of the women's movement, afraid it will end their only security before providing equal pay and equal opportunity.

Words like "oppression" and "exploitation" are not very romantic, but neither is the family as we know it particularly romantic. What might be freely given, built and shared by two equals, is instead demanded of the wife. What is wrong with the institution is, simply, that women are asked to do too much, rewarded too little, and have no alternatives.

Why do you think everyone's first response to the women's movement was the question: "But who will take care of the children?" Because no one else wanted to take care of the children, and if women were allowed the options of liberation we might quite wisely opt not to go on bearing the children and the burden of their care and the psychic burden of being expected to hold together the fabric of society, universally described as the Family. With options, women might choose to participate in the society instead of being fabric glue.

This reluctance to go on being the ones expected to raise the children did not spring from a reluctance to have the children. Most of us felt no primal repulsion at the notion of childbearing, and those of us who did were glad we could express it, and not respond to a social imperative to reproduce despite it. The reluctance sprang from the fact that more and more we were literally the only ones to raise the children. A natural source of supplementary skills would seem to be the fathers of the children, but that rather obvious notion has not yet gained very wide acceptance. Certainly I have not found many employers offering part-time jobs to their men employees (or even their women employees) so child care could be shared.

We are not talking about Alternative Life-Styles here. The suspect vocabulary of self-fulfillment skates too lightly above the institutional point. We are talking about women's enforced economic dependence. We are talking about the low value our society places on the provision of basic human services: care of the very young, the ill, the disabled, the old. And we are talking about attitudes toward women and the family as reflected in our public policies.

The individual, personal family is a cause of much continuing examination and anguish in America, but our collective policies show little comprehension that one family is only a unit of the society, which includes all families. Still less do we respect the idea that all the nation's children are the nation's future. Politician after politician promises to help the American Family, and the promises are quickly lost in bitter controversy. It turns out that there is no American Family, no sense of "we." There is only "us" versus "them." "Their" children, notably poor or black or native American or handicapped children, we think of as God's punishment to their parents for having done It, and therefore not our problem.

More specifically, those children, like all children, are considered their mothers' problem. But those children, like our own, will grow up to be the society we deserve. When advocates for children plead for help, they are answered by the men who make public policy, and who are strongly disinclined to spend money on a problem they think women should be solving, that the voters demand "realism," and that "the people don't want federal interference in their lives."

Money is, of course, still spent to help families. Pots of money, more than would be necessary for the purpose if the spending did not go around the point. Two hundred and sixty-eight federal programs in seventeen federal agencies provide direct financial assistance or services to individuals and families. One begins to suspect the existence of an infrastructure of vested interests when one discovers, in the somewhat murky tabulations of these agencies, that close to 500,000 children are in foster care at an average cost of $381 a month. Perhaps 440,000 children are in institutions at an average cost of $739 a month. But the average Aid to Families with Dependent Children payment is $254 a month. (The national average is not very helpful to a woman who lives in a state such as South Carolina, where payments average $88 a month.) Parents, most likely mothers, are distrusted, investigated, and generally held in contempt by the experts. It follows that those parents are not very much helped, which was supposed to be the point.

Twenty-five percent of our children live in poverty; there are fewer children now than there were in the 1960s, but more poor children; only half of the poor children in the United States receive any public assistance and four million children have two working parents and are still poor. Most of us, after serious reflection on those facts, can manage to see the virtues of such ideas as more voluntary day-care centers, prenatal care, nutritional assistance, and early diagnosis of handicaps. But can we keep ourselves from shrugging impatiently when publicly funded parent education programs are suggested?

Listen, knowing how to care for the baby does not come with the baby. Just as an example, many parents, living as we all do without the wisdom and support of an experienced extended family, literally do not know when a child might reasonably be expected to be toilet trained, and consequently bash the child in the hope that a little abuse will help. All families need help in raising children. All children, not just poor children, suffer from the chaos and inadequacies of our public programs of health care, education, and child care. The future of the entire country suffers. But poor children suffer the most.

———

When public policy chooses unemployment as more desirable than inflation, the effect on families is catastrophic. In 1976 Leonard Woodcock, then president of the United Automobile Workers, said: "Families are being broken up because of the incredible psychological strain—the loss of dignity and self-worth—that occurs when a worker can no longer bring home the paycheck that feeds and clothes the family." He described the rise of alcoholism, drug addiction, and child abuse that accompanies a rise in unemployment.

Woodcock was, at the time, talking about male heads of households, whose unemployment rate then was counted as 4.2 percent. Consider then the effect on households headed by women, whose unemployment rate in 1976 was 10.0 percent.

Every 1 percent of unemployment is estimated to cost $16 billion in welfare, unemployment insurance, and other forms of public support. The victims of unemployment are blamed for being a drain on the public till and treated to self-righteous speeches on the necessity of cutting back services. This approach is particularly unhelpful when unemployment does nothing at all to curb inflation.

One-fifth of the population in the United States owns three-quarters of the assets. Eleven percent of the population lives below poverty level. Obviously, whoever is benefiting from our economic policies, it is not the poor and powerless. It is not the workers and the families. It is probably only the top one-fifth.

A mother of six recently confided to a television audience that she did six or seven loads of wash a day. She also complained of feeling isolated. Remarkably, she did not seem to connect the two statements. In my mind, Mother of Six was an eloquent example of why privately owned washing machines must be abolished for the good of democracy.

I fully sympathize with those who feel this sacrifice is too great. All my life I have wanted a washing machine. Only recently has ideology become the reason I don't have one instead of the fact that in my apartment building the installation cost is twice the appliance cost. I love to browse through the washing-products section of my local supermarket. I take soap as a house gift when I am invited for weekends, and I beg to be allowed to do the family wash, reveling in the magic of dirty in—clean out. Wash and Dry and Delicate Cycles seem to me to be technology's highest achievement.

But washing machines have turned out to be another sad example of technological achievement being a mixed blessing. It is perfectly obvious that a woman who does six loads of wash a day has too many clothes or too large and lazy a family. She uses too much soap, water, and electricity. What is not so obvious is that she is at home with about $500 worth of inefficiently utilized machinery when she could be somewhere else being part of that desirable concept—a community.

We should build Laundromats the way the Romans built public baths. There should be a central, preferably vaulted hall full of washers and dryers and ironing boards. Other halls should be equipped as nurseries, gymnasiums, and pool halls. There could be bingo on Tuesdays and visits of political candidates on Thursdays. Perhaps even fish fries on Saturdays. Urban visionaries constantly suggest turning old railroad stations and warehouses into boutique complexes. Why not Laundromats instead?

The Laundromats we already have serve as effective community centers only in very poor rural or urban areas where the people have to hang around and do their own wash. After they have read the cards on bulletin boards offering free kittens, used baby beds, and shared life-styles, they sometimes talk, which makes Laundromats very good places for journalists to go to test public opinion.

But, community-center-wise, existing Laundromats are rarely comfortable and they are not very good places to plug into the world of ideas. In order to foster an intelligent and informed discussion of those issues crucial to a democratic society, it might also be a good idea to ban all television in the new Laundromats, and no one should be allowed to drop off wash for someone else to do.

It will be hardest for Americans to do without the television. Nations launder as they live. In the United States we have too many clothes, too many kittens, and too many private washing machines.

In Scotland the most nationally representative Laundromat I visited was in Edinburgh, where little old ladies called us one by one out of a waiting room as bleak as a county jail to take our turns at nice yellow secondhand American machines. There were no facilities for folding, apparently because the Scotch prefer to scurry modestly home with their wash unrevealed to prying eyes. Some scandal resulted from my willingness to display my clean knickers to the crowd.

In Paris scandal is an important part of the ambience. Every *laverie-automatique* always seems to have at least one romantic couple oblivious to the secrets told by their dirty linen. Usually they stand, arms entwined, gazing at the sheets twisting and turning behind the little window of the machines, as the couple themselves have apparently been doing only a short time before. A woman of sterner aspect always seems to be standing just behind them, starching collars.

In Italy the Laundromats are always on strike.

In Athens, conveniently for my theory, the newspapers while I was there were reporting a decline in community spirit in small Greek towns since the laying on of running water.

I know that Americans are not ready to give up running water, but I do believe we are ready for a symbolic return to the town pump. I have seen the most implausible people rediscover the joys of chatting while washing. I was assigned to write an article about a cruise on a Norwegian ship, the *Royal Viking Sea*. The *Sea* is one of the most elegant and technologically advanced merchant ships in the world. There are endless rooms, big and small, carefully designed to bring people together. But the most successful room is the launderette.

It is the most sociable place on the ship. American women encrusted with diamonds come to look and stay to talk. Husbands are brought in to inspect the mysteries of European washing machines. People who have not thought about their laundry for years hold cocktail parties while they iron their ball gowns and put a few pairs of socks through a rinse. Women, deprived by the isolation of the suburbs and money, learn the joys of beating someone else to the dryer.

One day the ship visited Odessa, and I asked the Intourist guide if I could see a public laundry. She expressed shock and surprise: "We do our *own* laundry in our *own* machines at home."

Communist Russia is probably not the best place to explain that we have tried the future and it doesn't work. Let them find out the hard way.

When Californians voted to cut property taxes through Proposition 13, they apparently believed they were voting to cut off welfare loafers. In other words, they believed they were voting to cease providing basic human services. The voters, as it happened, were wrong about which money goes where, but they did manage to cut out for a while a few things such as summer recreation programs, librarians, and school crossing guards. Several public officials were quoted as saying "the community will have to take care of these problems." I suspect that by "community" they meant women, who are presumed to be available for volunteer community betterment. Perhaps women are—after we get home from work. Perhaps the officials meant the women who were finally getting off welfare by holding some marginal public jobs, which they will lose if Proposition 13 cuts off the funding.

My dear, it's practically impossible to get a good service class these days.

In all the urgent meetings with mayors and governors, cabinet and Congress, one crucial point about welfare reform always fails to be clarified. That is the matter of who is actually on welfare. Ninety-seven percent of the people receiving Aid to Families with Dependent Children are three million women taking care of eight million children.

Welfare is a women's issue. Not those "other" women—lazy, not quite bright enough to keep a man to support them. All women. It can happen to any of us. A ten-year study of 5,000

American families conducted by the University of Michigan showed that a third of the women who were divorced and not remarried fell below the poverty line afterward, even counting alimony, child support, and welfare. Only 13 percent of divorced men suffered such a fate.

The suggestion that the government cease driving a man out of the home by denying benefits if he is there is commendable. In 1977, eighteen states had programs of aid with unemployed fathers at home. But in California, for example, less than a fourth of the families on welfare had a father at home. A man in the house does not solve welfare problems. The solution is to make women self-supporting.

The poor wish to work, and workers are still poor. Given the facts of who is on welfare, it would seem difficult—when planning public programs of jobs and income—to avoid the problem of day care. But administration after administration, Congress after Congress, has managed to avoid it. The favorite avoidance technique is to fund another study.

In 1977, during President Carter's ill-fated flurry of welfare-reform meetings, an assistant secretary of labor named Arnold Packer passed into feminist history by writing a memo advocating the oldest solution to female poverty of all: marry them off. Packer wrote: "One can think of the traditional American family structure with two partners and children in which the family head goes out to work and makes enough of a living to keep the family together. The major thrust of any program ought to be to support this as the predominant situation for Americans. Secondly, for families in which there are small children, and only one parent, there should be enough support for those families to live a dignified life. The incentives should be arranged so that individuals prefer the two-parent arrangement. The earnings at work should be sufficiently greater than the dole on welfare to encourage families to stay together or to encourage women who are single parents to remarry."

At it happens, only 7 percent of American families are in the "predominant situation" Packer blithely imagines. Furthermore, poor women do not fail to remarry because they have more fun single on welfare. They are often poor even when they are married and both spouses are working. Theirs are the marriages most likely to break up, not simply because of the inherent strains of an institution based on inequality, but because of the strains of the larger inequalities of the system—unemployment and low income. This sort of ignorance and disregard for poor women created our present custodial, paternalistic welfare system.

President Carter's "welfare-reform" program showed an attitude toward poor women that was also reflected in his insistence that they be denied Medicaid payment for abortion. Apparently he could not accept the notion of assisting poor women to control their own lives, either through control of their bodies or through control of their own economic destinies.

Real welfare reform depends on training women for better paying jobs, a national day-care program, and an end to the idea that a man is the solution to a woman's problems.

In December 1976 the Supreme Court decided that the 1964 Civil Rights Act did not require the inclusion of pregnancy in disability-insurance plans. The majority held that such plans do not discriminate against women.

The very best solution to the problem of discrimination against pregnant workers would be a new system under which pregnancy would be allocated more fairly between both sexes.

At present, pregnant workers are women, a fact of which Justice John Paul Stevens felt compelled to remind the Court after he had contemplated Justice William Rehnquist's majority opinion. In his dissent Justice Stevens said: " . . . the rule at issue places the risk of absence caused by pregnancy in a class by itself. By definition, such a rule discriminates on account of sex; for it is the capacity to become pregnant which primarily differentiates the female from the male."

The Supreme Court always reflects popular attitudes. And this society's attitude toward women—pregnant or not—is that women are still subject to injustice if it is more convenient for the system.

That December, Justice Rehnquist concluded that pregnancy disability would cost a lot, that denying payment is not discriminatory because pregnancy is not really a disease, and anyway it is "often a voluntarily undertaken and desired condition."

The voluntary nature of pregnancy (which the Court apparently found different from the voluntary nature of hair transplants, which are insured) seems to be a very important part of the generally hypocritical and bewildered attitude toward the reproduction of the species held by our society and its Supreme Court.

I find no particular difference between the majority opinion that held that pregnancy is voluntary and therefore the responsibility of no one but the volunteer, and nurses who once roamed maternity wards saying to women in labor: "Well, dearie, you had your fun, and now you've got to pay for it."

In fact, pregnancy is not always safe, not always voluntary, and always somewhat disabling—particularly in the United States, where we have inadequate contraceptive research and information programs, inadequate abortion facilities, strenuous efforts to re-outlaw abortion, and, in some states, no Medicaid assistance for first pregnancies.

In the United States the entire economy is run on selling through sex, but children are an unacceptable by-product of our marketing revolution. No one is responsible for them. Except their mothers. But she is denied full control over her body, and at the same time denied a chance to become economically independent. Because she might get pregnant.

Even if pregnancy were always entirely voluntary, desired, and uncomplicated, no one seems to remember anymore that it is the result of a voluntary act of two people and that the child is not a punishment for a sinful entertainment but part of the nation's future.

Justice William J. Brennan, Jr., in his wise dissent, said: "In dictating pregnancy coverage under Title VII, the Equal Employment Opportunity Commission's guideline merely settled upon a solution now accepted by every other Western industrial country." Those countries have all kinds of nifty programs of support, not only for the mother, but also for the father. Biology is no longer final destiny there, and certainly it is not penury as here. Surely it is time for the United States to recognize that women contribute to both the GNP and the population and should be encouraged to do both.

The problem of covering pregnancy under worker's-disability insurance was resolved in April of 1979 when a new federal law went into effect which forbids any employer with fifteen or more employees to treat pregnancy differently from any other disability. This law is not a complete solution, since the federal government is itself exempt from compliance and employers are not required to cover abortion—but it is an improvement. The problem of attitude in the Supreme Court is more difficult.

In a different decision two weeks after the pregnancy-disability case, the Court gave permission for men eighteen years old to buy 3.2 beer in Oklahoma. Women had been able to buy such beer at eighteen, but men had to wait until twenty-one. The Court considered this difference unjustified. The decision, while unlikely to cause any immediate revolutionary change in the lives of Oklahoma women (except, perhaps, for the women who wish to sell more beer, one of whom brought the case before the Court) had the effect of advancing the position of the Court to a constitutional middle ground. Thereafter, laws that make distinctions in treatment of men and women could no longer be acceptable on the grounds of "reasonability" but must be justified by "important" government policy aims. Such distinctions would not, however, be automatically suspected of discrimination (as laws that would allow different treatment of races are). In other words, women became slightly more equal under the law than before. But still not equal.

We need the Equal Rights Amendment and we need a woman on the Supreme Court. Just because men can't have babies doesn't mean they can't learn what it's like.

———

A few years ago it was stories about the Berlin Wall. Then it was poverty in Appalachia. Now the story being played for all the knee-jerk sentimentality it can get is "Inside the Abortion Clinic."

Many people do feel an ethical squeeze when they consider abortion, but a woman's right to choose to have an abortion is still a constitutional right, which is why these maudlin stories of pain and anguish are essentially fraudulent. Such hand-wringing would be better directed to a consideration of a much more complicated and difficult issue, which is the matter of health care—particularly maternal and child care—in the United States.

Where are the stories about "Inside a Maternity Ward"? Does everyone assume that maternity wards today are entirely filled with healthy babies and proud parents, the mothers sporting orchid corsages pinned to their bed jackets while they put the finishing touches on a hand-sewn layette?

The layette, just for a start, is one of the things those mothers are worried about. Very few states make any public-assistance payments for diapers or cribs. Every country in Western Europe gives every mother—not just poor mothers—some kind of assistance in providing for a newborn child. In Europe income supplements to families with children, maternity benefits and leaves for mothers (and, in Sweden, fathers), day care even for children whose mothers are not working, and universal child and maternal health programs are considered normal and desirable public policy.

In the United States we are apparently content to mouth pieties about family life and to go on ignoring the fact that we have the highest infant mortality rate of any industrialized nation. Our maternal mortality rate is twice that of West Germany and France.

We behave as though the reproductive process is a woman's whim, certainly not something basic to our lives or to the national good. One million U.S. teen-agers become pregnant every year— one out of ten young women. One-third of all United States abortions are performed on women under twenty. Yet, it is estimated that half of all sexually active teen-age girls have no access to effective birth-control services.

Only half the 9.9 million low- and marginal-income women in need of subsidized family-planning services are served under federal programs. Considering the mortal risks of the pill, one can wonder how well served that half is. But only .016 percent of the federal budget for fiscal year 1979 was allocated for development of safe and effective birth-control methods.

A new phrase is beginning to be heard on Capitol Hill. It is "abortion fraud." Naturally women will be blamed for fraud too, just as they are blamed for having babies. It is important to remember that abortion fraud refers to doctors who tell a woman she is pregnant when she is not and collect Medicaid for an abortion, or they perform an incomplete abortion—risking the woman's life—and then collect for another. The millions of dollars paid to criminally fraudulent doctors could pay for a lot of preventive and diagnostic medicine.

If, in spite of all the risks, a woman decides to have a baby, do we applaud her bravery? No. We don't even bother to tell her how. One-half of the women delivering babies in cities and one-third of all the women who deliver babies in public hospitals receive no prenatal care at all. In a city hospital in Brooklyn, New York, in the course of a month, only two women had had any prenatal instruction in childbirth and these had found the books and taught themselves. The assumption of public policy seems to be that the know-how comes with the baby, or else that having a baby is a fact of life so technically mysterious that only the doctor knows the secret. Prenatal care and such postnatal information as how to feed and care for the child are mere frills in the national budget.

Maybe this kind of distortion of priorities is inevitable in a country where the medical establishment and the politicians are still overwhelmingly white, authoritarian males. But all the inconsistencies, pieties, and deprivations add up to one thing. When you have a baby in this country, you are on your own.

———————

If women cannot decide when to have a baby, we cannot be said to control our lives.

If we can control our lives, can plan, but still cannot count on sharing the raising of children, we may decide not to have children.

This would not be a happy situation. I would prefer to believe that it will turn out differently, that the present resistance to the idea of women's autonomy—as manifested in the opposition to both abortion and birth-control—is the last shudder of biological determinism.

To think otherwise is to yield to the bleakest possibility—that men's power over women depends precisely on our inability to control our own lives and that men would prefer to enforce pregnancy rather than give up any power, even the power to refuse to care for the children. To accept that explanation is to retire from the field, defeated by the presumption that women can never be equal because we have the children.

So I would prefer to think that we are simply arguing within the context of a peculiar and particular historical moment: a threshold of scientific and social possibilities that could mean change so profound that half the country takes fright and wants to turn back.

We have been approaching and rejecting this threshold of reproductive control for a very long time, and the history of that approach does much to soften the moral absolutes of today. James Reed, in his book *From Private Vice to Public Virtue: The Birth Control Movement and American Society Since 1830*, and James C. Mohr, in *Abortion in America*, have traced the demographic shifts of the nineteenth and early twentieth centuries which affected and were affected by attitudes. In 1800 the average American woman had 7.04 children; by 1900 she had 3.56. The steepest drop occurred between 1840 and 1850, when the widespread practice of abortion became publicly acknowledged.

Then, as now, Americans tried to deal with a changing society by reading quantities of self-help books and evoking an image of an ideal, earlier time. They argued that birth control was unhealthy and possibly immoral, but they practiced it as far as they were able. Women had to reconcile themselves to the contradiction between a generally accepted ideology that all healthy women were willing multiple mothers, and the fact that every time an individual woman rolled over in bed she faced the real possibility of illness, pain, or death. Notions of equality and self-determination were bravely arrived at before anesthesia and antiseptics; before 1910, when Lane Bryant began marketing maternity clothes—thus ending "confinement"—and before 1920, when Kotex was invented.

The crusade against abortion between 1857 and 1880, which resulted in legislation that remained much the same until the 1973 Supreme Court decision making the choice of abortion a constitutional right, began as a doctors' issue, not a popular issue. After the Civil War doctors had the scientific knowledge to make abortion safe. Instead the newly organized American Medical Association used abortion as a rallying point to deploy legislative sanction against "unprofessional" competition (home remedies, quacks, nostrums), to create a sense of esprit de corps, and to recover what they saw as the doctors' rightful role as society's moral arbiters.

The arguments against birth control and abortion in the second half of the nineteenth century were based on the strong fear of the native Yankees that increasing immigration of "bad" stock would drive out the old, "good" stock. It might seem more reasonable today to have extended birth control and abortion services to the poor, but at the time it was far easier to enforce reproduction than to ensure limitation. The fear that "good" women might destroy society by refusing to breed was expressed by contemptuous references to women who wanted abortions for convenience. It is an emotion that both Mohr and Reed describe as springing from a society in which the men doubted their virility and feared betrayal by their own women.

The women were also busy fighting abortion and birth control as part of a general campaign against social evils, which they believed would be cured by the application of a higher moral standard, much higher than the old double standard—no recreational sex for either women *or* men. The elite of both sexes worried about the rapid reproduction of the poor, but it happened that the poor and their children provided the very pool of cheap labor that made it possible for the native stock to enjoy the opportunities of the American life that went along with having fewer children. The circularity of the situation was not clear at the time, and women of all classes came in for much blame. Luckily, before the turn of the century women themselves, led by Emma Goldman and Margaret Sanger, began to talk about sex, and health, and other forbidden subjects. Still, the dissemination of birth-control information remained widely illegal in the United States until 1960.

It is no surprise that we have not yet resolved the contradictions of the last century. The resolution, after all, involves allowing a very large number of people the chance to control their own lives. This chance has been resisted by the powerful of every century, including the present one.

There is a wide consensus in the United States that the person whose body does the work is the person who gets to decide whether she will continue with a pregnancy or not. All the polls indicate that although the American people do not all support federally funded abortions, the majority does support the 1973 Supreme Court decision giving women the unrestricted right to choose abortion in the first trimester of pregnancy.

Abortion is an emotional and moral dilemma that has become a political issue because the right-to-life minority is so extremely loud and tireless, and political, in their ceaseless efforts to protect the rights of the fertilized human egg. They have considerably less sympathy for the human being whose egg it is. As the right-to-life people see it, a woman harboring a fertilized human egg should lose certain constitutional rights such as the right to privacy and to freedom of religion. She should, in protection of the egg's presumed "personhood," lose her own personhood and become entirely subservient to her biological condition.

Most of us are quite willing to let them believe that, as long as we don't have to believe it too. But they are not willing to be so democratic. They impose their views at the state and local levels through restrictive laws and ordinances that require such stumbling points as parental consent to abortion for a minor, prior notification and/or consent of a spouse, waiting periods, and "informed consent" by the woman requiring an abortion—a process designed, in effect, to dramatize for her the notion that she is murdering a child. As harassment techniques these restrictions show a certain ingenuity. But as law most have been found, as they made their way through various court challenges, to be unconstitutional.

Right-to-life groups have an answer to what they see as the disappointingly wide latitude of personal freedom allowed by the United States Constitution. They plan to forbid abortions by amending the Constitution.

In the spring of 1976 the U.S. Senate was surprised to find itself debating whether or not to consider a constitutional amendment to forbid all abortions. It was Senator Birch Bayh's weary duty, as chairman of the Subcommittee on the Constitution, to remind the antichoice faction that abortion "is not an issue that can be properly or effectively dealt with in a constitutional context."

The afternoon was not without its illuminating moments, and they are preserved in the *Congressional Record* for the day. The principal illumination is that United States senators do not feel at home in discussions of human reproductivity, and many of them are ill at ease when reminded of women's role in the process. The discussion, only tangentially scientific, centered around notions of fertilization, implantation, and the start of life. No one knows when life begins—they can only believe—so no one persuaded anyone else. Senator Dewey Bartlett of Oklahoma suggested teen-age victims of rape and incest could get a D & C (dilation and curettage, or scraping of the womb) before implantation took place. Compounding the absurdity of his own argument, Senator Bartlett said: "During that period we do not know whether an abortion would be taking place or not. But it cannot be proved that it is, and I feel that that is the important fact."

The senators floundered on. Senator James Buckley made the customary right-to-life leap in logic from abortion to euthanasia. Wiser men rose to point out that no antiabortion amendment could ever be enforced. Almost everyone found time to express their personal abhorrence of abortion. Throughout the debate a pregnant woman's decision to abort was often referred to, with considerable contempt, as a matter of convenience. Bearing a child is an inconvenience no man has ever confronted. As Senator Bayh, the underappreciated champion of women's rights, said: "We are talking about whether a woman has the right to make that personal decision or whether we are going to make it for her or prohibit her from making it. Although I am prepared to make it as a man, I am not prepared to make it for a woman."

The Senate, that time, decided against an antiabortion amendment to the Constitution.

In January of 1977 the Senate enthusiastically confirmed Joseph Califano's appointment as secretary of the Department of Health, Education, and Welfare, now renamed the Department of Health and Human Services. (One cannot avoid describing a vote of 95 to 1 as enthusiastic.)

Senator Robert Packwood, R-Oregon, the lone voice crying out in the wilderness, voted against the appointment for a few perfectly good reasons, expressed lucidly in the congenial atmosphere of the Senate floor. He believed that Mr. Califano showed a "blatant disregard for the human needs of indigent women."

There is reason to doubt that the Senate floor is the best place to express anything lucidly. The senators are usually too busy to be affected. They no longer occupy themselves very much with snuff, still kept in two receptacles on the Senate floor. They were not, the day Mr. Califano came up for a vote, much engaged in the ritual inscribing of their names inside the bottom of their desk drawers, a traditional activity of long history.

They were, that afternoon, simply milling about, clasping each other's elbows and neck napes, assuming postures of power and importance (one hip slightly out, one fingertip to chin). Senators Moynihan and Hayakawa, in diplomatic *tailleur* and California color-coordinate respectively, were seated next to each other, each happy as a pig in clover. Senators Eastland and Sparkman shared a row, as no doubt they will in eternity.

To gaze upon the Senate is to understand patriarchy.

There are a few things it is important to remember as a background to the matter of Mr. Califano's being approved as secretary of Health, Education, and Welfare.

One: All of the members of the United States Senate were then men. One is now a woman.

Two: Women are the people who get pregnant.

Three: Abortion is legal in the United States.

Four: The United States Constitution demands separation of Church and State.

Mr. Califano, a Catholic, asserted with some vehemence during the hearings: "My views are as follows: I personally believe that abortion is wrong. Secondly, I believe that federal funds should not be used for the purpose of providing abortions." He then spoke warmly of improved provision of alternatives to abortion, such as day care, family planning and sex education, and foster care. He also said he would enforce the law, however repugnant to his personal morality, even if the law turns out to be that poor women are entitled to Medicaid payments for abortion.

Mr. Califano was pressed to admit that if the choice should be between the life of a mother and that of a fetus, then he believed it would be appropriate "for someone to make the decision to save the life of the mother."

He did not go so far as to suggest that that someone might be the mother.

He was voted in, with many expressions of admiration. As one of the good fellows on the Senate floor said to a woman lobbyist, "Oh, come on, you can't hold up a fellow's appointment over a little thing like abortion."

Eventually, Califano lost his job, not because of his views on abortion, but because his loyalty to President Carter was thought to be less than absolute. Some newspapers reported that he was fired because he believed cigarettes were unhealthy and that the University of North Carolina should make somewhat greater efforts to integrate. Which only goes to show that opposition to abortion won't help a man keep his political job.

In June of 1977 the U.S. House of Representatives began its annual consideration of the Labor—Health, Education, and Welfare appropriations bill. The money appropriated is the largest part of our national budget and much of it is spent, theoretically, to improve the the lives of the disadvantaged and powerless fifth of our nation.

The debate over appropriations is traditionally a time for powerful congressmen to speak of fiscal responsibility and public morality. They do so while offering schemes to limit school desegregation and while demanding deep cuts in programs for low-income families.

The most disadvantaged, least powerful, most consistently excluded people in the United States are poor, pregnant women. The infamous Hyde Amendment to the appropriations bill, first passed in 1976, which cut off federal funds for all abortions except in case of "life endangering" pregnancies, did much to perpetuate poor women's condition.

Congressman Henry Hyde of Illinois felt that the wording of the original bill—"life endangering"—could be too broadly interpreted. During the 1977 debate he called for tighter restrictions, admitting: "I certainly would like to prevent, if I could legally, anybody having an abortion, a rich woman, a middle-class woman, or a poor woman. Unfortunately, the only vehicle available is the HEW Medicaid bill."

It was indeed very unfortunate for those women who alone were vulnerable to Mr. Hyde's effort to control their lives—those too poor to choose an abortion without public assistance. Mr. Hyde justified his discrimination with a great deal of talk about "the slaughter of innocent children." He and his colleagues explained during the subsequent lengthy (and now annual) debates that they were also worried about fascism, decadence, and the meaning of life.

They are not, of course, the only people in America worried about such matters. Nor do they hold a firmer grip on righteousness than the rest of us. The congressmen who oppose Medicaid funding for abortions think that poor women are dishonest, immoral, promiscuous and somehow outside the general society. Or so I cannot help but interpreting the record of their public remarks made on the floor of the House. Their holy glow lost some of its luminosity when, for example, Mr. Rudd of Arizona rose to say: "The cliché we hear most often is: 'A woman has the right to control her own body.' I agree. Let her exercise control—before she gets pregnant. But do not ask the taxpayers of America to pay the price when there is a failure to exercise control by forcing taxpayers to subsidize the ending of lives of unborn children as a convenience to adult women."

No wonder that Mr. Allen of Tennessee said: " . . . I cannot but wonder if some of my colleagues here in the House who are preparing to vote for this bill realize the cruelty its literal enforcement would visit upon the poor, the sick, the mentally ill and the innocent victims of rape and incestuous pregnancies among welfare patients."

By September 1977, after months of debate, the antiabortion members of the House were no closer to a comprehension of cruelty. Mr. Conte of Massachusetts said, "The Senate version would allow Federal funding of abortions in the case of rape, incest, or other medical necessitites. In my opinion, the language is weak, overbroad, unnecessary and would lend itself to abuse."

The word "abuse" is always a signal that the nastiest side of legislators is about to be revealed. But the debate that September and October was nastier than usual. Mr. Hyde proclaimed: "The pregnant woman would not even have to claim she had a headache or athlete's foot to get an abortion under this language." He and Mr. Conte continued through the month to assert that the rape issue was a "red herring" because, they said, rape almost never results in pregnancy. Mr. Stokes of Ohio objected, reminding the House that as far as it is known, rape results in pregnancy at the same rate of any unprotected intercourse: 4 percent of the time.

But the House was preoccupied with discussing whether a victim of rape or incest could perhaps be allowed some sort of "morning after" treatment, if she reported the incident promptly.

Voices of reason were raised. Ms. Fenwick of New Jersey

spoke of pregnant teen-agers—"children in the seventh and eighth grades who were expecting babies not knowing even where they came from." She added: "Just do not be so sure you are right." Mr. Stokes reminded those members afraid of fraud that they "are actually acknowledging the desperation faced by women faced with unwanted pregnancies."

Mr. Hyde remained adamant. "We are offering a financial inducement to simply report a rape and we are putting a burden on the police department to investigate every one of these fraudulently reported rapes. We are inducing fraud: we will not stop abortions, because every woman who wants one will doubtless say she was raped by an unknown assailant."

If these are the opinions that appear on the record, one shudders to imagine what men like Hyde say off the record. Perhaps they openly express, in private, a philosophical discontent that women are capable of doing something very important which men cannot do—have babies.

By 1978 the number of abortions funded by Medicaid dropped to less than 1 percent—thanks to the Hyde Amendment.

More than a million women a year have an abortion. *Before* passage of the Hyde Amendment, only 17 percent of public hospitals offered abortion services, and only three out of every ten abortions were Medicaid federally funded. That means only about 300,000 poor women were affected, not a very large or important constituency. Perhaps those women found a cheap abortion somewhere, although it may not have been very safe—an ironic consequence of a bill that was designed overall to equalize access to health care. The medical complications of unsafe abortions made those same women, ironically, eligible for Medicaid. As a further irony, most of the congressmen trying to deny poor women abortions were demanding cutbacks in child-care spending.

From the point of view of society, the peculiarity of this policy is that Congress evidently believes that the children who *should* be born are those of the poorest, least healthy, and least educated people, those who have the least access to the opportunities of the society.

Perhaps the vast majority of Americans believe, with Congress, that poor women deserve what they get, which includes inadequate health care of any sort, inadequate contraceptive information, inadequate employment, and inadequate welfare. Perhaps the majority of Americans—who regulate their consumer habits by response to sexually motivating advertisements—believe that some women's morality should be publicly legislated and punished.

But the result does not seem to be a very fair or desirable allocation of breeding responsibilities. Adjustments will have to be made. Congress will have to say they have made a mistake (an unlikely event). Or they will have to see that the future mothers of America are lifted from poverty, educated, and made healthy, and their children made equal (an even more unlikely event). Or, they will have to march resolutely along the wrong fork they have chosen and declare that today's constitutional right has been superceded because they have now decided that the state has a compelling reason to encourage all women to bear children.

And that means me.

As it happens, in 1978 Congress turned its attention to me, and to all other middle-class women. They cut off health-insurance coverage for abortion for the 110,000 women on active duty in the armed forces, and the millions of women dependents of military personnel—and retired personnel—by adding the Hyde Amendment language to the Department of Defense appropriations bill. Abortion coverage for Peace Corps volunteers was forbidden as well. The Pregnancy Disability Bill was passed allowing employers to elect not to cover abortion in employee insurance plans.

During the closing nights of that year's congressional session, the right-to-life groups finally overplayed their hand. A series of amendments to the Health Services Bill, which would have required such things as parental consent before minors could receive abortion *or* contraceptive information, were offered. Congress, apparently recognizing an attack not only on abortion but also on the dissemination of contraceptive information and sex education, defeated all the amendments under the comfortable anonymity of a voice vote.

According to the National Abortion Rights Action League's analysis of the voting patterns of the 1977–78 Congress, there were 184 members who consistently opposed funding for abortion under any circumstances. Of that 184, over half, or 105, also voted consistently in 1976–77 against legislation that would indicate a concern for such basic human needs as food, shelter, and income.

The ugly congressional record on abortion was not entirely due to mean-spirited fanaticism (nor was it the record of the entire Congress). A certain amount of routine political buck-passing was involved. It seemed easier, no doubt, to placate the hordes of right-to-lifers tramping through the halls handing out red roses than to hold out for an invisible majority of American women who—let us admit—were not in daily attendance urging support for their poorer sisters' right to federally funded abortions. A politician's impulse in controversial matters (especially matters that cannot be viably legislated) is to go with the pressure and hope the courts will decide.

In January 1980 Judge John F. Dooling, Jr., of the Federal District Court in Brooklyn, New York, decided. He struck down the Hyde Amendment on the grounds that it violated both the equal protection guarantee of the Fifth Amendment and the religious freedom guarantee of the First Amendment. In June 1980 the Supreme Court overturned the Dooling decision and declared the Hyde Amendment constitutional. So much for the needs of poor women. Right-to-life groups will now redouble their efforts to add an antiabortion amendment to the Constitution. The U.S. Congress, sensibly acknowledging the futility of such an amendment (which would, after all, affect *all* women, not just poor women), has so far refused to pass one. But some state legislatures seem more eager to tamper with the Constitution. By the time of the Dooling decision sixteen states out of the necessary thirty-four had voted to convene a constitutional convention on the abortion issue. (Revisionism is in the air: thirty states have voted to convene to consider an amendment requiring a balanced budget.) If such an event takes place, it will not be a rerun of the wisdom of 1776.

———

In November of 1977 Connie Downey, then acting director of special project planning at the Department of Health, Education, and Welfare, wrote an "internal working paper" on alternatives to abortion that concluded: "Abortion is but one alternative solution to many of the 'problems.' It is an option, uniquely, which is exercised between conception and live birth. As such, the literal alternatives to it are suicide, motherhood and, some would add, madness. Consequently, there is some confusion, discomfort and cynicism greeting efforts to 'find' or 'emphasize' or 'identify' alternatives to abortion."

Some confusion resulted at HEW when Downey's report made its inevitable way into the news. Spokespersons at HEW urged that attention be paid to their much more important (they said) proposals concerning the problems of teen-age pregnancy. HEW wanted money for birth control, sex education, counseling, follow-up programs to avoid second pregnancies, and enforcement of civil right laws which would forbid expelling or segregating pregnant girls.

Those were all fine proposals and they were sure to be welcomed by Congress about as eagerly as budgets for child care and prenatal health clinics have always been welcomed. Which is, shall we say, not warmly. It would have been nice, while HEW was about it, if they had also proposed some plan for a society that would allow American females to arrive at their teen-age years with some more constructive vision of self-validation than having a baby before they are grown themselves.

Such a plan would be no more visionary than the search for alternatives to abortion. There are alternatives to getting pregnant, but once a woman is pregnant, the alternatives narrow down just as Downey describes. Motherhood is the obvious alternative, a role that in our society is entirely the mother's responsibility. Many women cannot face the responsibility for extremely good reasons that have nothing to do with "convenience." What are their alternatives? Surely something beyond madness and suicide.

Infanticide was the nineteenth-century answer—has been an answer throughout history. It was not a particularly good one, but it was the only answer available at the time. Dead babies are regularly discovered in trash bins even now. Some people think abortion is infanticide. Most of the country does not.

Nevertheless, the Congress of the United States has managed to decide that since some people do not approve of abortion, that alternative should be denied a fifteen-year-old girl from the inner city who is pregnant, perhaps because she has been having too much fun. Since her pregnancy in effect cuts off hope for the rest of her life, as perhaps her own birth kept her mother in poverty, someone must feel that denying Medicaid payments for abortion is a socially useful policy. A fifteen-year-old girl on welfare won't ever be very uppity. She won't ever pay taxes either, but that connection is never made.

Adoption! the alternative seekers cry, growing all dewy-eyed at the thought of large suburban homes waiting to be filled with the happy laughter of blond, blue-eyed children. The owners of the large suburban homes are willing to prove their love and capacity for parenting by offering large fees for babies with suitable backgrounds. Never mind the crowded institutional homes full of children who are handicapped, disturbed, older, racially mixed. Never mind the absolutely never remarked-on fact that nine months of pregnancy is not a trip to Palm Springs or a momentary displacement, something like having a cold.

Let's do think of alternatives even for the forty-one-year-old mother of four, happily married, relatively well off, just getting a job to help pay college fees for the oldest. She realizes another child will mean a nervous breakdown. Her alternative to abortion is to tell the children, "Don't worry, Mommy is going to be pregnant for a few months, but we will give it away." The children consider the prospect, and then suggest perhaps it would be better to give away Tommy, who never helps with the dishes.

How about the woman of thirty-two, self-supporting, single, who has gotten pregnant even though she knows better? The man is married (he knows better too). She decides single parenthood is too hard on the child. What is her alternative? To keep going to work, explaining to concerned friends that she will be giving the baby away so they don't need to knit booties? That is a public loss too terrible to inflict on friends. Better for her to inflict it on herself, alone. The only place to do that would be the Mary Magdalen Home for Unwed Mothers, where she can practice shame.

The one absolute alternative to the possibility of needing an abortion is to be born a man. An additional advantage of being born male is the time saved by not having to worry about becoming pregnant, which can be usefully spent acquiring public responsibility and making policies designed to keep women busy worrying.

THE PERSONAL

I used to laugh when I read that someone had been put in the hospital to recover from exhaustion. I assumed it meant that they didn't choose to testify before an embarrassingly nosy committee or that they were simply too inadequate to deal with modern life. Now I know it meant that when they noticed that their plants needed watering, they started to cry.

Would anyone like to adopt fifteen ugly but tenacious house-plants? How about a stubborn, moth-eaten but beguiling cairn ter-rier? Would anyone like to take a chance on getting a few bucks for the scrap paper in exchange for carting away the contents of the closet which contains the unsorted accumulation which repre-sents my life's work?

I am too exhausted to cope. The doctor says so. She says I should go away for a few days. At least if the doctor says so, I don't have to go on feeling so guilty about not carrying on, chin up, a real brick through the whole ghastly affair.

But as for going away for a few days, the trouble is, I have already been away for a few days. Fifteen wearing, fascinating, almost entirely sleepless days and nights in the remoter sections of Senegal and Mali. Eighteen of us were observing development, endlessly and arduously trying to understand other places, other cultures, their needs, our needs, ourselves.

Of course we all had a terrific time, but the temperature was usually 112 degrees and we returned mentally overloaded and physically underslept. On the plane the men confidently asserted that, even as we struggled to fill out customs declarations, their wives were at home warming up steaks, turning down beds, and warning the children that total silence would be required until their poor fathers had recovered from jet lag.

Everybody has to pay for a trip away from the family somehow, even men. The price may be only a few days of sulky silence or a major fight about something trivial or at least a detailed recounting of all the real and imagined domestic disorder during the traveler's absence. But how lovely it would be to have the accounting put off until after the steak has been served.

My household was as I expected it would be. No milk. No dog food. A visiting dog had ruined three rugs. One sprained ankle. One sulky love object. The painters only half through the house so all the furniture was in the front hall covered with sheets. The furniture that had not been covered with sheets was covered with paint. A man was waiting to cut off the electricity. The paid bill rested where I had left it, stamped and ready to mail, on the kitchen table. The baby-sitter had left a note saying she was exhausted and off to the beach. The plants were dying but, alas, not liberatingly dead.

My bed was turned down—sort of—just as I had left it unmade two weeks before. Slightly more so, since the dogs had been sleeping on it. I retired to consider the demands that surrounded me. I dreamt of a small white room with a mat in one corner and a typewriter in another. Someone was pushing trays of strawberry shortcake through the door and the right Mozart was playing without my having to select it. It was wonderful. Nothing and no one told me to hand-wash only, refrigerate after opening, pay in three days, respond, file, shut, etc.

My son, who has been a real brick through the whole ghastly affair, had a helpful solution. "Mom," he said, "what you need is to get back to work."

———————

I am getting a little bit tired of the children.

The summer days have been filled with picnics by the waterfall and trips to the granite quarry. Occasional forays to Laundromat and Supermart have been squeezed in as optional treats for the adults. Then back home again for the never-ending after-dinner puppet shows and postprandial games of Murder. There is much mingling of peer groups.

It is all perfectly charming, but I am beginning to yearn for some grown-up conversation. Perhaps it is because my son is not one of the children around. He seems to have grown up and to be off visiting more exotic relatives this summer. I expected him to grow up, but not quite yet. He has left me alone to test my convictions and to applaud other people's children's puppet shows (the sound of one hand clapping).

My convictions involve the notion that less peer-group exclusivity would vastly improve society.

In New York people do not gather, they entertain. And they do not often willingly entertain each other's children or grandmothers. Bringing either to a cocktail party would be an affront to the social decencies in New York. Children do not plan puppet shows and coerce adults into crawling around in the dark after dinner in New York. They watch television and the adults drink brandy. I have always believed it was a bad system. Children (and, by connection, the mothers of children) should not be treated as impediments to normal human contact and activities. Children should be able to go anywhere and everyone should share in the wonderful rewarding process of socializing the young. (I was particularly strong on this point when my son was very small.)

I do believe that no reliably human philosophy or policy can be formulated in an ivory tower that is completely guarded against interruptions from children. But I am not entirely sure that puppet shows every night are an absolute indicator that civilization is on the march.

After a full day of picnicking I wanted to hear about my friend's first term as a state representative. Her teen-age daughters declared that politics were boring. They wanted to talk about Life. So we talked about Life. When we began to connect politics and Life, they talked of rock groups.

A neighbor came to dinner. He has a scheme for the improvement of the Vermont economy we were anxious to hear about. But it turned out to be difficult to discuss with eighteen-month-old Ezra swinging from his father's arm. Ezra's mother was obviously snatched back from the brink of gibbering madness by the brief rest Ezra granted her arm and no doubt that was of more immediate concern than an economic scheme. But I could see, and am loath to admit it, why men are not eager to include children in their office plans.

Eight-year-old Eliza spent an entire day at an auction, whining that she wanted to go home because she was bored. I dimly remembered that my son, the perfect guest, had been wont to whine to the same tune. It never seemed to bother me very much at the time. But now I found myself saying aloud, in the general direction of Eliza, that a child who is bored at an auction is a child who would be bored anywhere and therefore she should shut up about it.

Shutting up seems to be expected only of the adults.

I would not mind the puppet shows so much if the parents of the little troupers did not also caution the adults during dinners, "Please don't talk about religion (death, families, taxes, politics, sex, etc.) in front of the children." Wasn't there supposed to be a compromise, something along the lines of initiating the children into the adult world, instead of locking us all into the children's world?

Obviously I am getting old. As soon as my son comes back and the conversation at my own house turns to rock groups and who will walk the dog, I will remember the summer as a time of total enrichment. After all, most of these endless puppet shows contain more intellectual content than the talk at an average New York City dinner party. And tomorrow night the children are going to let me work the strings for *Cinderella.*

———

Putting on and taking off snowsuits is a process that seems to infinitely lengthen the hours of the day, At the time, it does not seem possible that in the briefest twinkling of an eye the toddler will turn into a person who will not, under any circumstances, wear ski pants to school even if the blizzard of the century is raging outside.

It did not seem possible to me that I would ever turn into a mother who could stand, back to the front door, waving ski pants in the air and talking about pneumonia. I once kept a childhood diary titled *Things Never to Do When I Am a Mother,* and I am sure the first entry was, "Never argue about what to wear in the snow."

Many of my friends find that as their children turn into adolescents, they themselves turn into their own parents. "When you have learned something about the value of money we will discuss a ten-speed bike," said Walter despite himself, despite his visible efforts to say something else. He had expected to say something about shared costs and feasible expectations, and yet what came out was a primal scream, the voice of his father, and his father before him.

After one of those frightening, reflexive moments, the people in the middle generation—that is, the parents of teen-agers—tend to fall into black depressions and to brood alone in their rooms about the sins of the fathers (and mothers) being handed on, apparently forever. It begins to seem a miracle that anyone has ever had a new idea, much less actually changed because of it.

The young are expected to have new ideas, which they present in the most contentious possible terms at the family dinner table, thus causing much shouting, recrimination, mutal denouncement, slamming of doors, and general turmoil. This upheaval is called "having an adolescent in the house." The experts' explanation for this generational clash has been that the teen-agers are searching for their own way of going about things and the parents are offended because they feel their values are being rejected.

I think that the real cause of the trouble is that even as the parents discover themselves turning into their own parents, they discover that their children are growing up to be like themselves. Most parents hoped that their children would be different, and, of course, better. Instead, the children turn out, most of the time, to be no better than could have been expected.

It is easy to cope with something new and strange, compared with the almost impossible task of accepting in a child what you have always hated in yourself. Mona tells me she can't bear her daughter's slovenly habits. I have known Mona for twenty years and she has never hung up her clothes. She throws them on the bottom of the closet.

Susan is very worried because her fourteen-year-old daughter thought Porthault sheets would be appropriate to take to camp. "She seems awfully materialistic," says Susan, whom I remember insisting on seeing the stock portfolios of the men who wanted to marry her.

Greg's father complains that the boy will never get into Harvard Law School if he doesn't cure his obsessive compulsion to rebuild bicycles. Greg is fifteen, and his father hated Harvard Law School, hates being a lawyer, and is happy only when rebuilding boats.

My own son writes history papers at 2:00 A.M. He says I work at night; why shouldn't he? Because I want him to be more reasonable. I, unreasonable, forget that he gets up in the morning, which I don't. I not only want him to be better, I want to define "better." At this rate I'll be lucky if he settles for door-slamming and doesn't run away to sea.

Now that I think of it, I wanted to run away to sea when I was fifteen.

———————

I realize that I have to get rid of my television set. Given the role it plays in my family and in most American families, that is a little like saying I realize I have to get a divorce. It is going to be painful and wrenching and I am not sure I have the courage to do it. But I have to.

I want to be disconnected. I read *The Plug-in Drug: Television, Children and the Family,* by Marie Winn. It is an important, well-written book which I hope will change my life. I read it with growing horror as Winn carefully confirmed my worst fears about the effects of television addiction on children. And adults.

First of all, she asserts that while the content of programs is more often bad than good, it is not even the content that is the primary problem. "It is easy to overlook a deceptively simple fact: one is always watching television rather than having any other experience."

Preschool children in America are spending more than a third of their waking hours watching television, which requires nothing of them but passivity. To the child the real world reflects television, instead of the other way around. The child has no experience to compare television with. The child does not even have a chance to use such meager information as television imparts.

Worse, the child is not eager to acquire any experience. Ms. Winn offers extensive evidence to suggest that the visual and neurological effect of too much television is literally addictive. She describes children who become frantic when the set is finally turned off, who wander dazed through the house if the set is broken, who will stare at a blank screen until they are shaken awake.

Television is the new member of the family. It has replaced grandmothers and uncles of the extended family, and given Mother—who inherited single-handedly all the housekeeping chores the extended family once did cooperatively—some peace and quiet. Unfortunately the peace and quiet eventually means dependent, unhelpful older children, who never learn to help.

Television is the present destructive answer to the need for day-care centers, family community centers, flexible working hours for parents, and the isolation of both urban and suburban nuclear-family housing. Winn's immediate answer to the problem she elucidates so persuasively is to turn the darn thing off. It is a start.

My son is addicted.

Last night he asked me to serve dinner on a tray in front of "Star Trek."

Last night I unplugged him. He has been the fourth Stooge long enough.

One night not too long ago I realized that the "baby" was upstairs in another apartment, earning more than a dollar an hour by watching over a real baby. Meanwhile, the "baby-sitter" residing in my house was rehearsing a play with five friends—four of them equipped with tap shoes—in my living room.

It seemed time for some domestic rearranging. I decided Linda would be the last baby-sitter. When I look into her empty room, I feel a touch of empty-nest syndrome. That room has been painted purple, pink, royal blue, and dark gray, according to the whims of the incumbents. It has been decorated with dance charts, diet charts, musical scales, and a life-size Robert Redford. At the moment the "baby," nearing fifteen, is using the room for a science experiment involving fifty-six sunflower plants. I miss Linda, but she comes back to see us whenever things don't work out with her boyfriend. She is, after all, a member of the family now.

We have had fifteen baby-sitters and they were all—or most of them—members of the family. Perhaps it wasn't a nuclear family, or even an extended family, but it was an adaptation to the demands of life, which seems to be what a family has in fact always been.

On an anthropological chart of my family there would be Mother, reliably at her typewriter, tending to the Band-Aids and hamburgers, but dreaming her secret girlhood ambition to be a trench-coated foreign correspondent. Probably Mother is around too much, just like most middle-class mothers. Father is a constant figure too, although this is supposed to be a broken home. In place of grandparents and aunts and uncles there would be the nuclear apartment building, inhabited by great numbers of people willing to tell stories, buy circus tickets, and help Mother in emergencies. And then, to complete this strange but viable kinship system, there would be the baby-sitters—friends, tutors, siblings, and (at the least) experiences.

Annie arrived at the front door one day carrying a three-day-old puppy and a large plant. I remember her as being barefoot, but I must be wrong, although it was at the height of the reign of the flower children. I was desperate, so I hired her. The dog grew into a mastiff, she taught my son to play the guitar and to meditate, and she told us both about what it was like to hitchhike to New York from California. Eventually, she took the dog to a commune in Vermont.

We hoped we had found another Annie when we hired Lottie, but we were wrong. She taught my son to recognize symptoms of amphetamine addiction and taught me how to get someone out of jail after she has been busted for possession. When I called her mother to say that Lottie had hepatitis, her mother said she didn't care.

When Katya tried to kill herself during the Christmas holidays of her third year with us, my friends advised me to get rid of her. They said her depression would be bad for the child. I thought the notion of disposable people would be bad for the child, and I was glad I had been so firm about it a month later when the child went into the hospital and Katya took over the entire household.

I miss Katya, and I miss Nan, who stayed for two years. She taught my son everything he knows about math, and she spent most of her time, when she wasn't in dance class, bringing me cups of tea.

I was busy lying on the floor and crying those years, so I could hardly blame her when she wrote me a mean letter after she left to live on her own. I felt better when I compared her letter with one I had written my mother some twenty years before and discovered that at least two young girls leaving a place they consider home felt they had to burn it down before it would be left.

Bless her heart. She wrote me a thank-you note. I smiled at the envelope, reflecting that the writer's mother, my best friend, had obviously done a better job of inculcating the social niceties in her seventeen-year-old daughter than I had in my sixteen-year-old son. I carried the note down the hall to use as a threatening example. Then I opened the note. "Thanks for letting us visit. Your house was as refreshingly chaotic as usual." Hmmm. "Refreshingly chaotic." Well now.

As I recall, three arrived at the door when I had expected only one. "Hi," said Beth. "This is Lisa and Sonia. Can they stay too?" I had not actually finished saying yes before all three had regrouped in front of the refrigerator. "We're starving," they said, and three days of careful menu planning disappeared. The milk, the cold chicken, the ham, the special Stilton cheese (wrapped and marked "mine"), the pumpernickel that has to be imported from sixteen blocks away, the jar of sweet peppers in oil I canned last August and was saving for a special event.

Everyone knows that adolescents consume their weight in food every day. Still it comes as a surprise when it happens to one's own refrigerator. In fact, adolescence comes as a surprise when it happens to one's own child. That is why I always welcome adolescent visitors. They serve as a reality check. I discover such useful and reassuring things as the fact that my own adolescent is not the only one in the world who believes that carrying his plate to the sink is the same thing as clearing the table.

Adolescent houseguests expect very little. No small dinners with interesting guests or tours of the city are required. They ask only for sleeping-bag room, a working hair dryer, and a full refrigerator.

Perhaps it was because of my bad back, but I found myself growing slightly impatient during Beth, Lisa, and Sonia's visit. The first couple of days there was a vague air of bewilderment around the house, especially at suppertime. A hopeful flutter around the kitchen door subsided when I ordered in Chinese food. Finally, after a few days, they realized I was not cooking because I couldn't walk. I persuaded one to travel to the grocery store. They cooked dinner happily. But they forget to cook any for me. To put it briefly, they (and I include, embarrassedly, my son) appeared ignorant of all realities of domestic management.

"Why?" I asked Beth's mother, my friend. She replied with a sigh, "They think we are grown-ups. They think we are so organized that food simply appears. They have no idea that every meal takes planning and time."

Suddenly, I remembered myself at that age: the households I adopted, the meals I ate without noticing, the cookies I assumed were baked just for me, the family evenings I interrupted with long soliloquies on my problems with college admissions (or, oh shudder to recall, love's woes).

But then, another friend of mine pointed out a crucial difference. "When we were growing up," she said, "the mothers we knew did not work. They were, in fact, organized. They had time to shop and plan and run a house." Maybe they even had time to renew the pumpernickel. Then again, maybe meals were provided at the cost of hysterics upstairs. But we never knew. Mothers provided and we expected.

Now things are different. We provide and our children expect. We, who grew up to be the generation of working mothers, seem to have followed our mothers' examples instead of working out new systems. It happens to be impossible to provide nourishment for the neighborhood *and* work, unless everyone in the family is part of the organization, but by trying to achieve the impossible ourselves, we have passed on the task of reassigning responsibilities to our children.

Poor Beth. How cross she will be when she discovers that true liberation does not depend on her ability to become a construction worker or a doctor, but on her skill at persuading her family that milk does not walk through the door and jump into the refrigerator by itself.

———

One day my friend Helena found me sitting in my study, weeping and tearing my hair. She wasn't too alarmed at first because I weep and tear my hair the way other people jog—it seems to clear my system and recharge my energies for the day's activities. But this time I didn't seem to be reaching the refreshment point.

"What can I do to help?" she said, patting my shoulder.

"Waaaaah," I wailed, "bills, soot, work deadlines, interpersonal relationships, urban woes, the meaning of life, inflation, equal rights, the human condition, woe, etc."

"Here, take my car keys," said my friend, "and go to Vermont."

Two days later at seven in the morning I found a herd of stray heifers breakfasting in my day lilies. Two neighbors passing by stopped to help me round them up. We saved the day lilies but we knocked down a corner of the porch. The neighbors have promised to come by this afternoon to help prop the porch up again. Until then I plan to pick raspberries. In other words, a perfect day.

Thank you, Helena. Thank you, kind fate for giving me friends who, when they say, "What can I do to help?" mean it.

In my particular corner of the human condition people have had a bad spring and a worse summer. They have been suffering through burglaries, assaults, accidents, runaway children, death, car crashes, psychotic episodes, and cancer. In the course of it all, we have learned a lot about what can be done to help.

The first thing is, don't ever ask, "What can I do to help?" without being prepared to do it, whatever it might be.

If time or resources are limited, offer only what is possible, and offer it without a lengthy explanation of your schedule to the people in trouble. They are in no position to worry about your baby-sitter or your job.

Sometimes it is just as useful to help the helpers. In any emergency people call each other up to fret and wonder what they can do. They don't seem to realize they can coordinate for maximum efficiency. For example, if C baby-sits for B's children, then B can go to the hospital with A.

If the person in trouble is a good friend (the sort of friend, for example, who says, "No, no, I don't need help," and you know she does), then rush right over. Clean the house, walk the dog, water the plants, go to the grocery store, change the beds, drive the bill collectors away from the door. Keep daily life intact. Vacuuming someone's house can be the grand gesture that will keep them from feeling that chaos is closing in.

Offer money or credit cards, if possible.

Answer the telephone for the people in trouble. Keep messages, coordinate information, help turn aside the ghouls and parcel out the problems to be solved. Find the family's personal telephone book, and make sure everyone knows where it is.

Don't call up and vaguely mention a doctor or hot line or funeral home you've heard about. Do all the research first: cost, qualifications, hours, theories. The local crisis hot line will give you information to pass on to the person in trouble.

If you have taken on a responsibility, find your own reliable replacement. Don't disappear after the immediate crisis.

The people I cherish most are the ones who take on the job of soothing the relatives or friends who have every right to be in the house, but cause trouble. A person who will take the dominating mother for a drive, listen to the meddlesome aunt describe the last four family funerals, or tactfully remove the crazy brother-in-law is a person who will be rewarded in eternity.

Do not, ever, explain how the crisis could have been avoided. Any sentence beginning "If only" should never be finished.

Do not confuse worrying with helping. Calling up the person in trouble or even the friends of the person in trouble to talk about how worried you are is a hollow exercise.

Do not expect to be thanked.

IV.

If Women Work

There are times when the problem of who will take care of the children seems less immediate than the problem of who will take care of me. I live on the flip side of the work ethic, where the corollary mottoes are "No wife of mine will ever work" and "fear of success." At least once a day, sometimes all day on bad days, I look around the house and am surprised and furious to find no rich husband paying the bills. I do not want to shuffle down the hall to my typewriter. I want to take a taxi to Bendel's and charge things to a rich husband. I want to take a private plane to Vermont and direct many contractors in the rebuilding of kitchens and cellars at the expense of a rich husband.

This vision is, apparently, my lingering notion of the natural order. It does not often occur to me to imagine that if I were not someone who can shuffle down the hall to a typewriter, I might be someone living in a fifth-hand trailer on a dirt road, washing overalls in a tin tub, and wondering how I could afford new teeth. I am an American and we do not look around and count our blessings. We look above and complain.

It does sometimes cross my mind that the gilded lilies I know—they toil not, neither do they spin, instead they spend—live in constant terror of losing their jobs, of being fired by their rich husbands. What else but an overexaggerated need to prove their worth as a decorative possession could explain the false-fingernail industry?

Certainly, had I ever had a rich husband, I would long since have been turned in for a more amenable new wife. Because, while

I do not enjoy supporting myself, I do not want the rich husband to interfere in any way with my life.

Perhaps it would be nice if I had a rich husband who wished only to remove the burden of daily care so that I might devote myself to My Work? No. The truth is, my devotion to My Work would expire the very moment I realized I no longer had to pay the electric bill myself. I feel no internal compulsion to work (at least, I don't think I do, and I doubt that I will ever have enough money to test the assertion). Instead, I feel a strong, permanent, instinctive, and continuous desire to stop working. I resent having to work. I feel sorry for myself. I pity younger women even as I encourage them to think in terms of career planning instead of rich husbands.

Resentment, self-pity, and an inertia bordering on paralysis are poor career-planning tools. My attitude is a character defect, my secret vice, a devil riding on my shoulder hissing and tempting: "What's a nice middle-class girl like you doing, having to support yourself? What a pity, tsk-tsk." I do not admit easily to this failing. I would rather say: "Oh, I *always* expected to take care of myself." Except I didn't.

We are tracking change here, not cataloging grievances. It has been a bewilderingly abrupt transition for most women, and it continues to be simultaneous instead of sequential. The woman lawyers who bring suit in the cause of other women workers feel the same creeping sense of "What am I doing here?" as the women in displaced homemaker centers who are learning to say "I can do this job" instead of "I don't know how to do anything." My own life is so much at odds with what I expected that I have just spent two months in bed with a bad back—and still no rich husband arrived to take care of me. I can walk through brick walls, but it hurts.

I have spent years in dread of the typewriter. I thought all the time about the moment I would be finished working and could lie

down and read mysteries. Since freelance writers are never finished working, I read mysteries before finishing and felt guilty. I
always worked at night and on weekends, and spent the daytime
making phone calls and cooking. I have never yet owned a proper
desk and only last month I bought a new typewriter to replace the
one I got in a pawnshop ten years ago.

I envied men writers a lot because, unlike them, I have never
had a full-time secretary and I do not lunch at Elaine's and meet
with my lawyers and agents after lunch, before going on to sign
movie contracts. The men writers I know have offices, to which
they withdraw after their wives cook them breakfast. We women
writers, until very recently, never stayed in hotels on expense
accounts, and we carried rolls of dimes to make our business phone
calls from coffee shops.

I have lived with my roll of dimes for years, earning my living, my son's living, and my intermittent baby-sitters' living. Every
woman writer I know who does not go to a regular office job
arranged her professional life in that weird way. It has been a
hand-to-mouth living (hand-to-mouth beats nine-to-five is my personal motto, and perhaps my personal problem). But, more important for all of us, it has been a basic evasion of reality. We were
evading the fact that we worked, diffidently denying ourselves
necessities like secretaries and pretending that the real satisfactions
and duties were domestic.

No wonder life was not very satisfying. I wrote because I had
to, and was lucky enough to like it, but I didn't know I liked it
because I thought of it as work, and work was a bad thing for a
woman to have to do.

Those of us who grew up feeling we would be taking men's
jobs and thus subverting the economy and the natural order if we
worked, also feel that we have been gypped if we have to work.
We usually are being gypped if we work and we are women, but
not because life has not provided us with a nice rich lawyer.
Women working full time earn 40 percent less than men working
full time. If we take into account women's shorter lifetime working
experience, we still earn 20 percent less and the gap is due to pure
discrimination.

Marabel Morgan suggests, in her best-selling book *The Total Woman*, that women greet their working husbands in costume at the end of a long day. A Bunny costume, she suggests, is a good start. Two-thirds of the women in the United States are either widowed, divorced, separated, or have husbands with incomes less than $10,000. What does Ms. Morgan suggest we wear to the welfare office when we need money and are unfit for the labor market?

———

We were sitting around the dinner table—my son, the babysitter, and I. The dog was crouched under the table, staring hopefully at my son's plate. I was describing a meeting I had just been to in which a large part of the staff of a magazine I often worked for had decided to quit their jobs in protest.

"It is a very hard decision for people to make," I said. "After all, a lot of those men have families to support."

My family, including the dog, stared at me in silence. I reached for more salad. They went on staring at me. Finally my son realized I wasn't going to get the point without a little help.

"But, Mom," he said, "some of those people are women with families to support. In fact, *you* have a family to support."

Click!

I sat there at my dinner table, feeling foolish and facing a few facts. Not only do I have a family to support, a good part of the time I do it by writing about women's issues: equal pay, equal opportunity, equal access. I have repeated and repeated the statistics. The one statistic our daughters should be repeating daily is: by the time women are middle-aged we have a fifty-fifty chance of being divorced, widowed, separated, or single. The lesson is perfectly obvious: women have to take care of themselves. And yet, our national policies of employment and welfare still presume that a woman will be taken care of by a man.

The collective wisdom is still that women do not need to work. Therefore, we do not really need equal pay, do not need the education and experience that would make it possible for us to move up, do not really need child-care arrangements, do not really need pensions and job-protection benefits. It is an assumption that has kept millions of women, and their children, who are not lucky enough to be supported by a successful man, in poverty.

I thought I understood that perfectly well. But at my dinner table, when my mind went Click!, I realized how far most of us have to go. Even I, well stocked with numbers and experience, had never taken the matter seriously. After all those years of consciousness raising and independence I apparently still felt, down deep where the subconscious meets socialization, that I was only marking time until the proper order of things reestablished itself. A man would come home, bringing bacon. A ship would come in, a lottery ticket would pay off, a mythical rich uncle would die and leave me millions. In the meantime, it never occurred to me to congratulate myself on my accomplishment, much less plan to meet the challenge.

No wonder I curse an unkind fate (instead of my own irresponsibility, or inflation) whenever I cannot meet the bills. It is dreadful to consider the energy I have wasted feeling angry and petulant because I have to work. (After all, men generally assume they will have to work, and they make the most of it.) No wonder I have never bothered to learn about credit and investments. I still put off working at my desk until I have finished working at the housework. After years and years of trying to change, I *still* think making the bed is more important.

It is not so surprising, I suppose, that I expect things to be as I was taught they would be, instead of as they are. After all, I belong to a generation that was brought up to believe that preparation for the proper order of things involved sending the boys to college and urging the girls to learn shorthand and typing to fall back on "in case something happens." Girls got clothes allowances, boys got money for cars and dates. Marriage was a woman's meal ticket.

"Something" did happen, and here we are, stranded. There is not much point in complaining that we were ill prepared, but we might reserve a bit of grumpiness over our mothers' lack of foresight. "Something"—the Depression and the war—happened to them, and they failed to warn us.

Women are not wondering anymore whether working mothers are bad mothers and wives, or whether women are qualified, or whether women really want to be aggressive enough to demand the important jobs. The questions are no longer "if," but "how." The first answer to "how?" seems to come with that little Click! in the mind when we realize the ways we shape our lives by our attitudes toward money.

In a coffee shop in Topeka, Kansas, last summer, I met a woman who said she had no independent income, that she did not work. Her husband said: "What do you mean? You work for me, one day a week. I pay you."

"Oh," she said, "isn't that odd, I never thought of that as earning money." She went on talking for a while, about children and vacations, and then she suddenly said: "Wait a minute. I work for you seven days a week. At home. How come I think of that one day's pay as the only money I have any right to decide about spending?" Click!

Lucia, divorced and remarried to a man with another family to support, always comforted herself with the knowledge that she was rich. After all, when she was eighteen her father had given each of his children some money, saying: "This is all there is going to be." For years and years she felt safe. This year she went to her accountant and discovered that her great, big, massive fortune was $20,000, of which $4,000 had to be paid in taxes. The rest, these days, is not even enough to send her daughter to college. "Finally I faced that fact that I have no options, and no more time to waste," she said. Click!

Her story is not really so different from the doctor's wife I visited in Chicago. Every time her marriage rocked, which was often, she remembered that she had $500. Then, one day their hot-water heater broke and a new one cost $1,500. "I realized that five hundred dollars wouldn't get me to next month if I had to get there alone," she said. "I'm only beginning to understand that my standard of living is conditional. I try to remember that I can't expect to be kept this way forever, but I'm a long way from doing anything to prepare for it. I still talk about 'my' money, and 'our' money. I know I'm entitled to think of 'our' money because of my contributions at home, but the real fact is that 'our' money is 'his' money." Click!

In Colorado I watched two elderly couples come into a gift shop to look around. The men walked to the back of the store. One of the women picked up some turquoise earrings and said to her friend: "Buy them quick, the old man's gone." With a kind of sly urgency she pushed the earrings toward the salesperson.

The woman I was with, who is about sixty and owns a motel with her husband, stared at the other couples in horror. "I used to act like that. Then one day I went into the bank to get a loan for some television sets for our motel. Even though the credit laws have been changed and I should have been able to get a loan right away on my own, the bank wanted my husband to sign and take responsibility. I started thinking about all the hours I spend running that place, and I got madder and madder—at myself and at the bank. It was my money, and my responsibility, and they were treating me as though I scarcely knew how to tie my shoes. And I had been being cute about it for thirty years." Click!

Women think of money in nickel-and-dime terms. The grander schemes of investment and mortgages, and even savings, often escape us. We do not have much experience with expense accounts, tax shelters, and pension plans. We do not plan much at all, probably because we expect someone else to come along. And, worst of all, we think it is feminine not to know.

"So many women make a weapon and an escape out of not knowing," a woman who had had to give up her job when her husband's job moved to another city told me. "Couples only fight about money when they don't both understand the reality of the situation. Too many women—and men—use not knowing and not telling as an excuse for infuriating behavior, for extravagant spending or martyred penny-pinching. I run our household and at least I make sure I know the financial facts. But it is still not *my* money. Anyone who says it doesn't make a difference if you earn your own money, no matter how much your husband has, is crazy."

A neighbor of mine in Vermont said: "Do I wish I had money

of my own? Do I think money is the key to power in a relationship? Does it make a difference who handles the money? Yes. Yes to all of the above. Control of the money equals control. The money I earned from time to time always seemed to have to go to pay off emergency bills. One day I was having my car fixed and I took a bus home from the garage so my husband would have to pick it up and pay for it. I was paying him back for all the times he said things like: 'Hon, close out your savings account so we can pay the taxes.' Then I thought the whole thing was ridiculous. We were tricking each other all the time. I decided I didn't want to be sly about money anymore. If we were going to fight, we were going to fight about reality. And guess what? Once we got it all laid out, we didn't fight anymore." Click!

Some women—very few—have had moments of truth when they suddenly started making more money than their husbands. A woman I know, married to a high school teacher, said: "We always threw our money in the same pot and I never worried about whose was whose. But all of a sudden I sold a book, and I started talking about *my* kitchen and *my* car. The day I heard myself saying '*My* bill for *my* daughter's orthodontia,' something went off in my head. I realized I was being insufferable. In fact, I was acting like the kind of patriarchal man I most dislike."

It seems to be as hard for most women to adapt to making money as it is for their husbands. Some men, of course, hate to lose the power of being the total provider, but most of them have always been more generous with the notion of "our" money than their wives. They have, after all, been taught about money; they expect calamities like broken hot-water heaters. Women, still thinking in terms of small change, find they regress to dependence when a big expenditure suddenly arises.

A real estate broker in Arizona started making more money than her husband. They had always had a family car, but she decided she wanted "a little Cadillac" because she spent so much time on the road. "All of a sudden it was *my* car," she said, "and I was expected to pay for it, buy the plates, keep it up. I felt my husband was punishing me for buying my own car. Finally I realized it *is* my own car, and my own responsibility. I was just traveling along in the same old rut, thinking he should be in charge of all the big stuff."

Sometimes the Click! that signals a financial moment of truth turns on a big neon sign in the head reading RESPONSIBILITY. Not just responsibility for budgeting and cutting corners and all those things women are supposed to be good at, but responsibility for knowing what is going on with all the money.

Allison is a woman I met in Illinois. She said: "I was working as a waitress, and my husband had a job in a hardware store. We had two kids. One day he simply disappeared. Left the country. And I found out we owed twenty thousand dollars. Can you imagine? Twenty thousand dollars, and my name was on everything. How could I have been so stupid, not to notice what I was signing? I couldn't believe I had to pay if off, but I did. It took me fifteen years. And at the same time I put myself through school and raised the kids.

"Now I'm married again, and even though we are not struggling, I still feel like I am. A Click! doesn't begin to describe how I felt when I found out about those debts. But it has been almost as bad lately. I've begun to realize that my husband and I are equally qualified, and there is no way I am ever going to make as much money as he is, because I am a woman. I've learned the lesson that I can't expect someone else to take care of me, but try telling that to an employer."

The lesson is a painful one to learn.

Marriage—the beginning of a marriage or the end of one, or even just the notion of marriage—is the time when a woman's sense of responsibility for herself always falters. A newly married thirty-five-year-old woman said to me: "Last night my husband asked me if I would mind helping out with the mortgage payment this month, and I clicked. I'd been letting him pay for everything, and I have been buying fancy clothes for myself. I had turned my salary into a special occasions fund, even though I have always supported myself, and I have always expected to."

Even being truly rich is no guarantee against moments of

financial truth. A very, very rich woman in Chicago told me: "I became a feminist the day I went to see the family lawyers because I wanted to adopt a Korean orphan. I learned that any child I adopted, or had out of wedlock, could not inherit my money. And then I learned that my money isn't really mine, but is all held in trust. My brother's money, on the other hand, is his absolutely. I'm going to break that trust if it is the last thing I ever do."

I realized I had better find out about retirement plans.

But then I fell in love, and spent a lot of time making new curtains instead of working. I forgot to practice what I preach. And so I ended up at my own dinner table, feeling foolish. The lesson I learned from that Click! is the lesson I am pasting on my own bathroom mirror.

If I did not realize I have a family to support, then I was not facing reality. I was not yet competent to deal with my situation in life. I was not planning, saving, ordering my time. I was not taking responsibility for myself. I *need* to be equal, but I never will be until I take it seriously myself.

No one is going to do it for me.

It was raining in Maine, and I settled down by the fire with a nice thick book. My hostess insisted that the book's entrails would reveal omens and portents for society. Unlike the Delphic oracle, she was quite clear about what the omens mean. Women, she said, turn out to be the sacrificial lambs.

The book was the Twenty-fifth Anniversary Report of the Harvard Class of 1952. It is four inches thick and contains a thousand more or less self-serving self-portraits gathered from a class of 1,401 men. They were the elite of the Togetherness Generation: 97 percent of them married and 76 percent are still married to their first wives. They have 2.88 children each.

The question on "wife's occupation" elicited the first signs of confusion in a time of change. "Housewife," some replied, sure of their ground. Others wrote "dietician," "lawyer," "flower arranger," "potter," or "teacher," as circumstances seemed to indicate. But some, out of bravado or perhaps bewilderment, elaborated: "multitalented family facilitator," "homemaker and citizen," "volunteer and intensive homemaker," "aspiring artist," "domestic engineer and pleasurer."

The average age of the wives is 35–44, so it is odd to see the number of times "student" is put down as an occupation: 56 percent of the wives are getting some kind of degree. Thirty-nine percent have a B.A. already; 22 percent have a master's degree. The wives, like their husbands, went to schools that theoretically prepared them for the fullest possible lives: Vassar, Radcliffe, Wellesley, etc.

A full life is a very personal notion, as the members of the class amply demonstrate in their individual reports. Self-actualization at forty-seven seems to depend on such variables as an introduction to Jesus, coming out of the closet, and resignation to fate. None of the class seems to have felt that money, as a source of satisfaction, was worth mentioning, despite the revelation that one-half of the Harvard Class of 1952 was earning, twenty-five years later, more than $40,000 a year. That was $20,000 a year above the national median income for men forty-seven years old. Only 7.3 percent earned less than $15,000 a year.

The female group described as "Wives-Partners of '52" apparently did feel that income was a matter worth taking up. They expressed themselves so forcefully in their own part of the class questionnaire that the compiler felt moved to remark that the source of women's rage might be found in their own earnings report.

Of the women who answered, 62 percent earned less than $5,000 a year. Two percent earned more than $30,000 a year. Only 26 percent worked full time, 30 percent part time, and 25 percent as volunteers. Of the Ph.D.'s in this group of women, 86 percent were working, but only 37 percent earned more than $20,000 a year, and 25 percent earned less than $5,000. In answer to "How do you feel about yourself" only 19 percent of the Ph.D.'s felt "blessed," and most of them felt "disappointed." Of the women earning less than $15,000, 53 percent said they were less interested in sex than they had been when young, but 74 percent of the women earning more said they were more interested.

My host insisted that a polemic cannot be fairly constructed from these figures. He wanted me to compare full-time workers with Ph.D.'s, for example. Okay, let's compare some full-time workers. A woman with five years of college earns less than a man with four years of high school.

I wanted my host to recognize the effects of social expectations on a group of people who were at graduation similar in all respects except sex. He wanted to argue. According to the class report most arguments between Classmates and Wives-Partners are about Children, Money, Diet, Sex, In-Laws, Friends, Life Goals, Politics, and Religion. In that order. One woman pointed out the questioners had omitted the women's movement as a possibility.

Frankly, my polemic was slightly sidetracked by the inclusion of diet as a cause of domestic disorder. Obviously if diet is a personal issue of that magnitude, the Class of '52 could not be expected to find time to consider problems of opportunity and equality.

———

Caroline Bird has suggested that the two-paycheck family also liberates men, frees both workers to redefine work in human terms. The thought is pleasant, but a worker's paradise will emerge only if women keep their wits about them. At the moment far too many men seem to view the presence of a working woman in their lives as a chance to emulate the Greek model: the women do the work and care for the children and the men keep the power and sit in cafés discussing politics all day.

———

It is quite wonderful, the way men continue to devise new rules to perpetuate old problems, keeping the world the same safe, comfortable place they have always known. One of the most diverting examples is the rush of advice on what women should wear to be successful.

I don't mind the advice. After all, the coat and suit business needs a market, publishers need books, magazines need layouts that will attract advertisements. What I am afraid of is that women seem to be believing the advice instead of simply choosing some new clothes according to need, size, and price.

On Park Avenue during lunch hour one day the sidewalks were filled with young women wearing things dark and tailored with fluffy neck-tie objects at the neck. I felt as though time were rushing backward to the dark ages before August 27, 1966.

That was the day I first stepped out on the streets of downtown New York City wearing blue jeans. To my astonishment no lightning bolt struck me down because I was not "dressed for town." The world had changed. I could put away the dark cotton, white gloves, and black pumps. The era of pin curls, waist cinchers, and girdles had ended.

I have looked perfectly dreadful ever since. Luckily, "perfectly dreadful" is the success look for freelance journalists. I am certainly not ideologically opposed to being well dressed. Whenever I am going to interview someone who might have a paneled office, I try to wear a dress. I understand that most women do not even want to try to get away with looking like someone delivering pizza.

On the other hand, they must not be led to believe that they can't get away with anything other than dark and tailored with a fluffy tie at the neck. John T. Molloy, author of a book called *The Woman's Dress for Success Book*, must be kidding when he writes: "There is one firm and dramatic step women can take toward professional equality with men. They can adopt a business uniform."

Uniforms are useful. They solve the problem of choice in the morning, reducing the options to the fluffy neck object. Very businessmanlike. Very school-uniform-like. (How about blazers for everybody with patches reading IBM or USDA on the pockets?) But uniforms have nothing at all to do with firm and dramatic steps toward equality with men.

They have to do with telling women that we are inferior forms of the superior model and we should go back to square one and learn to copy the real thing. We will continue to fall short, naturally enough, but our search for the right suit will distract us from filing suit because of job discrimination.

If we don't find our own rules pretty quickly, we will be left with the dictim: never carry a pocketbook with a briefcase, or so warned Michael Korda, author of *Success*. In fact, most women carry huge satchels to work because they might have to get groceries on the way home. New rules would allow men to carry shopping bags and deal with the groceries and pick up their own dry cleaning during the lunch hour. After that, they might even abolish all-male lunch clubs.

And then, after a while, the millennium might arrive. Women might be allowed to stop feeling guilty if someone in the office finds them sexy. After all, everyone is sexy to someone; it is one of the miracles of life. If women are not taken seriously because they are considered sexy, surely that is the men's problem, not the women's? Especially since the men are simultaneously telling each other that those women whom they do not think are sexy are tough broads. Which isn't exactly being taken seriously either.

The fact is, women in offices who take themselves seriously are threatening to men, no matter what they wear.

Dressing for success, even being a success, is not necessarily the same thing as being a feminist. Feminism is a conscious and continous effort to improve the lives of all women, an effort which requires changing the system that defines success merely as making a lot of money.

A man I know told me a story. He had just gotten a glimpse of the Big Picture—the oppression-of-women picture—while he was lunching in the executive dining room of a very large New York corporation. Twelve heads of departments, two of them women, one of the women sitting next to the Chief, were there.

"The two guys sitting next to me spent the entire hour speculating juicily on how the woman next to the Chief felt. They described his powerful knee rubbing against her middle-aged knee under the table," my friend said. "They said women are all turned on by power." But they were the ones turned on. Vulgarizing a woman who has as much power as they do makes them feel more powerful.

"And those guys," my friend went on, "are the same ones who write 'How does she look in a bikini?' on a woman's job application, and the ones who drive the secretaries crazy by offering back rubs. No wonder eighty-five percent of the women in that company are in the lowest paying jobs. No wonder they had to sue before the company promoted any women."

My friend wandered off, muttering "no wonder," and I called another friend, who happened to be the woman whose knee was the subject of such speculation. "Oh, I know that locker-room style," she said. "It's their way of making me feel confused, slightly guilty about being where they don't think I should be. It is psychological harassment, but it is no different from a man who threatens to fire his secretary if she won't sleep with him, and then does fire her if she complains. It's not sex, it's a power play."

Sexual harassment on the job is becoming a big issue, not because it is a new issue, but because women are beginning to talk about it. What women once saw as an individual, isolated problem—probably her own fault, she should never have left home—is now beginning to be seen as inexcusable and inappropriate behavior that should be subject to penalties.

Working Women United Institute found in a preliminary survey that 70 percent of the women sampled had experienced sexual harassment at least once. They were women of all ages, marital status, and job categories, although women in lower paying jobs were more subject to physical harassment than purely verbal. If the harassment was ignored, it did not stop, and those who complained were penalized.

Ellen Cassedy, of Nine to Five, a Boston organization of working women, advises women who are being harassed to treat the problem objectively. It is not a sexual problem, it is a job hazard, a matter of being able to earn a living. Make your refusal absolutely clear and start keeping a notebook of what happened, where, and when. Ask other women in the office if it has happened to them. It is far easier to speak to the management in a group, but if that is impossible, inform your supervisor yourself.

Keep a record of whom you have told. Records objectify and make it easier to deal with the always lingering feeling that you somehow are guilty. The records are also useful if your company has no grievance procedures, or management has no standards (in other words, all the guys club together in the locker room and decide you are crazy). Then the records go into a statement to your Equal Employment Opportunity officer, into your personnel file, and—if worse comes to worst—to your state attorney general, Fair Employment Practices Commission or Human Rights Agency, or state Equal Employment Opportunity Commission. Records also may prove eligibility for unemployment insurance if you are fired.

Cases have been accepted, and sometimes won, by those organizations. It varies from state to state. (To find out the most likely place to turn for help in your area, write to Working Women United Institute, 593 Park Avenue, New York, N.Y. 10021.)

Organizations of working women are growing, and they are important, because they form a support system for even the most vulnerable women, such as waitresses. After all, "In unity there is strength" is a motto that works just as well outside the locker room as inside.

———

Inflation is a women's issue. Women earn, on the average, fifty-nine cents for every dollar men earn. A 7 percent (or 12 percent, or 20 percent—who can keep up?) reduction in real spending power because of inflation is felt more painfully by people earning only fifty-nine cents on the dollar.

Women are now 41.7 percent of the entire labor force. However, 80 percent of those women are concentrated in jobs at the low end of the pay scale: in service industries, clerical occupations, retail stores, factories, and plants. A "low-paid" job is also a job without benefits, security, and is usually nonunionized.

Women's unemployment rate—7.2 percent in 1978—is higher than men's. For minority women the unemployment rate was 13.1 percent, and for minority teen-age women it was a staggering 38.4 percent. Furthermore, women make up two-thirds of the discouraged labor force: the people who need jobs but have given up looking and are not counted in the unemployment figures. Government programs designed to solve the unemployment problems of white men do not solve the unemployment problem.

The persistent illusion that millions of women out of work are somehow not part of the problem, that they somewhere have a man to take care of them, is only one of the reasons that affirmative action programs in employment are enforced with something less than absolute rigidity. (The other reasons are cost, confusion, and prejudice.)

Discrimination against women and minorities in wages, hiring, promotion, and benefits is illegal in all federally assisted programs. Employers who get federal money are supposed to first supply some proof of positive action to wipe out such discrimination. The more usual practice has been for the employers to supply assurances that after they have gotten the money, they will certainly do something about affirmative action, and meanwhile they will be providing jobs (for unemployed white men, but after all a job is a job—and so back to start).

If all the affirmative-action laws were enforced tomorrow, there would be a major upheaval, not just of a few women moving into supervisors' jobs. *One-third* of the national labor force depends on federal procurement expenditures for their jobs. Some 250,000 organizations (including universities) have been awarded government contracts to provide the paper clips, B-1 bombers, books, training programs, research and development that our government buys with our tax money. It would be nice if our money did not go to companies that continue to discriminate against women.

Meanwhile, women remain poor. Another persistent illusion of economic policy planners is that "the poor" are somehow neuter.

This is a usefully depersonalizing attitude to hold during the debates about cutting services to "the poor" out of each year's budget, but in fact the vast majority of "the poor" are women and children. Well over a third of all families headed by women live below the poverty line. Only one out of eighteen families headed by men live in poverty.

Women work to survive, to cushion the effects of inflation on our families—because we need to work. The most extraordinary social dislocation of the last decade has been women's entry into the job market. We took any job we could get, and in the process rediscovered systemic discrimination. The original fight—equal pay for equal work—turned into an organized movement for equal opportunity, for an end to barriers based on sex, and for the formulation of new policies and programs that would help women become equal, independent members of American society.

We have hardly begun to define the problems and the goals, but now we are told the well has run dry. The government, instead of taking into account the fact that women need to work and are working and that such a change requires major far-reaching changes in public policy, has created bits and pieces in response to women's demands. A bit of CETA here, a piece of HEW there, a soupçon of affirmative action over there. Now it seems easiest to hack away at the bits and pieces and hope such snips will fight inflation.

Politicians snarl about corruption in CETA programs. Women were not the people being rehired with CETA funds for long-standing city hall jobs. Women in CETA programs were getting, as usual, the short-term low-paying jobs.

Politicians growl about social services (those services women, now working, once performed for free). Women are now paid minimally to provide child care, nursing-home aid, school lunches, health services, and family planning which also help women. Those programs were created to meet needs.

The bureaucracy must be cut, they say. One-fifth of all women on nonfarm payrolls are employed by some level of government. Seventy-three point six percent of federal jobs in the low GS 1–6 categories are filled by women. Only 6.3 percent of the much better paid GS-13 and higher jobs are held by women. Guess which parts of the bureaucracy will be fired?

The Joint Council on Economic Education warns: "We all pay part of the cost of discrimination because we are denied the full value of what [women] could be producing. Indeed, because of discrimination, our Gross National Product is many billions of dollars less than it should be."

Women are 70 percent of hospital workers, but 90 percent of all doctors are men.

Women are 67 percent of public-school teachers, but in 1972—the last year the data was broken down to show the position of women—only 2 percent of secondary-school principals and 18 percent of primary-school principals were women.

Women are 31.1 percent of federal workers, but only 0.3 percent hold jobs rated GS-15 and above (that is, top ranked government service jobs).

Women are one-third of bank employees, but 80 percent of bank officers and administrators are men.

Women are 98 percent of all clerical workers.

Only 3.1 percent of construction apprenticeship jobs are held by women. "But why would a woman want to go into construction?" a well-meaning white, male liberal once asked me. Not because they want to sit on girders and whistle at men. Because of the money, which is at least double that of the traditional jobs they are offered.

Women are only 15 percent of the trustees and regents on university and college governing boards.

Women are only ten of the 6,400 officers and directors of the 1300 largest companies in the United States. Yes, ten.

This scant intrusion by women upon the upper ranks of the

working world is not because of our stupidity, our lack of self-confidence, or our poorly developed work ethic. It is because, as Rosabeth Kanter, author of *Men and Women of the Corporation*, has neatly put it: "It's hard to be a team player when they don't want you on their team."

V.

Inside
the Clubhouse

Their team is called the Establishment. They play the game of Power and Patriarchy by the rules of Upward Failure.

They do not call it Upward Failure. They never use words like "failure" or "ruin" or "disgrace" or "dishonor," thus accommodating failure by refusing to admit it. They do recognize failure elsewhere; minorities, women, and the poor are the assigned and expected failures, and we serve in that capacity as a kind of self-protection for the system.

Upward Failure is an exclusive prerogative, a gentleman's agreement, an old school tie, a good ol' boy operation, a dirty little secret.

Upward Failure explains why nothing works in this country.

Upward Failure explains why some of our most permanently prominent successes are in fact either corrupt charlatans and thugs, or merely discredited, mediocre, and out of date.

The rules of Upward Failure are:

1. *Be born white and male, preferably WASP.* Adequate planning in this regard will not guarantee success, but it will guarantee lack of failure.
2. *Never admit failure.* If it should become impossible to continue calling a spade a club, call a spade a spade and blame someone else.

3. *Always surround yourself with people so distin-
guished they must promote you in order to protect
themselves.* Admission of failure, by anyone, gives
the game away. Could the Establishment have
afforded to let William Bundy wander up and down
the East Coast handing out résumés that might read
"former assistant secretary of state for Southeast
Asia, special field of expertise the domino theory"?
Certainly not. To let Bill Bundy go jobless would be
to admit that the Establishment itself suspected it
had been arrogant, stubborn, wrong. The march of
the clay feet. So they made Bill Bundy editor of
Foreign Affairs, house organ of the foreign-policy
Establishment.

4. *Be loyal to your team.* George Bush so well illus-
trates the rewards of loyalty that he has become the
basic case. As Richard Nixon's national chairman of
the Republican Party from 1973 to 1974, and as
director of the Central Intelligence Agency from
1976 to 1977, he remained ever the gentleman, even
as the nation woke each morning to fresh reports of
scandal, subversion of the Constitution, abuse of
civil liberties, and murderous intervention in foreign countries. Such doubts as he now claims to have
had about the activities of his team mates were, at
the time, extremely private. Question not, and ye
shall not be questioned. Instead, ye will be considered "experienced" and hailed as a possible candidate for president of the United States.

5. *Dissent is almost never effective, and worse, it will
get you booted out of the club.* Who honors Walter
Hickel for leaving the Nixon Cabinet, complaining
loudly about policies toward the war and demon-
strators? He was considered some kind of nut. John
Gardner, on the other hand, left the Carnegie Foun-

dation to become secretary of Health, Education, and Welfare under Johnson. (Note the significant routing: secretary of HEW is the chief administrative post of the University-Government-Foundation Upward Failure network.) Gardner left the Johnson administration for "personal" reasons, and formed Common Cause, an organization that asks the rest of us to make a public moral commitment. Walter Hickel is still in Alaska.

6. *There is no such thing as bad publicity.* Richard Nixon, an example of Upward Failure in its rarest and most spectacular form, carried this maxim to its logical extreme and eventually established the uppermost limit to the entire system.

7. *Be mobile.* The ability to get out before they catch you, and to arrive at the next place full of chutzpah and big plans, is the fundamental skill of American corporate life. Similar nimble footwork is practiced by television anchormen and university professors. Urban consultants in traffic, sewage, and schools skip from city to city, and so do dozens of sports managers, coaches, and indeed entire teams.

8. *If you are outside the Establishment try to work at something no one really understands.* Something like Decision-Making or Movie-Making, or Management, or something "creative" like publishing will do. If no one can define what "success" might be, or if they are unwilling to admit how large a part luck plays, then no one can recognize failure either.

9. *There are individual possibilities in every collective disaster, especially in political disasters.* The ticket on your steamer trunk reading "Goldwater Campaign" or "McGovern Campaign" or any loser's campaign does not mean you are a loser too. Take the heartwarming examples of Gary Hart and Pat

Caddell, who were boy geniuses of the McGovern campaign, which carried one (one) state. Gary Hart is now a United States senator and Pat Caddell has found employment identifying a "national malaise" for Jimmy Carter.

10. *You will know if you have reached the top.* You will be appointed Director of a Major Foundation, or to a prestigious Presidential Commission. Certain jobs are simply understood to be reserved for a major failure requiring promotion up and out, or for someone at the end of a long career.

11. *Jobs can always be found, or invented, inside the system.* If you do not reach the top, you will never be abandoned if you have followed the rules. Jobs as University President were once reserved for successful failures, but the universities have recently tended to object. Honorific posts with public television or cultural institutions await the faithful. Businesses still set up inadequate colleagues in consulting firms, although "consultant" is a word so overworked it automatically conjures up visions of unemployment. Law firms anxious to honor someone but not to share the graft will appoint a fellow lawyer "of counsel" or shuffle him off to a client. Chairman of the Board, even to a gullible public, signals senility and approaching death, or managerial chaos undergoing reform.

12. *The more important the title, the more self-important the person, the greater the amount of time spent on the Eastern shuttle, the more suspicious the man and the less vitality in the organization.* Smugness reinforces Upward Failure, and both are the particular marks of corrupt and decadent institutions, whether they are baseball teams, city governments, or political parties.

Several years after I attempted this clarification of the Establishment rules for the benefit of puzzled feminists who were having trouble believing the evidence of their own experience, I learned that William Zinsser had offered a variation of the same analysis in 1972, in a column in the old *Life* magazine. He, too, called the rules "Upward Failure." I was delighted to discover that his wisdom had preceded mine because it meant: a) that I must be right, and b) if a man could notice Upward Failure and find it a system worthy of derision, then not all men consider it a Sacred Code, and therefore the possibility of an improved future exists.

In Washington, power is perceived as something to acquire, a sort of inert object that might be held in the lap. Few of the men who have power have any really imaginative ideas—good or bad—about what to do with it. Instead they tend to think in rather banal terms, often along the lines of demanding bigger limousines.

Why isn't power ever defined as having a higher standard of living, or a lower infant mortality rate, or feeding the old and the poor? Could it really be because feeding the old and the poor would mean fewer powerless?

Is it true that women define power as having control over our own lives? And that men define power as having control over other peoples' lives? Probably it is not true but merely a comforting oversimplification. Probably men really see power as a game of musical chairs (deep, leather chairs in paneled rooms), and the fun depends on making sure there are not enough chairs to go around. Washington reporters like to refer to this activity, when it takes place in the United States, as "a peaceful transfer of power."

We do peacefully transfer power, very decorously, from white male to white male. It gets kind of boring for the people who find they can't get into the circle. I used to entertain myself at dull dinner parties by asking the host if any of the many corporate boards he sat upon included women. The host invariably would express his deep commitment to the idea of granting women access to the paneled rooms of power and prestige. But, he would add, he couldn't find any suitable women to cross the threshold.

Some hosts meant they were waiting for a suitable woman to appear in a dream and leave a calling card on the pillow. I gathered from their description that the name on the card would be prefixed H.Q., for Highly Qualified, instead of Miss, Mrs., or Ms. Sometimes the hosts meant that Margaret Mead, Jacqueline Kennedy, and Barbara Jordan had refused their invitation. Therefore they considered every avenue had been exhausted.

If I had had my wits about me, I would have worked up a list of Highly Qualifieds before the dinner. If I had really had my wits about me. I would have charged a large fee for my list, after skillfully leading the conversation around to a discussion of the penalties for evasion of the equal rights acts.

However, the penalties for evasion are neither very severe nor immediate and my wits are seldom with me. I used to join the murmurings about "Where are the qualified women?" As we murmured, we would all gaze about the room, up toward the chandelier, into the corner behind the potted palm, under the napkin, hoping perhaps that qualified women would pop out like leprechauns.

In 1976 the National Women's Political Caucus presented newly elected President Carter's transition office with a list. The quality and quantity of qualified women available for jobs in the new administration surprised the feminists who made up the list only slightly less than it surprised the administration. Former commerce Secretary Juanita Kreps's observation that more qualified women might be found if more women were doing the looking proved true. Presumably her axiom will continue to apply as the women who were certified "Qualified" by the Carter administration move on to the next step, influence in the real world. Because, never forget, while it is very nice to be part of a new administration and to devote oneself heart and soul to saving the world, the ultimate reward is that such a job is a direct route to the paneled rooms.

Which is why the men in any new administration—the men who know that a deputy assistantship at the Treasury Department means a sure partnership in a rich law firm—do not exactly roll out the red carpet when women (and blacks, and Latins, and Indians—half of whom are women) arrive at transition headquarters demanding jobs. Like Leprechauns.

It looked, not too long ago, as though women would be elected to public office only after it became absolutely clear that there were no men left who could do the job—or wanted the job. But in 1978 the number of women running for office began to increase, and the number of women holding seats in state legislatures rose for the first time to 10 percent. Social-change buffs may reasonably point out that 10 percent since women got the vote in 1920 is not exactly the revolution the suffragettes had in mind. But optimists will smile bravely and point out that for the last twenty-five years women held only 3 to 4 percent of all state seats. Now women have stopped waiting for permission, are getting organized, even donating money (which means women have some money). We have learned not to begin speeches with a self-deprecating "I don't really know much about this issue"—an important transformation if the personal is to become political.

What difference will it make? Well, for one thing, the presence of women in our elected assemblies affirms the possibility of a democratic society. Women in office, helping to determine public policy, might invent a welfare system that actually helps recipients get off welfare, instead of spending huge sums to distinguish the worthies from the unworthies (those designated unworthy usually turn out to be women). Maybe women would doubt the wisdom of subsidizing arms sales to people whose interest in defending the free world is distinctly less than their interest in destroying their neighbors (whom we have usually also armed). Maybe women would see to it that affirmative-action laws are enforced and think of ways to allow day-care centers in office buildings as tax shelters.

I am fairly certain that most women would consider it immoral, as well as bad policy, for the United States to train experts in torture, and to let them loose upon the world. I cannot help but hope that women are slightly more likely to understand that American women are not yet equal and to think equality is a good idea, both because I want to be equal and because a society's attitude toward women indicates its capacity to understand and to change those systems that oppress and limit some of its people and much of its potential.

I am not saying that women in power *will* make a difference. I am only saying we should. Margaret Thatcher, Indira Gandhi, Madame Bandaranaike, are always mentioned at this point, and so I add, with some sorrow, that I never said being a woman was the same thing as being a feminist. A feminist is a person—man or woman—who understands and wishes to change the injustices of patriarchal systems. It is very unlikely that such a person would, at the present time, have risen to the top of such a system.

What is remarkable, considering the way the Establishment has set up the rules of the Game, is not that there are so few women in power, but that there are any at all.

Take, for example, the Supreme Court. There are not very many women working at any great distance from a mop or a steno pad in the Supreme Court. Of the group of law clerks that arrives annually to spend a year working for individual justices, only 14 percent have been women since 1975. Before that, it was hardly worth counting: Justice William O. Douglas, a great man, hired the first woman law clerk in 1944. Three more slipped in over the years, and in 1972 Justice Douglas repeated his original experiment and hired two more, bringing the grand total to six.

Supreme Court law clerks process petitions and do research. The work may not be as varied or interesting as clerking for another kind of judge, but it carries a certain cachet. Perhaps even carnet to the future. Justice Rehnquist clerked for Justice Jackson, Justice White for Justice Vinson, Dean Acheson for Justice Brandeis, Elliot Richardson and former Transportation Secretary Coleman for Justice Frankfurter. Members of the law faculties of Harvard and Yale have been Supreme Court clerks. New clerks are hired by committees of former clerks. The whole process is a nice example of how the Establishment works.

One is not necessarily being oversensitive if the atmosphere at the Supreme Court seems somewhat excessively male: the usual leather chairs and a rather antique perception of the role of women in American life. Nor is one being oversensitive if one objects to being accused of demanding conspicuous tokenism when, in fact, one is simply suggesting a woman Justice of the Supreme Court. She would be a token (*of course* a Highly Qualified token) that women are at last recognized as equal, as Justices Taney, Brandeis, and Marshall were appointed as Catholic, Jewish, and Black tokens of equality.

In 1971 Professors John D. Johnston, Jr., and Charles L. Knapp, both of New York University School of Law, wrote an article in the NYU *Law Review* titled: "Sex Discrimination by Law: A Study in Judicial Perspective," which examined the difficulties male judges have in understanding women's problems. They do not, to put it in the vernacular, understand where women are at. Perhaps more women judges, including Supreme Court judges, would enlarge the male judge's ability to empathize. Men and women empathizing back and forth might equalize the problems and the solutions. Admittedly it is extremely unlikely that such a feast of sweet reason will occur. But it certainly won't if no women are appointed.

Institutions do change. Even the American Bar Association has changed as more and more women become lawyers. Ten years ago less than 3 percent of the country's lawyers were women. Now 26 percent of law students are women, the greatest increase in any of the professions. One reason there are not more women lawyers, and not more gloriously "qualified" candidates for the Supreme Court, is because law schools such as Harvard started graduating women only in 1953, after years of offering such evasions as concern about plumbing facilities. (More likely they were afraid women would learn how to sue academic institutions. They were right.)

It has been a long, slow march from 1875, when Myra Bradwell passed the Illinois bar exam, but was refused admission. The United States Supreme Court, in a famous and infamous decision, sides with Illinois on the grounds of natural law and the sanctity of the family.

"The natural and proper timidity and delicacy which belongs to the female sex evidently unfits it for many of the occupations of civil life," the Court opined, and "the civil law as well as nature herself has always recognized a wide difference in the respective spheres and destinies of man and woman. Man is, or should be, woman's protector and defender."

Well, obviously that notion of natural law didn't hold up. We might as well try equality.

———

Seventy-eight percent of all the nation's college and university faculties are men, and they will apparently go to any lengths to keep it that way.

Consider, for example, the fact that Brown University deemed it worthwhile to spend close to one million dollars of its meager resources fighting a sex discrimination suit brought by anthropologist Louise Lamphere. Denied tenure in May 1974, Lamphere took her grievance through all the appropriate channels, from the Brown Faculty Policy Group, which found certain procedural violations, to the Boston Equal Employment Opportunity Commission, which found cause to bring suit, to the U.S. District Court, where she claimed sex discrimination under Title VII of the Civil Rights Act.

The court, in July 1976, certified her suit as a class action, which meant that Lamphere (and three other women at Brown, who later joined the suit) represented all women faculty at Brown, present, future, and past since 1972.

Hundreds of academic institutions are fighting, by fair means or foul, sex-discrimination suits. But the Lamphere case was considered "the best" by the women's Equity Action League, which provided expertise, because it covered discrimination in every area of faculty employment.

Brown University felt it was defending a basic principle: that the integrity of the university depends on the faculty's right to decide whom they shall hire. A few of the faculty defended the principle to the point of being fined nearly $8,000 in 1977 for contempt of court displayed by lengthy delays in turning over papers.

Brown said that in a period of declining student enrollment and reduced federal funding, tenure should go only to the very best. Lamphere's scholarly work was criticized for "theoretical weaknesses," and the direction of her future work was said not to fit into the department's long-term goals. Her lecturing was said to be sloppy.

The people supporting Lamphere felt that the tenure system is The System that keeps out women and minorities. They cited statistics showing discriminatory patterns at Brown. The "future direction" of her work happened to be feminist. She was co-editor and contributor to an important book, *Women, Culture and Society*. The faculty at Brown was then 97 percent male. They had difficulty, as do all university faculty men, with the notion of women in society as a valid scholarly field. Lamphere's earlier work dealt with the more acceptable Navaho Indians.

Lamphere admitted she prefered working with students more directly than lecturing, and indeed she worked very hard, especially for change within the university. Universities do not like change.

Somehow, by using words like "quota" and making accusations of preferential treatment, academic males have persuaded the public that they are pleading fairness when they are in fact protecting their privileges.

Since 1970, when the first academic institution was investigated for failure to comply with affirmative-action regulations, the money gap between men and women in all types of institutions, at all ranks, has remained the same. More women are employed in the lower ranks, but fewer in the upper ranks. Women and minorities, in a time of retrenchment, are retrenched most. Even where there are declared affirmative-action programs, there is little change. Rules without enforcement are paper tigers, and the institutions know it.

"You can always go to court," people say. Yes, if you don't mind losing all your friends, several years running bake sales for money while facing corporate law firms, and hearing that you were never smart and have a rotten personality. And then, even if you win or settle, being treated as a pariah. It takes more strength than spite can give: it takes commitment to principle.

Sometimes principle wins. Louise Lamphere won tenure and two other women were given tenure and back pay. Brown was required to set up a fund of $400,000 to pay other possible claims of sex discrimination. The court settlement also requires far-reaching goals and objectives to assure the hiring of more women and the awarding of more tenure slots to women.

Brown complained: "These nuisance suits make it very difficult for institutions." Why not make it easier? Why not stop discriminating?

An institution, to remain an institution, must take itself absolutely seriously. There must never be a moment's doubt that the institution knows best and does right. A challenge to the institution's rectitude must never be allowed to become an opportunity to examine the procedures of the institution, but must instead be blamed on faulty understanding of the "Right Way" on the part of the challenger.

The mark of a truly successful institution is the degree to which those connected with it lower their voices when speaking of it, as in The Church, The Bank, and The Junior Cotillion. So, too, do people who work for the *New York Times* lower their voices when saying "The *Times*."

The women who work for the *Times* lower their voices as reverentially as do the men. They say, without blushing, "I love the *Times*." In 1974, when eighty separate women from all departments of the paper filed complaints with the Equal Employment Opportunity Commission, it was not simply because they wished to end personal discrimination in their professional lives. It was also because they hoped to make a great newspaper even better.

If a newspaper pays its women employees on the average of thousands of dollars less for the same work than its men employees, if 70 percent of its women employees are clustered in the lowest job categories, if its evaluating memos include descriptions of women employees' figures—as subsequent records gathered by the *Times*' complainants revealed—the thought was that that newspaper's attitude toward the women it employs will be reflected in its coverage of issues involving women. Equal opportunity for women working for the paper will result in a less biased, more objective, and thus even better paper.

The *Times*, bristling with institutional rectitude, did not see the logic of the argument. The women's case, represented by Harriet Rabb and Howard Rubin, was declared a class action in 1977. Depositions were taken and records turned over. The depositions often showed an attitude of malevolent contempt toward women which surprised and horrified even those New York media watchers who are unsympathetic to women.

In 1978 the *Times* agreed to settle. The *Times* said the women agreed to settle. A *Times* press release read: "The settlement . . . is one which, in all respects, imposes so few new obligations on The *Times* that it would have been vindictive not to accept it."

In private, *Times* executives expressed their views of the case less becomingly—more or less on the lines of: "Nyah, nyah, they settled so we won." It was possible, one imagines, for the women to have said the same thing, and in fact Ms. Rabb's press release indicated that because the *Times* had agreed to everything the women would have asked for if the case had come to trial, the women were happy to settle.

The *Times* idea of no new obligations was $233,500 in annuities. The *Times* insisted on the word "annuities" although, since they were cashable immediately, the women tended to call them "back pay." The *Times* press release said, "This annuity program, which will compensate some women for societal discrimination. . . ."

"Societal" is a nice touch, a pleasantly objective way of describing what the women who were getting the money felt was small compensation for years of discrimination by the *Times* in its hiring and promotion policies.

The *Times*, while insisting it had had an affirmative-action program all along, also agreed to what it described as "the modified affirmative action" program. The essential modification was that the much more stringent goals, reaching much higher in the company, must thereafter be enforced under threat of contempt of court.

The most astonishing argument in the depositions and briefs of the *Times* was the argument of market value—that women will work for less, therefore can be paid less. This is the argument Title VII of the 1964 Civil Rights Act was passed to counteract. It was embarrassing to see it made by a great, liberal, unbiased institution.

The point of the Establishment game is to deny, to most of the population, access to money and power. A successful challenge to the Establishment always involves a transfer of money and power. This rule applies to the political, professional, and institutional branches of the Establishment, and applies as well to that segment of the business branch that Flo Kennedy has named the Jockocracy—the sports industry.

The one nice thing about sports is that they prove men do have emotions and are not afraid to show them. In 1972 the Civil

Rights Act was amended. Title IX of those amendments prohibits sex discrimination in federally assisted education programs—and that includes sports. The outraged reaction suggested that men know how to weep for what they hold dear. Title IX regulations became effective in 1975, and there were men who believed it would mean the end of college sports as we know them.

There were women who thought that would not be a bad thing. Some of the things women in sports wanted to see changed were outlined in a 1975 report prepared by the Association of American Colleges' Project on the Status and Education of Women. A random selection of examples included the fact that women were sometimes prohibited from taking coaching courses and so, upon graduation, were not "qualified" to coach teams and were thus effectively barred from a common career ladder that moves from physical education instructor on up to principal. Women's teams regularly relied on bake sales and bazaars to get traveling funds, while men's teams roamed around in university-chartered busses.

Reordering such traditional discrepancies is a revolutionary effort at social change. Luckily, nobody put it quite that way in 1972 when the educational amendments were being pushed through Congress. Back then, equality was just a nice word, and anyone against it sounded as preposterous as the Connecticut judge who in 1971 denied women the right to participate on a cross-country team with the words: "The present generation of our younger male population has not become so decadent that boys will experience a thrill in defeating girls in running contests. . . . Athletic competition builds character in our boys; we do not need that kind of character in our girls, the women of tomorrow."

The uproar over Title IX is not simply a sentimental response to the abhorrent thought that the mothers-of-tomorrow might learn aggressiveness on the playing fields of today. The uproar is over money, and it is usually phrased: "But we don't possibly have enough money to provide equal budgets for women's sports." One solution might be to give less money to men's sports and more money to women. That is not, however, the solution the men of the nation's collegiate sports industry have found. As Title IX has turned out so far, they have managed to get more money and more jobs—for men.

True, the flagrant, previously unquestioned kinds of discrimination detailed in the Association of American Colleges' 1975 report have begun to change. In 1974 the average annual budget for women's sports at the 150 biggest institutions (Michigan, Nebraska, Missouri, Stanford, etc.) was $27,000, and the budget for men's sports was $1,200,000. By 1979, the average women's budget at the same institutions had increased to $276,000. But, the men's budgets had increased to $1,650,000. In other words, men's budgets had increased nearly twice as much as the total women's increases. In the same period, the average football team budget increased from $793,000 to $1,045,000.

Furthermore, in 1972 only 6 percent of the same institutions had merged men and women's sport departments. By 1979, 64 percent had merged. Curiously, in 1979, not one of those departments was headed by a woman, and the number of men holding jobs as head coaches of women's teams had increased 137 percent, while the number of women holding such jobs had decreased 20 percent.

Women, and a lot of men in such sports as lacrosse, tennis, and golf, hold on to the tenuous illusion that sports is part of education. Football and basketball coaches understand the situation differently. They know they are in business.

1978: Does the fact that women sports reporters are now allowed to enter the Yankee locker room mean the end of civilization as we know it?

Probably.

Or so the Yankees, and baseball commissioneer Bowie Kuhn, seemed to think. They argued heatedly before the court that it would be an invasion of the players' right to privacy if one woman reporter had been let in after the 1977 World Series.

The woman reporter argued that exclusion from the locker room meant a severe handicap to the performance of her job.

Judge Constance Baker Motley, a black woman veteran of the civil-rights movement with a deep understanding of what it means to be excluded because of race or sex, ruled that as long as some reporters—albeit, men—were allowed in, so must all reporters—even women.

The argument raises several important questions about the state of civilization as we now know it.

Is there not, for example, a slight suggestion of false modesty in the Yankees' claim that their privacy would be invaded by the presence of a few women in the huge locker-room throng? After all, many of those same players gladly appear before millions of American television viewers in situations of the most remarkable intimacy. They demonstrate cures for body odor, itching afflictions, and uninteresting underpants. No doubt the money they are paid helps to soothe their boyish blushes.

Is there suspicion that once women are allowed in to report on the game in the traditional locker-room style, they might want to actually play the game? Those little girls who successfully sued for the right to play on Little League teams are growing fast, and perhaps the male players fear competition. They should not worry. Teams may not expand indefinitely, but the entrance of women into the great American sport will mean a vast increase in embarrassing advertising possibilities.

Why do women want to work as sports reporters? For the money, of course. And for the fun of it. Most of them like sports. Probably they also enjoy the same things that male reporters have enjoyed for years: things like free drinks in the press room, swell computer printouts of sports statistics supplied by the management, and proximity to greatness. The excuse that men offer for not eagerly welcoming women into the great fraternity of sportswriters is that no woman could become Howard Cosell.

The most important question to be asked about the issue of women reporters in locker rooms is: Why are there any reporters in the locker room? Why is it considered interesting to watch someone—male or female—ask a professional athlete clad in a towel what he thought about the game? The person in the towel invariably feels fine about the game, or hopes for better luck next time. He is almost never seen slumped in tears against the shower-room wall, or expressing himself in some fascinating manner such as punching a hole in the locker-room wall.

Professional athletes are professionals, and the first thing professionals learn is to recognize a reporter and watch out. If they have, in the past, proven themselves too professional to punch a pushy male reporter who insists on asking dumb questions at the end of a hard day's work, they are certainly not going to be unnerved by the presence of pushy female reporters.

So, civilization as we know it is slightly absurd. Luckily the hard-pressed Yankees have come up with a compromise. All reporters—male and female—will now be asked to wait outside until the players are dressed. Surely they could have thought of that without going to court.

———

When the editorial pages of America cry out in one agitated chorus: "Absurd! Ludicrous! Nonsensical! Madness!" it usually means that the writers have been caught off guard by social change.

When recommending an improved society, they speak in the soberest and most well-considered terms. But when improvement actually occurs, their first reaction is to ridicule. The change tends to be not quite what they meant.

They did not, for example, ever imagine that laws designed to withhold federal support from institutions that discriminate on the basis of sex would mean that the Scottsdale, Arizona, school system would have to give up its father-son banquets and its mother-daughter teas.

The Office of Civil Rights of the Department of Health, Education, and Welfare, with its 1976 Scottsdale edict, provided every politician, paper, and pundit in the country with an opportunity for some fine midsummer moralizing. Father-son banquets seemed so trivial an issue that everyone felt free to energetically excoriate the pointy-headed Washington bureaucrats.

As it happens, the issue was not trivial.

No one whom I read or heard stopped to ask why HEW made its decision. Everyone assumed that one-parent exclusive school events are good things, and HEW wrong and stupid. The assumption indicated how lightly people skim over the implications of equality for women.

No one would have dismissed as not worth arguing about charges that separate events for black and white students are illegal and harmful. But the idea of women's equality had President Ford bounding up from his breakfast table angrily demanding that traditional American family-oriented events not be interfered with.

Traditionally, the president of the United States is a white male.

Traditionally, social policy and social attitudes in the United States have been formed by the entrenched image of a middle-class nuclear family. In reality, 12.6 percent of the white children and 42.6 percent of the black children under age eighteen live in fatherless homes.

Forty-five percent of all American children, will, at some time, live in a single-parent home for an average of four years. A fatherless home does not mean a fatherless child. But too many children are excluded and caused pain by the insensitivities that underlie a father-son or father-daughter or even mother-child event. Parent-child seems the obvious solution, but everyone exept HEW dismissed it. Something, traditionally, must be unacceptable about the idea of both parents sharing a role.

Traditionally, father-child events have been the only way to coerce fathers into participating in their children's education. If mothers were invited, fathers didn't go. Child rearing has been, traditionally, women's work.

Traditionally, as Scottsdale school officials and President Ford pointed out at the time, father-son banquets have been community-building events. Indeed they have been. Men's community. They have been great places to sell insurance. To meet the mayor and the president of the bank.

Traditionally, mother-daughter teas have been nice times for a fashion show or a food demonstration.

Traditionally, girls have been discriminated against in school budgets, in access to courses, and in expectations. Title IX is designed to interfere with those traditional systems and structures of discrimination.

Eventually, equal sports budgets will mean equal awards and equal public interest. Equal access to courses and colleges will mean equal intellectual efforts. Daughters will have a future too. And mothers will have a present. Women and men will be selling insurance. Men and women will be serving coffee.

Eventually, women may even get equal pay.

No wonder they tried to make a bureaucratic joke out of it. But she who laughs last laughs best.

———

One drawback of living by the rules of Upward Failure is that, while a man may never feel like a failure, he may never feel successful either.

I had planned a small reunion. Tom was in town from London. Nearly twenty-five years ago he had been at Harvard with John. John had recently married Abby, one of my best friends. Nearly fifteen years ago Abby had not married Tom. Sometime in between I had briefly wondered if I should have wanted to marry Tom.

It is, as they say, a small world.

At any rate, Tom and John had not seen each other for twenty-five years. It seemed a good idea to have dinner together. There was a bit of awkwardness when they met. It would have been kinder if John had also lost his hair.

The conversation quickly settled into a recounting. "Whatever happened to so and so?" Divorce, suicide, bankruptcy, were the answers. Nothing particularly unusual. After twenty-five years, it becomes fairly clear that the sorrows which into every life must fall are a good bit more random and inevitable than we expected.

The true heart of the matter eventually emerged. What both men were really interested in was: Who won?

"What about M.?" one asked.

"Oh, he's president of a college, never quite measured up to what we expected."

"What about S.?"

"Editor of an intellectual monthly. Bit of a disappointment."

"And T.?"

"Went around the world on a ketch, wrote a few books, started an international charity. Never did become governor."

"Remember P.? Spoke five languages? What about him?"

"Ah yes, P., what a bore he was. There's another one who never became what we hoped for. Just chairman of his department."

It was really a very peculiar conversation, made even more peculiar by the extreme formality and deference each man exhibited toward the other. "Ah! But you, as a figure of prominence . . ." one would bow, passing the salad. "Ah! But you, as a member of the Establishment . . ." the other would concede, pouring some wine.

In fact, one is head of international operations for a huge corporation, and the other is indeed a member of the Establishment. And both see themselves as underrealized; the other as the one who measured up, became what they had all hoped for.

I asked them, if they and M. and S. and T. and P. were not successes, what on earth would success be? And they finally agreed that success, to their class at Harvard, would be a combination of president of the United States, Jesus Christ, and Robert Lowell.

America is run by men like Tom and John, perfectly decent men, most of them, doing the best they can, but the best they can is never going to be enough. They will always be catching up, fulfilling some insane vision of success, competing with each other. If they cannot recognize achievement in themselves or in each other, how can they recognize real failure? If the men at the top, like them, are always looking ahead, worrying about their place in the race, how can they ever see below, or even around? No wonder they resist the claims of the excluded. They feel they are part of the excluded.

No wonder they are amazed and confused when women want to get into the race too. Twenty-five years ago there were no women to speak of in law school or medical school or business school. If men happened to find women at their college, the women gracefully married them and retired from the field.

The way Tom and John talked about the women they had known was even odder than the way they talked about themselves. "What about L.?" "She's a state legislator." "No! How amazing, what a success. I wouldn't have expected it!" It isn't that they don't think women should be legislators, they simply didn't expect it.

At the moment, women support and encourage each other, surprised as we are by possibility and delighted by unexpected accomplishment. What a terrible waste of time the woman's movement will have been if we end up like Tom and John, competing in a shadow world of unrealizable, elitist visions of success.

Once upon a time, men of Tom and John's class had wives who, in addition to all the usual wifely duties such as remembering to pick up cleaning and guarding two-year-olds, were expected to produce and direct elaborate pageants known as dinner parties. These spectacles involved days of work and were thought to be "good for his career" and, in Washington, "the place where all the really important stuff goes on." Neither assumption was ever proven true, but the illusion that it might be true was sustained by the supreme hostessing ritual: after dessert the hostess would herd all the ladies off to the bathroom so the men might more comfortably unroll conventional wisdom over brandy and cigars.

My son finds my descriptions of those parties (" . . . and then your father, to accompanying murmurs of dismay, complained that I had forgotten the salad plates") as hilariously implausible as I find memoirs of summers in Newport during the 1890s. But, in fact, it was only in 1966, after a digesting male strolled forth from my dining room and kindly inquired: "Have you ever heard of de Tocqueville?" that I began to find something rather bizarre about the system. And it was only about 1972 that I began to realize that what we wives were, even sitting amongst our heaps of privately owned, perfectly polished sterling silver knives and salad forks, was the servant class. It was about the same time that my sister, who was spending most of her day in a car fetching and delivering through the Connecticut suburbs, made the same connection. "It is widely held in the suburbs," she reported, "that the proper place of women is barefoot and pregnant behind a steering wheel."

I should mention that my sister and I were both also trying to keep paying jobs. We had almost unlimited opportunities for service, and damn little for advancement.

Women have their place in the Establishment scheme of things. A woman in Washington once described our place: "The world is still too full of too many men who think that all a woman wants is a tight sweater, a loose girdle and a warm place to type." The United States Congress is still much, much too full of such men.

I guess, if I had to choose, I would say that my favorite part of the Elizabeth Ray–Wayne Hays story was the euphemism "sexual favors." It seemed so appropriately archaic for the particular arrangement alleged to have been reached by the former rental-car clerk and the congressman from Ohio.

The fun of the story was that most of us feared that old-fashioned things like sex scandals, mistresses, and fears of further disclosures had disappeared forever. These revelations were a brief return to the good old pre-Watergate days, when right was right and sex was the only thing wrong.

There was a minor debate over the use of the word "mistress." Some people held out for the view that a steady income constituted the more respectable "being kept," and others maintained that because of Miss Ray's avowed dislike of her provider, she should have been described by a less flattering term. Hays himself seemed to favor "hysterical" (the female equivalent for "ill-tempered bully," which is what he was called), and no amount of colorful reporting was able to support Miss Ray's self-presentation as a pitiful victim of a rotten system. Both seem to be equally unpleasant, which may or may not be a step forward for equality.

There are several reasons that being the mistress—or whatever—of a powerful man is a notion that still lurks appealingly in the back of many women's heads. In the first place, it seems it would be more fun than honest labor. We imagine lying about before a fire on a white rug, eating bonbons and trying on furs, arranging flowers and keeping large dolls on embroidered bed pillows.

It seems—on the face of it—to beat heavy lifting. We tend to forget the price that has to be paid. Having dinner with Wayne Hays at the Marriott would be a dreary duty, about equal to the meager glamour available on $14,000 a year in Washington, D.C.

The rewards of honest labor on Capitol Hill are not, after all, particularly rewarding for women. In 1975, of the people earning above $18,000 a year by working in senatorial offices, 75.4 percent were men. But 64.1 percent of the total employees were women.

So, while it was regrettable that Elizabeth Ray may have accepted public funds for private favors, it is also regrettable that public funds are being paid to sustain economic discrimination against women who work. It was understandably irritating to the women on Capitol Hill when a great deal of energy and noise was suddenly expended to smoke out alleged other women loafing about on the public rolls in exchange for sexual favors. The jokes, which all seemed to be about "the girls" on Capitol Hill, and none at all about goatish congressmen, did not seem funny.

There was once a girl who worked on Capitol Hill—more than one girl, to tell the truth—and her name was Marilyn, or

Cheryl, or possibly Brenda. She made a mistake and was banished. She was young and naive and she had Misunderstood the Situation. Misinterpreting dalliance as intention she asked the Member, her employer, to come home to share Thanksgiving dinner with her parents. Zip! She was sent to the Folding Room.

According to mythic tradition, the Folding Room is where "they," the rejected, are sent to find useful employment when they threaten to become embarrassing or boring. "They" is the word Hill Women use to describe a sister whose bosom is too big or whose eyelashes are too long or whose clothing is too often adorned with substances that glitter. "They" implies groupies, and it is true that sometimes their apparent lack of intellectual credentials suggest they have been hired to please the eye of whoever happens to pass the open door of a member's office.

However, being sent to the Folding Room sounded too horrible to be true. I imagined it as a room where hundreds of girls who had wanted only to look like Farrah Fawcett were interned, wearing white pinafores, laboring for their sins at folding. Folding what? Towels? Sheets? Doors? Whatever they were folding, I expected them to be doing it next to the room where The Wives are said to roll bandages.

I decided to visit this realm of lost hopes, to interview the seduced and abandoned, if possible to arouse them from their wisful lethargy and to send them forth, Donna Anna–like, to serenade their Don Giovannis out of office. (It is a thought *très charmant*, is it not?) I went to the basement of the Longworth Building. The corridors seemed to me to be suffused with an aura of sex. Perhaps it was the effect of the stories I had been hearing about life on Capitol Hill. My informants may have confused my interest in sexism with an interest in sex.

Or perhaps I mistook the feeling in the corridors for romantic sex when it was only Washington sex. In this city, as in most cities, it is taken for granted that the office is a natural place for sex, but here everyone assumes the sex means something. No one admits it might just mean fun, companionship, lust, or affection.

I was disappointed in the workaday appearance of the women walking up and down the basement corridors. They may experience private raptures, but at noon they look like people who have paid careful attention to the advice of *Glamour* magazine, and having achieved a pleasant appearance have turned their minds to other topics. They did not look like "they." Not in the cafeteria. Not in the stationery room. And absolutely, certainly, not in the Folding Room.

Most of the women in the Folding Room were black, all gave the impression of being respectable smock-wearing matrons, and they worked at their desirable patronage jobs under the supervision of several men who advised me I would have to clear any conversations with the Speaker or Chairman Hays. (By a happy coincidence, the sort of coincidence one so often finds where power is exercised, Wayne Hays himself, as chair of the House Administration Committee, was then in charge of the Folding Room.)

The Folding Room, also known as the Publications Distribution Service, did not look like a very amusing place to work, not so much because it is at the end of a dark hall that might be a loading platform, but because it involves spending the day running machines that fold and insert such wit and wisdom as congressional newsletters, agricultural reports to constituents, and calendars decorated with the Constitution (a good idea, the Constitution).

So, if "they" (for which, it turns out, it is better to read "we") are not sent to the Folding Room, where are they sent? Well, they are traded in the cloak room, auctioned off at committee meetings, ejected by wives from offices, and snapped up by others. Tangled webs of liaison tend to accrue, but at the same time so does a lot of competence and experience. Only a few will ever achieve, or want to achieve, the ultimate promotion to wife.

Most would settle for equal pay. The pay scale on Capitol Hill resembles the financial structure of South America: a few of the males have most of the money. In 1975 the Capitol Hill Women's Political Caucus hired a computer that printed out a very nice visual display of discrimination; page after page listing each senator's staff by title and salary, the salary listed under female or male. Almost every page showed a neat but small block at the top of the scale under male, and the rest, much larger and poorer group, under female.

Also like South America, the women have no place to take their grievances, since Congress exempted itself from the coverage of the Equal Pay Act of 1963 and of Title VII of the Civil Rights Act of 1964, which bans discrimination in employment because of race, or sex. Corporations across America have been taking a keen interest in Congress's reluctance to do as they tell others to do.

I have always thought it would be highly entertaining, and possibly instructive, if all the women in Washington went on strike. There would be no dinner parties and no dinners, no clean laundry, no phone calls placed and logged, no messages taken, no letters opened or typed, no files retrieved, no appointments made and remembered. There would also be no baby-sitters, housekeepers, or day-care center workers, which would serve as a salutary reminder to the few women who have achieved a place in the system the extent to which they, too, depend upon other women, even as the system depends upon women—to serve.

A man who thinks of women only as occasions of sin, or sainted mothers, is going to have a lot of trouble imagining a woman as secretary of state or Supreme Court Justice.

Jimmy Carter's remarks about sin and sex were so embarrassing one didn't know where to look. I mean, who wants to vote for a man who thinks women are occasions of sin? There one was, riding along quite peacefully on the IND uptown line, speculating about day care and equal pay. Suddenly, one noticed that the headlines were all about Jimmy Carter lusting after women in his heart, but resting secure in the knowledge that God had forgiven him. It was an unwelcome glimpse back along the road out of the swamp.

Carter's remarks, as reported, embarrassed and irritated women. Not because he was vulgar, or too sincere, or aesthetically icky. Not because he had failed to be hip, or had been too frank. He was all of those things and none of it mattered a lot. What did matter to women was something Carter had obviously never thought of, and his very sincerity made it much worse.

He spoke of not thinking ill of another man whose sexual behavior did not match his own moral standards, but he said absolutely nothing to indicate he recognized that women are equally responsible partners in the relationship. He appeared to be depersonalizing women.

What Carter said was a clear and painful reminder of the kind of dark, bottomless prejudice women face, of how far we have to go before we obliterate the myths of Lilith, of Woman as seducer and destroyer.

Maybe we are being too sensitive.

Maybe Carter didn't mean to be so insensitive to our sensitivities.

Of course he didn't mean it. That's what insensitivity is. He doesn't even seem to have noticed that *Playboy* magazine is ever so slightly an odd place to reaffirm the belief that sexual fantasy is sin.

God was spoken of as providing temptation but understanding lapses. Men were spoken of as shacking up, or worse. Women's role in this moral struggle seemed by omission to boil down to being either the temptation provided, or the wife to whom loyalty is owed. The choice, madonna or whore, is somewhat limiting, which is the point.

Some women would choose to be priests. This choice is impossible, according to Pope John Paul II, the top priest of his established system, because of "tradition." It is a tradition I know something about. In the early 1950s I attended, along with most of the Catholic schoolgirls in St. Louis, the organizing rally of SDS. Not the SDS you are thinking of. This SDS stood for Students for a Decent Society. We planned to achieve our goal by making a single bold pledge: we would never wear strapless evening gowns. Those indecent creations, we were assured, provoked occasions of sin, *for the boys*. Henceforth, our shoulders would be veiled in pink tulle and white eyelet.

Years passed. In the spring of 1979 I found myself in Tehran watching fifty thousand women who were counterdemonstrating against the women who had been marching earlier in opposition to enforced wearing of the traditional veil—the enveloping, fantastically hindering *chador*. I was one of perhaps five women who were not veiled, and so I received quite a lot of literature from passersby. One placard, handwritten in Farsi, I keep framed on my wall next to a chart titled "Federal laws and regulations prohibiting sex discrimination." The placard reads: "Sister, I value your modesty above the blood I have given." The earnest young man who gave me this message assured me that he did not consider me a CIA whore like the women who had been marching to protest the veil. But, he explained, without a veil, the breasts (in this context, breasts begin at the collarbone) and legs show, and men have corrupt thoughts. As it happened, his views were identical with the Ayatollah Khomeini's.

There are certain flaws in these arguments, these invocations of "tradition," flaws that have prompted some of our more elaborate psychological, anthropological, and philosophical investigations into the myth, magic, and mystery of women. I am more interested here in the results of traditional thought than in the roots. The results are breathtakingly efficient: women are the troublemakers and can be denied power, identity, and control over their own lives—for the good of society.

Upward Failure Rule #13: *Blame the victims of the system, not the system.* Only a few years ago it was considered reasonable to blame society for criminal acts. The theory suffered from the observable fact that the majority of the people who had been most victimized by society were not robbing, raping, mugging, and murdering.

A new theory was needed. Unfortunately, the theory that seems to have caught the public imagination at present is the old notion that the victims somehow brought the trouble on themselves.

The corner grocery-store owner who is robbed is told he should not have kept money in his cash register.

The woman who is raped is told she should not have been hitchhiking, or wearing a T-shirt, or walking down the street.

The old lady who is mugged is told she should not have been carrying a pocketbook and should not have gotten into her elevator without first looking.

Someone who is murdered should not have been riding a bicycle in the park at noon, or should not have been walking down a street where some men decided to shoot it out with the police.

Women are more likely to be blamed than are men for a crime against themselves. Recently a friend of mine was coming home to her tenth-floor apartment, carrying two bags of groceries, in the middle of the afternoon. A couple of boxes of previously delivered groceries were waiting outside her door. She opened the door and started to pull in the boxes, and at that point two people descended the stairs next to her door, pushed her into her apartment, and—when she fought back—kicked and punched her, dragged her into her bedroom, tied her up, undressed her ("so you won't run for help"), and put a pillow over her head.

One of the attackers was a man in his twenties, the other was a boy about ten. My friend, while she could still talk, directed them to everything in the apartment that could be considered portable and valuable. She was afraid that (a) they would kill her, and (b) they would hurt her children, who were due home any minute.

Finally they left, her son came home and cut her loose (I gloss over the details of his reaction), and the police were called. They responded rather sympathetically.

The sympathy of most of the staff of the building and many of the tenants proved to be short-lived. At first they were extremely alarmed. How could it have happened in a supposedly secure building with a buzzer system on the door and elevator men theoretically primed to obstruct intruders.?

A simple desire not to be blamed for leaving the front door open, or for not stopping strangers, cannot fully explain why some members of the building staff—and some tenants—insisted that nothing had happened. Oh, yes, it was true that she had been hurt and humiliated, but "nothing" had really happened. It was just a

"weird incident." Within a day there began to be hints that perhaps literally nothing had happened. One tenant, another woman,
said she had not seen "many" bruises on my friend.

My friend was quite brave and calm for several days, even
carefully writing out a report so the tenants would know exactly
what happened. Rape crisis centers warn that the victim of an
attack will, after a numb period, feel furiously angry and want to
strike back. Anyone with the slightest capacity for compassionate
imagination could figure that out, and indeed many tenants did
understand when my friend broke down in the elevator a few
nights later and punched and shouted at a young man operator.

The elevator operator hit her back. The building manager
later suggested my friend apologize to the operator. The tenants
who were in the elevator with her got out and left her alone with
the operator, although they knew what she had been through,
because, "Well, she was very offensive," "She used dreadful language." They implied that, because she had lost control, she probably deserved the first incident. "Perhaps she wanted to relive the
event," one woman offered as her psychiatrist husband's explanation. My friend's pain was invalidated by her own natural reaction,
her "bad manners." Everyone could forget about it.

In other words, a woman who goes out of the house deserves
what she gets.

VI.

Incognita

Most of the time I feel invisible, like something living under a dust sheet. I mean, I know who men are. They are the people pictured in the newspapers as meeting with the president, holding hearings on the CIA, being given state funerals, and controlling from football huddles the hearts and minds of large metropolitan areas.

But who am I? Where are the women? We are the people who lose our names when we marry, the also-rans of recorded history, the unidentified half of "mankind." We travel incognita in our culture, looking for affirmation of our experience. No wonder, wrapped as we are in a cloud of categorical mystery, we so often acquiesce in the idea of ourselves as the unknowable, somehow lesser, other.

When I was born, my parents went through a brief fit of sentimentality during which they considered naming me April—for the month. April O'Reilly! (Oh, really.) Then they toyed with the idea of Marcha, an endearing—to them—combination of their own names. Fortunately, tradition prevailed and I was named Jane, for my paternal grandmother, and Conway, for my mother's maiden name. I still have my christening mug, which formally identifies me as Jane Conway O'Reilly.

Not, perhaps, a name that runs like a chiming brook over the tongue, or even one that unites easily with any sort of stylish penmanship. But mine. Traceable and evocative within the family circle. I have cousins named Elaine and Marion, and while their names are syllabically more euphonious, they were not named after my grandmother and mother, which was their loss. On the other hand, it was my loss not to be named with the initials *M.E.* as my sister was, a fact that later entitled her to inherit an enormous quantity of family silver that happened to be marked *ME*.

I understood early that people should be named with meaning. The important thing is not simply to settle on whatever stray Kimberly or Christopher is floating through the public consciousness at the time. Lately, many people have decided to choose their own names, and while I very much admire the choice of poet Verandah Porche, other names like Mother Earth and Running Water seem as much a cliché as Kimberly Ann. Besides, I've never been able to think of an alternative for myself other than Writer's Block.

Alternatives have been thrust upon me. At one time I thought it a great deal of fun to be able to call up department stores and complain in menacing tones that I, Mrs. John Jones, demanded immediate satisfaction. My name was not Jones, as it was not later on Mrs. Smith, but I have changed the names to protect the innocent and to leave anonymous the name I still hide behind when I want to be someone else. And that fact makes my point. When we change our names, we become in some odd metaphysical way someone else. People who met me as Jane Jones do not think of me the same way people who knew me as Jane O'Reilly or Jane Smith do.

And, of course, the initial fun of being Mrs. Jones was that I was someone else: a grown-up, certifiably married, socially acceptable woman—someone department stores gave charge accounts to. The trouble was, Jane Jones was not the same person as Jane O'Reilly, something I realized when my first article was printed with the by-line Jane Jones. Jane didn't mean my Jane without my own particular last name.

I reclaimed my name when I got divorced. My friends, being free from old-fashioned hang-ups about etiquette, did not address letters to me as Mrs. O'Reilly Jones. They addressed me as Jane

O'Reilly Jones O'Reilly. Ha ha. Then I became Mrs. Smith. Not instead of Jane O'Reilly, but at the same time, two people running concurrently. It was very confusing, but after I got divorced the second time, it became surrealistic. I decided not to revert to plain O'Reilly because my son was named Smith. But his father, for identity reasons of his own, decided he and my son would revert to the original spelling of his name. So now my son is named Smythe, and I am legally named Smith, a name that no longer has anything to do with anyone connected to me.

If I ever marry again, I will have to legally drop Smith before stating my intention of continuing to use my maiden name. Perhaps I could ask my husband to take my name. Imagine introducing someone as "My husband, Fred O'Reilly"! Né Fred Adams, formerly person, now Fred "adjunct" O'Reilly. What pure absurdity the whole process takes on when it is put the other way. What a ludicrous possessive act. I would be embarrassed to suggest giving my name to another person.

But what about the children? rises a voice in the back of the room. I don't know. Maybe they will all do what the young are doing, de facto, these days. "Lucy-with-the-green-car" and "Jerry-who-plays-the-guitar" will become Lucy Greencar and Jerry Player and by the time they marry and have children, we will all be identified by numbers anyway.

———

I pinch myself. It hurts, therefore I am. What I am is a journalist, sitting in a banquet hall with five hundred other journalists. It is our job to delineate the realities of our culture. The man who has the final word on whether the collective efforts of these five hundred people will reflect myth or reality is speaking of the future. "Beyond a certain point," he warns, "equality can be enforced only by tyranny." The men at the high table nod. The men retiring from power nod. The men being raised to power nod. There are no women in those groups to nod. There are no women in the subgroups that will eventually rise to power. Is this benevolent selective blindness or is it tyranny exercising its privilege of defining tyranny? Does it matter which?

If I fell on the table, if I howled aloud, if I shouted: "Please, can we first approach the point before declaring that equality has gone too far?"—would it make any difference? How can I explain what it meant to feel the edge of the dust sheet lift when I saw in my son's algebra textbook: "A pilot wants to maintain a course of 31° and ground speed of 400 mph against a 41 mph headwind from 343°. What should her heading and air speed be?" And when, in 1979, the *Wall Street Journal* quite casually referred to "politically important women's groups." And when, in the summer of the same year, a very serious male journalist moderating a panel at the Washington Press Club worried: "Can we find a man who can do the job of the presidency?" And Senator Gary Hart replied: "I would not discount the possibility of finding a woman who could do the job." And Senator Charles Mathias added, "We have twice as much talent as some people seem to think." What might it take to persuade a man who can speak about the "tyranny of equality" that hundreds of thousands of other women feel the same absurd shock of relief when, at last, our own perceptions—and existence— are reported?

An angel with a flaming sword blocking his limousine on Fifth Avenue might be a fairly effective persuader. Barring that, we will just have to go on trying to make sure more feminists are doing the reporting.

1976: The American Society of Newspaper Editors convened in Washington for four days of good fellowship and solemn consideration of such topics as "The American Condition" and "Editor Power."

I use the word "fellowship" because it was so entirely appropriate for the occasion. Only 5 percent of all policymaking jobs on newspapers were then held by women. The ASNE had then eight hundred members. Only sixteen of them women. As far as I could see, only one member was black, a man. The participants in the convention's program included only two women. Michael O'Neill, executive editor of the *New York Daily News* and program chairman, said to me: "We should have more women on the program. Sometimes you don't get what you hope for. I asked my wife for a list of interesting women." The *New York Daily News* had then the largest circulation of any daily newspaper in America and one might reasonably hope that it very soon managed to draw up its own list of all-occasion interesting women.

There were no women members of the ASNE board of directors nor were any nominated. The problem was widely discussed, and considerable regret was expressed that there were not enough women with enough experience in the organization to be nominated. At this point the entire history of women working on newspapers tended to flash through one's mind: the systematic exclusion of women from the newsroom where the *real* newspapermen hang out and have all the crisis-covering fun; the inability to imagine that an editor of any rank could be drawn from the women's pages because those editors (who, oddly enough, are usually women) haven't had experience dealing with crisis (which, oddly enough, is not in that case viewed as a skill which can be learned).

Consequently, there were (and are) very few women editors, therefore few women eligible for membership in ASNE, therefore none with experience enough to be elected to the board. The truth of this history is demonstrated by the large number of recent lawsuits brought successfully against newspapers for discrimination in hiring, advancement, pay, etc.

Any woman not actually longing to become a female newspaper editor will by now be wondering why we should care about ASNE. Why not let the white, male dears get on with their drinking undistrubed? Because: those particular conventioneers edit the newspapers we read, and what we read influences the way we think. The way we think should, theoretically, be influenced by the reporting of reality. I would not claim that men editors cannot understand the reality of women's issues today. But judging by the treatment of the issues in their own papers, and from the example of their own organization, I think it is safe to say that most of them don't, or won't.

It used to be that a woman who wished to be thought a lady made certain that her name appeared in the public print only when she married and died. Then women began to become chairmen, mailmen, newsmen. This usage was a slight distortion of reality, a fact apparent even to the nation's editors. They chose for a while to underscore reality, as in "Chairwoman Gonzales, a brunette," and "Prime Minister Golda Meir, a grandmother," and "even though a woman, Mrs. Smith manages a factory." In 1977, the Associated Press and United Press International, wire services with 16,500 foreign and domestic newspaper, television, and radio subscribers, decided to revise their stylebooks. Much acrimonious debate preceded the final concessions: "reporters" might thereafter be used instead of "newsmen," "humanity" instead of "mankind," and so forth. It was even suggested that Miss, Mrs., or Ms. could all be suitable courtesy titles for women. Many editors, notably those at the *New York Times*, rejected the suggestion, declaring *Ms.* to be outrageously unacceptable to the general public. In other words, they still believe the most important thing about a woman is whether or not she is married.

The man at the party was expressing his doubts about the women's movement. "Don't get me wrong," he said, thoughtfully extracting a toothpick from his blue cheese mini-quiche. "I was all for women in the beginning, I really supported the libbers, but they have gone too far now."

I chose a slice of salami wrapped in puff pastry and disconsolately chewed it as I waited to hear which particular outrage had caused him to draw the line. Demands for space on the pages of his newspaper? Demands for tenure at his university? Demands for equal pay at his corporation?

None of the above. He exchanged an empty glass for a full

tumbler of Scotch, fixed me with a glare of accusation, and said: "They are distorting the language."

Oh, wow, I flashed on that. I mean, you know, I could really get behind that particular form of alienation, as soon as we prioritize the agenda and develop the data required to proceduralize the preliminary results.

"How?" I asked.

He chewed up an ice cube and a fraction of the plastic tumbler and then, spitting out particles of both substances, he explained: "This nonsense about man and woman. Everyone knows the word *man* is supposed to include women."

Naturally, I spent the rest of the evening crouched over the *Oxford English Dictionary*. As far as I could tell (the magnifying glass was smeared with puff pastry and salami), the English language once included a word for women, *wif*, and a word for men, *wer*, and yet another word for human beings, *mann*. These useful distinctions disappeared by about the fourteenth century, replaced by "woman," "man," and "man." According to the dictionary: "In modern apprehension man as thus used" [in the sense of "person"] "primarily denotes the male sex, though by implication referring also to women."

I am not sure that "by implication" fully expresses the degree to which I wish to feel included in the human race. If language is a reflection of reality, then I do not feel my reality is properly taken into account by the word "mankind." Men, in the specific sense, think it is a small problem, but then, no one has ever told men to just "consider" themselves referred to when sweeping generalizations are made about womankind.

Would you, if you are a man, feel that your opinions had been considered if you read about a poll taken of the attitudes of the common woman on the upcoming elections?

If the woman-on-the-street were described as being angry about inflation would you, as a man, feel that your passage on the thoroughfares had also been observed?

If the people who report on such matters issued reports about woman-hours clocked and the condition of the working woman, would you, as a man, not feel a slight suspicion that your efforts were not being added into the general economic picture?

If the inspirational documentary film began with "The advances of technology have ever enlarged and enriched the life of modern woman," wouldn't you, as a man, feel left behind on the long march from the cave? If the book celebrating that march were titled *The Ascent of Woman*, wouldn't it make you feel slightly cross? If the world that has been so enlarged were defined in books of maps titled *Woman's World: An Atlas*, wouldn't you begin to think about starting your own publishing house?

A sailor may never cry "woman overboard," even if the sailor is the best woman for the job, and the person accused of pushing someone overboard may never be convicted for womanslaughter—and it probably does not matter.

But. If the advertisement read "Fly Eastern, the Wings of Woman," wouldn't you, as a man feel left out?

Furthermore, and in conclusion, how would you, as a man, like to be called a career man?

1976: It seems to me worth wondering why there were no reports of rape in Angola and Lebanon. Either women were being raped and it was dismissed as an unnewsworthy incidental or there was in fact no noteworthy raping going on. If there was none, the fact was remarkably worth reporting. Rape has always been part of war.

"It's funny about man's attitude toward rape in war. Unquestionably there shall be some raping. Unconscionable but nevertheless inevitable," says Susan Brownmiller in her book, *Against Our Will*. By documenting rape in war, including Bangladesh, Nanking, and Vietnam, the author forever persuades us that rape is an act of terror, a deliberately degrading assault of the powerful against the powerless. The unacknowledged enemies, victims, and seized property of war are women. "The attitude of historians toward this kind of documentation has usually been to ignore it as tangential, inconsequential or as possessing dubious validity," Ms. Brownmiller writes. The experiences of women are considered suspect, the facts, which seem too horrible to be true, are eventually dismissed as only propaganda.

I asked people who should know about reports of rape in Angola and Lebanon. Some of them laughed out loud. Some thought it "kind of a strange question." Some, suspicious, wanted to know what I wanted to know for. Most had never thought to inquire into the subject. I would definitely say that the question was not considered consequential or valid.

At the Associated Press neither the world nor cable desks recalled anything filed from either country on rape. The office of former Senator Richard C. Clark, D-Iowa, who led the fight against American intervention in Angola with Senator John V. Tunney, D-California, knew "nothing" about rapes there. An aide of Senator Tunney's who had just returned from Angola sounded incredulous and slightly amused by the question. "No," he snorted, "it wasn't one of the things I looked into. Rape was a subject that never came up."

An African expert at the United Methodist office at the United Nations, a black woman, said with some hostility: "In what sense do you mean rape?" The sense she feared was symbolic, to be used against her in arguments about anti-Africanism, globalism versus tribalism, racism, settlers versus natives, good guys versus bad guys. She did not, she said, tend to think to ask about literal rape.

A reliable source from the State Department said that months of daily situation reports from Lebanon had never mentioned rape. He offered, as explanation, the notion of a religious war—a suggestion that showed a fine disregard for history. "Hmm," he began to muse, "it is interesting. Why hasn't abuse of women become an issue?"

A genial aide in the office of Senator James G. Abourezk, D-South Dakota, chuckled at the question. "Heh, heh," he said, "this is a real dandy." Later he reported back that the senator, who is of Lebanese descent and was being beseiged by anxious American relatives of Lebanese, had heard of no incidents: "The Lebanese are great lovers; they wouldn't bother with rape," explained the aide. "It is just a piss-poor technique, right?"

A man holding a responsible position with the United States government said to me: "I can't understand the lack of reports. All the women can't be ugly."

1976: Three weeks later. After several readers of the above column sent me clippings of a story by Michael Parks which had appeared three months earlier in the *Baltimore Sun*. In it, he reported from Beirut that the war in Lebanon had involved incidents of kidnap, rape, mutilation, castration, children thrown out of third-floor windows, pregnant women bayonated in the stomach, and retaliation by "slicing." A hospital reported treating thirty-five rape victims one week after part of a district was overrun by the other side. "These accounts," wrote Parks, "verified by eye witnesses, government security forces and hospitals are of the more grisly incidents last week."

My reliable source from the State Department called back to report second thoughts. "It's interesting," said the reliable source. "Unless it's forced on them, people don't usually look at that aspect of things. The Pentagon would know the body count right away but we don't have briefing books for rape so we tend to think it isn't important. But if you think about it, it can be important politically. In Bangladesh the grudges and scars of the men whose wives were raped there are one of the main reasons it is still unsettled." He added, "These things tend to always get phrased in the body-count language that came out of Vietnam. It almost gets treated clinically, not just by the government, but by the media too."

The "thing" I happen to be interested in here is rape. It could be orphans or mutilation or the people's opinion. The semantic obliteration of the particular makes it impossible to begin to grasp the reality. Crimes against humanity depend upon the denial of the victims' humanity. Women—invisible, depersonalized, powerless—are the permanent victims.

1975: I went to see the Marx Brothers in *Coconuts* and *Monkey Business* at the Biograph Theatre in Washington. During the break between features, the theater ran a teaser for *Ilsa, She Wolf of the SS.*

The teaser showed young women being tortured to death, screaming in agony, blood welling up out of their mouths. It showed women attached to wooden platforms being flayed with whips by other bare-breasted women. There were scenes of shooting, explosions, and Nazi salutes. A man, clamped to a table, was being castrated by Ilsa and her henchwomen. Blood was shown flowing into a drainage trough. There were torture scenes of cutting, wounding, and attaching of electrodes or fuses to nipples.

Alan Rubin, one of the owners of the Biograph, said that the original teaser for *Ilsa* was X-rated, and was sent back and exchanged for a General Audience teaser. Rubin decided to black out part of the poster that advertises the Biograph's weekend, midnight screenings of the movie. He thought the block of print on the poster that read "Ilsa . . . she made her lovers into lampshades" was "in poor taste, and didn't happen in the movie." The Biograph originally screened the film for the theater manager's birthday party.

"It did pretty well the first weekend," Rubin said. The audience was mostly college kids. Ten people left, the usher reported to Rubin, and the rest laughed hysterically.

Vincent Canby, writing in the Arts and Leisure section of the *New York Times,* said: "This could possibly be the worst soft-core sex-and-violence film of the decade—and the funniest."

Ilsa, She Wolf of the SS is not a funny film.

John Simon of *New York* magazine had recently been prompted to examine pornographic films by the sight of matrons with shopping bags crowding in to see the X-rated *Exhibition.* Simon wrote on and on about the aesthetic of pornography. He quoted Susan Sontag's intellectualisms on sex and violence: "Tamed as it may be, sexuality remains one of the demonic forces in human consciousness—pushing us at intervals close to taboo and dangerous desires, which range from the impulse to commit sudden arbitrary violence upon another person to the voluptuous yearning for the extinction of one's consciousness. . . ."

Very briefly, Simon stumbled across the more exact and uglier point: "If George Orwell is right, and the typical pornographic work is ultimately about 'the pursuit of power' and, by implication, its complement, the pursuit of being over-powered, sadism and masochism are what all pornography tends toward." But then Simon retreated back to clouds of abstractions, concluding weakly with the thought that these films may be interesting to the psychologists, and assures us he is "certainly not for suppressing anything."

I am for suppressing films like *Ilsa*.

When I say that sex and violence in movies should be banned, all my friends immediately assume their tolerant expression. They purse their liberal lips and murmur about the problem of "Who shall decide?" "Certainly," they muse from the depths of their comfortable chairs, "one would not want the State to judge." They speak of solution through education and studies. But the children laughing at *Ilsa* were the children whose responses to violence on television were found, in studies never acted upon, potentially dangerous. The market for violent pornography is, in itself, a symptom of the failure of education in America.

My troubled friends murmur: "But would you ban *Coriolanus* or *Macbeth?*" The argument does not apply. Shakespeare explicates, moves us closer to an understanding of morality. *Ilsa* exploits, diminishes the distinction between right and wrong.

These kinds of movies are not a modern response to the sexual revolution. They are part of the long tradition of using pornography to dehumanize an enemy. The worst such propaganda ever yet produced was the work of Julius Streicher, Nazi Germany's most fanatical anti-Semite, whose depraved, sadistic Third Reich paper, *Der Stümer*, by its continual fabricated stories of Jewish sexual crimes and ritual murders, constituted, William L. Shirer believes, one of the strongest encouragements for the behavior and ideology of the Nazis.

Pamela Hansford Johnson, in her book *On Iniquity: Some*

Personal Reflections Arising out of the Moors Murder Trial, makes a clear connection between pornography—which leads to sadism—and fascism. The moors murders were committed by a couple who collected sadistic pornography, glorified Hitler, and tortured and killed children.

Violent pornographic movies of the last few years have followed the tradition of using crude propaganda stereotypes. Prison camps are favorite locales—Cuban camps, Nazi camps, Japanese camps. But more and more, women are becoming the victims and the villains. Susan Brownmiller believes these movies are anti-women propaganda. She suggests that the civil libertarians consider how long they could worry about banning books and movies that featured, as entertainment, the lynching of blacks or the gassing of Jews. But the torture of women can somehow be described as funny.

Pornography, even without violence, dehumanizes, exploits, and ultimately numbs human responses. That I have not always believed that point was embarrassingly clear in the pages of the now-defunct *Viva* magazine where I appeared as a book reviewer. I had even, according to one editor, "given *Viva* credibility." That it had occurred to me that anyone who would read a book would probably not read *Viva* is about as bad an example of a failure of standards, both professional and moral, as I can think of. Vincent Canby's ability to declare *Ilsa* funny seems to me a petty lapse by comparison.

Pornography is not camp. It is not funny. It is not even boring, as so many fashionable people announce after a visit to the skin flicks. Vincent Canby and I and all the rest of the culture mongers have been deliberately confusing trendy with vile. We have been in effect encouraging that which is worst, not only in our society, but in human history.

VII.

It's Hard to Be a Feminist If You Are a Woman

I am often tired of being a feminist.

I'm not even sure I am a feminist.

Probably I am just tired. I'm tired of earning my own living, paying my own bills, raising my own child. I'm tired of the sound of my own voice crying out in the wilderness, raving on about equality and justice and a new social order. I wasn't raised to take care of myself. Self-sufficiency is exhausting. Autonomy is lonely.

It is so hard to be a feminist if you are a woman.

Every time I get another layer of my consciousness raised, I find another, stubborner, layer beneath. Never mind that I know self-sufficiency is the only answer, that I know none of us is going to be taken care of by anyone else. Never mind that I have, comparatively, nothing to complain about. Nevertheless, whenever I read *Vogue*, whenever someone I know buys a house at the seashore, whenever I can't pay my bills, whenever I am not taken seriously, then I want to marry a rich lawyer and work needlepoint pillows. Clunk.

I have been married. Twice. Marriage doesn't mean not hav-

ing to work. (Although it can mean not having to work as hard.)
And yet, contrary to all experience and observation, the myth lurks
just at the line of awareness, tantalizing and demoralizing, something that makes me go—Clunk.

No wonder we go Clunk. We thought that the pointing out of
absurdities and insecurities would result in improvement. That
women would begin to get equal pay. We thought that because the
majority of people agreed with the Supreme Court decision that
abortion is a matter of individual choice, women, including poor
women, would be able to get abortions.

Oh, well, I guess we were all a bit naive and trusting. I was
willing to skirmish, even to face a battle. But I wasn't really prepared for a siege. So I am sometimes so tired of being a feminist.

And I am so afraid that being tired means I am not a feminist
at all.

Clunk.

We have all felt that tangible sensation of the tumblers falling
into place in our heads, the Click! that signals a permanent recognition that the women's movement is . . . me. That *I* am one of
those people oppressed, embarrassed, enraged, inconvenienced,
and generally irritated by attitudes and patterns that the world
would be well rid of. It is the click of tiny doors opening in the
mind, and they never shut again—even though they may swing a
bit in the breeze.

Clicks are enraging and stimulating and tend to strengthen us
for the task of making straight the path of reform. The trouble is,
we tend to forget that the path is not very well marked. We've
been trying—for how long this time? Five or ten years?—to right
the wrongs of four thousand years. It seems to me we get unrea-
sonably dispirited and embarrassed by minor failures. Those are
the moments when we do not Click!—we Clunk. As in: "I have a
wonderful new doctor," says my friend. "Oh?" I say, "what's his
name?" "She is a woman," answers my friend. Clunk.

I went down to Washington to cover the women lobbying for
the Equal Rights Amendment. I walked all over Capitol Hill looking for funny political ladies in hats, and in the process I chanced

to remark to a colleague: "Gee, some of these women are amazingly well informed on the issues." There were, by the way, no hats. Clunk.

At lunch with some newswomen I found myself arguing that women's news should be covered only when it deserves coverage. I realized I was defining "deserves" as outstanding, remarkable, and astounding—instead of run-of-the-mill coverage such as labor or television people get. Clunk.

I try to remember it's better to be a lawyer than to marry one, but, alas, the truth is no lawyer wants to marry me. I once wrote that I confidently expected that someone would like me, even love me, as soon as I liked myself. Perhaps I haven't yet reached the necessary liking myself plateau, but all the men I meet retire from the field murmuring: "I can't handle it."

They can't handle it? How about me? I'm trying to get onto the path of equality and mutuality before the final resolution of such problems as he-has-an-expense-account-and-I-don't. So I insist on paying for my drinks, but I run out of money before the drinking is over. He buys the last round, which spoils the entire effect.

I turned on the television set to watch a soap opera. It crossed my mind that a man would watch an important program. I am assuming that what men watch, and read, and write, is nobler than what women watch. Baseball is not nobler. What if it were? So what? Clunk.

Last fall I worked in an out-of-town office for a few weeks. I loved going out to drink with the fellows after work. I never wondered why the women didn't come along. Should I feel guilty because I never noticed? Guiltier because I never noticed that they worked harder than the men, and then went home to run their households? Clunk? Yes, Clunk. On the other hand, the men asked me out for drinks and the women didn't. Perhaps the women should feel guilty. Maybe they didn't like me and should feel guilty about not liking another woman. Plainly, that is ridiculous. Lots of women are not likable. Especially those who are twenty years younger than I am and flirting with the man I am talking to at a party.

Clunk.

What if a woman is not only twenty years younger but has just sold the paperback rights to her first novel for $250,000? Is it a Clunk if I hate her?

I could sit right here and worry about competitiveness until next Christmas, but eventually, if the effort is to be at all useful, I will have to get out of my chair and apply what I think. Theory is not always the best goal. I recently spoke to a woman in Washington whom I admire very much. Her work in the field of family and child care has contributed an enormous amount toward finding answers to a crucial feminist question: "Who will take care of the children?" And yet she told me that she didn't consider herself part of the women's movement, that she didn't like to "join things." She was surprised when I told her she was a leader of the women's movement by virtue of her work, her attitudes, her influence.

The worst Clunk of all is to worry about clunks too much. Trying to be a perfect feminist, with daily examinations of conscience, is not really a big improvement on trying to be a perfect wife, mother, and lady. Backsliding is undesirable, but giving up because you can't meet the standards is much worse. It helps if you feel a deep impatience with the way the world is presently arranged and try to question any manifestations of the systems that oppress people. But as for standards . . . well, the guidelines are still flexible. Inflexible guidelines are probably antifeminist by definition.

I think narrow discussions of who is and who is not adopting the correct political stance are usually arrogant and excluding. No one is entrusted with the final truth about feminism—because feminism is about autonomy: finding out what we as individuals (not as sex roles) really want and can do. There is no oracle, no entrails to yield up their secrets. Dogma is too easy. It is also the death of imagination, and we have a very long span of history for which to imagine an alternative. The cure for clunks—from the minor slip into socialized instincts to the major political error—is imagination, intellectual curiosity, experimentation, the continuing attempts to define the personal so as to discover the universal.

It also helps to laugh. There is, after all, a certain inherent humor in being on the cutting edge of a social revolution. It is funny, actually, to be unsure of what you feel more offended by: the guests ignoring your opinions or not complimenting you on your soufflé.

Women have an apologizing problem.

We should learn to count to ten before taking the blame.

Yesterday, I staggered around the corner in a supermarket aisle and pushed my cart directly into another woman's foot. Before I could gasp, before I could spring forward with a crumpled Kleenex to staunch the wound, even before I could finish rolling the cart off her foot, she spoke.

"I'm sorry," she said.

"Why are you sorry?" I asked, as I patted her ankle with my Kleenex. She said: "I should have seen you coming. I shouldn't have been in the middle of the aisle. Oh, I'm terribly sorry. I usually carry a Band-Aid in my purse, but I didn't today." She limped off down the aisle, muttering, "I'm sorry."

She had utterly defeated me in the *mea culpa* competition, but still I ran after her, repeating: "I'm sorry." I bumped into six more women. All of them said, "I'm sorry."

I once saw my best friend apologize to a dining-room chair when she kicked it by mistake. When my dog trips me up in hallways, I become overly abject and I apologize to him. My sainted mother has not written me a letter in twenty years without apologizing for the weather, whatever it has been, wherever I have been. "I'm sorry it has been so cold (or hot) in New York," she writes, adding, "I'm still so sorry that it was too cold for you to swim while you were here" (or, too hot to do anything but swim). I have never heard a man make a personal apology for the weather.

Women seem to feel responsible for all environmental problems and for everything else that might affect the happiness, comfort, and well-being of our loved ones. We are sorry our husbands are tired, and we are sorry our children have too much homework. I think we mean to say we sympathize, but what we actually do is apologize, and that puts us in quite a different position.

Yesterday I apologized to a neighbor because the shoes she bought six months ago at a store I recommended are now falling apart. This evening I apologized because the movie I picked turned out to be not terrific. Tomorrow I know I will apologize if the baseball game on television is not exciting. The worst two weeks I can remember were the weeks we spent at a vacation spot I chose that my family wasn't especially crazy about. The fact that I liked it only made me feel worse.

We drown out compliments with covering apologies such as "this article won't be very good because I haven't felt well, I'm sorry." At work we cover ourselves in advance: "This report really isn't finished. . . . I'm sorry." Men know how to fake certainty. Women apologize, especially when we are certain we are right.

At home, in the area of "feminine" skills, we become positively rude in our effort to avoid praise. "What? You like the living room? It's not the right color yet; I'm sorry it isn't finished." "You like the dessert? Actually it is supposed to be fluffier; I'm sorry it isn't as good as it should be."

Any woman who would sincerely apologize to her guests in a restaurant because the waitress brought the coffee with the wrong course is a natural patsy. I am that woman (but I know I am not the only one). I also apologize for rings around the collars. It is only a slight shuffle and a tug on the forelock from that to worrying about being shrill over equal rights, to blaming ourselves for being raped.

Feeling guilty is the most debilitating form of the urge to apologize. A friend's teen-age son drove a car into a tree and was dreadfully hurt. As it happened, the accident was the result of his own carelessness; but his mother kept saying over and over, "Oh, I feel so guilty about it, I feel it was my fault, I feel so guilty." In fact, she had nothing to feel guilty about, but her son did; and he should have been allowed to learn from the results of his carelessness instead of being told that somehow, mysteriously, his all-powerful mother was guilty.

If we are going to speed up the tempo of the long march from the cave to human freedom, we are going to have to stop this idiotic apologizing for things we can't possibly control and for things we shouldn't be spending our time feeling responsible about. Taking the blame because the sun doesn't shine is a pointless waste of energy that could be better spent writing angry letters to Congress about pollution. A ring around any collar not our own should be considered the fault of the person who failed to wash his or her neck. Apologizing in advance for the dessert is manipulation, a technique that could be more usefully applied to improving your local school board.

Apologizing too much is probably part of women's fear of success. It reflects guilt, low self-esteem, a touch of misplaced arrogance. God is actually in charge of the weather; and, if we assume the task of apologizing for God, how will we ever be able to notice when we really are wrong, and should apologize?

Maybe we should try some Gestalt therapy and make a tangible object of whatever we feel most guilty about. The trouble is, most of us would then make a collage of dirty collars, children's report cards, manuscripts, burned dinners, etc., turn it into a household god, and apologize for not keeping it dusted.

Every time I hire someone else to help clean my house I have to go through a crisis of conscience. Is it ideologically incorrect, even if I pay a living wage? Would it be better if I hired a man, or would that still be class exploitation?

Anyway, a woman cleans for me. Or she did until last week. She started coming hours late and did not take kindly to advice. One day I pointed out the curls of dust under the sofa.

"I didn't put that dust there," she protested. "That dust was there when I came. I'm not responsible for that dust." It was an interesting point of view, but I found it incompatible with the job description and I fired her. She carried her protests to the apartment next door, where I heard her furiously denouncing me. "That Miss O'Reilly may be liberated," she said, "but she wants a slave."

There is nothing more infuriating than having one's preaching turned against one. I mean, it was all very well when we raised the consciousness of the nation's secretaries and they began to refuse to get coffee and buy anniversary presents for their employers. But it is quite another thing when they won't bring me coffee either.

For example. I have some dealings with an office in which everything of importance—messages, mail, location, scheduling—is handled by the receptionist. For twenty years one woman faithfully carried out those duties. They were dull, dreary, deadening duties but they were essential and she was paid to perform them. One year ago, sensing something missing in her life, the receptionist began going to a radical-feminist encounter group. There she learned that she was exploited.

She has now enlivened her life. Not by finding more entertaining and less exploitive employment, but by refusing to perform any of the chores for which she is paid. No coffee, no messages, no mail forwarded, and above all no going to look for people who are needed in an emergency. Most interesting of all, she has turned first on the other women. Naturally. She has no respect for women.

I was a secretary once myself. I was a terrible secretary. I sulked and scowled and—wrongly—considered myself too good for the task. But at least I had the decency to grovel when clients called. Now many secretaries seem to be in the interim phase. They growl, but don't grovel.

So far, I have only met one person who has the new balance just right. She seems to think we are all cooperating to get something done, instead of engaged in a class war. I wasn't cooperating. I was furious. I stomped and shouted and all the men in the office did a really nice imitation of cowering and placating and treating me like a star. But my friend the woman editor said, when I threatened to quit: "Why don't you just quit, then, and save us all a lot of inconvenience?"

So I settled right down and tried harder. She and I are almost certainly both victims of the system, but I will think about that tomorrow.

Sometimes I lose my grip on the point. The long-range goal is blurred by the constant necessities of hand to mouth. I'm scared and I'm tired. So I think about courage, and three friends of mine who have shown me what courage can do.

A. is a woman of about forty. When I met her ten years ago she was an excellent mother of four and wife of one. She still is. Ten years ago she had the best analytical and political mind I had ever encountered and she still does. But ten years ago, and even five years ago, she had become psychically paralyzed by the conflict between her instinctive desire to take charge and make things better and her society's firm instruction that that is better done by men. She wouldn't drive at night and didn't venture out much by day. A strong-willed dentist reduced her, and her teeth, to a shambles. She limited her wardrobe to a couple of pairs of painter's overalls, unsuitable even for a trip to the drugstore.

Last year she took over her town government, and conducted an investigation with total probity, skill, and equanimity in the face of bitter opposition. No one, except her mother, minded the painter's overalls.

B. is thirty-five. She had a real nervous breakdown, the kind during which custody of children is lost and pills are taken with no particular concern about effects. We watched her pick up the pieces of her life and assemble them. It was a little like watching a two-year-old with a Tinker Toy set turn into Frank Lloyd Wright. She decided that she wanted to write about money, and she learned how and she insisted on being allowed to do it. She also learned how to be happily married. I've never been so proud of anyone.

Except, perhaps, of C. At thirty-six she decided to be a doctor. It took three years of special courses before she was even allowed to apply to medical school, and when she did apply, they laughed. When she finally was accepted, the students laughed and spent their time talking about the money they were going to make while C. investigated preventive medicine programs.

In the course of medical school she married a man who was writing a book. They both survived this impossible professional conjunction, and succeeded. When I recently visited her, in a large city hospital where she is an intern, she had just performed a pleural tap. She had thirty patients. Her father wonders why she couldn't have chosen a more pleasant hospital, which gives you some idea of where she started.

I think about all the women I have met in the last ten years. I think of a woman who sued to be given a job working on a city subway construction project, and, after she got the job, the men workers first stole her tools and then broke her thumb—but she went on working. I think of the women I have interviewed who started shelters for battered wives and counseling centers and job-training programs so that other women could learn the courage to take control of their own lives.

I don't know where those women, and all the other women who have dared to question the system, got their bravery, what sustained and motivated them. I only know they help sustain me.

It is the fate of heroines to be laughed at. By questioning the established order, they automatically become figures of fun. History is on their side, but history's judgment is poor recompense for not being taken seriously. Consider Abigail Adams. She was never sent to school, because in her youth, she explained: "It was fashionable to ridicule female learning." She taught herself to read and write, and later, in her letters to her husband, John Adams, she recorded the long years in which she managed the family farm and finances, raised the children, and reported on political feeling among the people. In 1776 she advised her husband: "I desire you would remember the Ladies and be more generous and favorable to them than your ancestors. Do not put such unlimited power into the hands of Husbands. Remember all Men would be tyrants if they could. If particular care and attention is not paid to the Ladies, we are determined to foment a Rebelion [*sic*], and will not hold ourselves bound by any Laws in which we have no voice, or Representation."

To which her loving husband replied: "As to your extraordinary Code of Laws, I cannot but laugh." He further joked: "Depend on it. We know better than to repeal our Masculine systems."

The hymn of choice at state funerals is "Let Us Now Praise Famous Men." I look forward to the day when an amended version is necessary.

Only Martha Mitchell could have prompted someone to send to her funeral as a final tribute a motto made from flowers reading: "Martha Was Right." In death, as in life, she evoked the meretricious, the overdone, the heartfelt, the desperate gesture.

She was the Cassandra of our time. Someday an opera will be written about her. I can see Beverly Sills in the part, in Harlequin sunglasses, singing tragic arias on a darkened stage with a spotlight focused on the telephone in her hand. There could be magnificent confrontation scenes before a Fifth Avenue apartment house, with passersby and media hounds in the role of tragic chorus.

I am not kidding about the opera, or the tragedy. Classical tragedy is always a story of the results of the sin of overweening pride. Martha Mitchell, and the Nixon administration's pride, transformed into catharsis, into art, into Beverly Sills on the stage, would be a sign that we were beginning to get a grip on what happened to us during Watergate.

Martha's role should be considerably nobler than it in fact was. I would like to see her at least as grand as Aeschylus made Cassandra, who said as she went forth to her death:

"Behold Apollo stripping me himself of my prophetic raiment, regarding me.

"Clad in his robes, a public laughing stock.

"Of Friend and enemy, one who has endured.

"The names of witch, waif, beggar, castaway."

Cassandra was another woman used and callously discarded by men. Apollo made her a prophet. When she rejected him, he blighted the gift. She would see the future, but no one would ever believe her. So she moves through Greek myth, stumbling through Troy, crying out about blood and death and sorrow, and the people say, in effect, "Poor old Cassandra, there she goes again, loony as a hoot owl." Probably they thought she had been drinking.

Of course, Richard Nixon, who gave Martha Mitchell her voice, is a bit less appealing than Apollo. He had his own problems with pride and fate. But that is no excuse (pride and fate are never an excuse) for leading her to believe she was cute and important when she was encouraging the crucifixion of Senator William Fulbright and the tearing of limb from limb of war protestors and then having her put away as soon as she began to declare that Nixon and his cohorts were rotten from the bottom to the top.

Helen Thomas of United Press International, the person who was kindest on the other end of Martha's telephone, wrote in her obituary: "She knew she was loved and a symbol to many women." I hope she knew that she was loved, but I hope she never knew that she was a symbol of everything women fear the most, of the way we are supposed to behave in this country and how we are punished when we break the rules.

She obliged the mores of Pine Bluff, Arkansas, by growing up sugar and spice and everything nice. She obliged her man by goading his political opposition. Perhaps she even thought Nixon and Mitchell and the others took her opinions seriously. How dreadful, then, to discover that no one took her seriously, even when it became very serious.

Women are not often taken seriously, especially when they are crying treason. We start calm and reasonable. When nobody listens we simper and giggle, which is inappropriate when discussing the subversion of the Constitution. Or we get louder and more aggressive, which is put down as strident and masculine. Usually we try a combination of simpering and shouting, which is called being hysterical.

Martha Mitchell was called hysterical. It was said she was loosing her looks. She was menopausal. She was making her husband look bad. She had gone too far. She was responding emotionally. No doubt kinder friends worried that she was projecting neurosis, had no inside knowledge, and misunderstood the situation. Worst of all, worst to all of us, she made a spectacle of herself. She lost her husband, her child, and her money. That is how women are punished.

Most men, and unfortunately many women, cannot distinguish between a hysterical reaction and a legitimate concern if it comes from a woman. But at least Martha Mitchell never spoke of Watergate as "a growth experience," as the other Watergate wives did. She did not settle for vague, sulky disillusionment. She called sin and corruption just that.

And so, Martha was right.

Bella Abzug may be the first politician in history whose devotion to both principles and constituents could be dismissed because of unladylike behavior. She was considered by her colleagues, according to a *U.S. News & World Report* poll, to be one of the three most influential members of Congress. The Gallup poll discovered she was counted as one of the ten most influential leaders in the world. But in the drawing rooms where power gathers in New York City she was declared to be "abrasive." The wives of the powerful echoed "abrasive," and thus avoided seeming pushy themselves, which might have upset their velvet-lined apple carts.

Bella herself would never speak so scathingly of other women. She would smile her ravishing smile and say gently: "Well, you see, they are afraid. It is hard for them. But change is happening." She brought jobs and money to her city, worked tirelessly for civil rights, for peace, for women, and for those niceties of the political process which make government function for the people. She never gives up. I call her "brave."

My niece is fourteen, and she does not yet know that bravery is what she will need most if her life is to be what she expects. I asked her what she wants to be when she grows up.

"Well," she said, "I want the kind of job that is interesting but doesn't take very much time."

I am a responsible aunt, and so I pointed out that there are no such jobs. I also explained that a woman can expect to work at least twenty-five years of her life, and probably more. In other words, no young girl can afford to grow up expecting someone to take care of her and thinking of work as a secondary part of life.

But I had good news too. "My child, all this can be yours someday," I said, waving my arms to indicate the island of Manhattan and surrounding territories. "If you keep in mind that what you want is money and power."

She shrank away from me, horrified by my use of the forbidden words. Polite liberal circles do not now speak of money and power, as they once did not speak of sex and death, or religion and politics. But sooner or later (and fourteen is certainly not too soon) facts have to be faced. Women are never going to get anywhere in this country until we have an equal share of the power and money.

If she succeeds, think of the fun she and her friends will have. They will have money to give the Girls' Clubs of America, so the organization will no longer struggle along on a quarter of the donations the Boys' Clubs get.

How satisfying it will be to hold elective office, and to make sure that half the patronage jobs go to women. It might be nice if they do away with patronage jobs altogether, but no doubt they will continue to be aware of the political realities. Luckily, by then they will themselves be a political reality to be considered.

How pleasant it will be to sit on the boards of all the generals (Foods, Motors, Mills, Pentagon, etc.) and say without fear of contradiction: "I think we will just have day-care centers everywhere we have working mothers as employees." (Which, by then, will be everywhere.)

I was really telling my niece to try to make a difference, which is very old advice, but a new way of thinking about it for girls. Of course, she won't have much fun getting to that point. She will have to study finance, marketing, engineering, and math. Role models do not exactly abound for her. She will have to invent her own role model, become her own heroine. She will, in her turn, have to find the courage to file suits, speak up, endure.

For my niece then, I repeat the following record of courage.

Susan B. Anthony lived from 1820 to 1906. She spent fifty of her eighty-six years dedicated to winning women's rights. Her colleague, Carrie Chapman Catt, calculated that women's suffrage took:

52 years of campaigning

56 referenda to male voters

480 efforts to get state legislatures to submit suffrage amendments

227 campaigns to get state party conventions to include women's-suffrage planks

47 campaigns to get state constitutional conventions to write women's suffrage into state constitutions

30 campaigns to get presidential party conventions to adopt women's-suffrage planks into party platforms

19 successive campaigns with nineteen successive Congresses

Catt wrote, three years after the Nineteenth Amendment was ratified: "It is doubtful if any man . . . ever realized what the suffrage struggle came to mean to women . . . how much of time and patience, how much of work, energy, aspiration, how much faith, how much hope, how much despair went into it. It leaves its mark on one, such a struggle."

Susan B. Anthony's motto was "failure is impossible."

VIII.

Being Serious

I have been thinking that I would like to become a Star. As I understand it, being a Star means that the gossip columns would take note of where I was seen last night and with whom. I am, at present, usually seen at night in the park, with my dog, but I would be willing to change that. If I were seen at night in Studio 54 with Warren Beatty I am not sure I would really want everyone to know, but it might be worth it.

It might be worth it because, if what I have been led to believe about Stardom is correct, I would be making more money. Large sums of cash would arrive from all over, sent to me because I would be famous. I would like that because it would mean I could catch up on the orthodontist's bill.

Becoming a Star will not be easy. A woman of my age, with my opinions, who lacks tap-dancing skills, will not often be chosen as cheerleader for the Dallas Cowboys. Besides, I am not blond. However, I have an idea.

I will announce the death of the women's movement.

I will explain that the passage of the Equal Rights Amendment is in trouble because the women of the country don't want it, and because those few radical women who did want it were unable to demonstrate political skills.

I will point to women serving on boards of large corporations and ask why, if those women succeeded, all women can't succeed if they are willing to get out there and play by the rules.

Then I will wonder about a woman's right to choose to have an abortion, and I will devote a lot of space to thoughtful considerations of men's problems in a changing world. Finally, I will yearn for the old custom of men opening doors for women, and I will reveal my secret desire to be just a housewife and mother. I will admit, with a rather offhand charm, that the energy has gone out of the women's movement. And no one will suggest that I am really saying that the novelty has worn off, for me.

Instead, I will be invited to appear on talk shows, my opinion will be sought by people in need of a damaging quote, large literary advances will be offered for books that will be advertised as, "At last! The truth about the movement that failed." I will be cited for bravery, a willingness to speak up, and general courage because I will, in fact, have taken the point of view popular with the men who anoint Stars. I will be famous for my allotted fifteen minutes, which—as I figure it—will be enough to pay off the orthodontist.

The only trouble is, none of it will be true. The women's movement is not dead. Women in Iowa and Florida, Idaho and Vermont now sound like the wild-eyed radicals of ten years ago. They refuse to take their husband's names; they object to being included when the word *mankind* is used; they make their families share the housework.

All over the country, women are struggling for power in labor unions, beating on the doors of their state legislatures, explaining to school boards what a nonsexist curriculum would include. They are holding down "men's" jobs as construction workers and truck drivers, and demanding comparable pay for the equal work done in their "women's" jobs as clerical workers. They no longer retire in confusion when they are accused of meddling in foreign policy or told that the economy is not a women's issue. They know that "women's issues" are all issues. They have made the connection between the personal and the political.

All that energy is not just part of change, or directed toward change: it is the result of change. Every woman who is now determined to be taken seriously, to get equal pay, to pass the Equal Rights Amendment, to imagine an alternative to injustice, first had to decide that she was not the only person in the family who could do the housework. Before she could believe those things were worth fighting for, she had to change herself.

The horrible fact that women are further away from equal pay, and from the Equal Rights Amendment, than we were in 1972 does not mean the women's movement has failed. It probably means backlash—a mark of success. It certainly does not mean that women are going to change back. Not even to pay the orthodontist's bill.

———

A person who signs her letter "Proud in Chicago" writes to tell me: "America is already an immoral, socialistic state. The Equal Rights Amendment, if passed, would complete the job, and by the way they've already installed coed bathrooms in New York." She encloses several pamphlets that list the other things she fears would follow passage of the ERA. The tracts "Proud" relies upon for her world view predict that the ERA will bring the federal government into all aspects of our lives, transfer power away from the states, destroy the family, take housewives out of the home and jobs away from men, compel federal child care for all children, draft women, allow homosexual marriages, and cause chaos in the courts. Furthermore, housewives will lose their privileges, and the ERA—as a scheme for massive redistribution of the wealth—will destroy the free-enterprise system. *And* there will be coed toilets.

Frankly, I don't want to argue about any of this stuff. Especially about the toilet issue. I don't even want to argue about the Equal Rights Amendment. The whole subject exhausts me. The ERA was first introduced in Congress in 1923. In 1972 Congress, finally persuaded that equality might be a good idea, passed the ERA and sent it to the states for ratification. In 1978 the amendment was still three states short of the thirty-eight needed for ratification, and Congress, again responsive to the argument that equality for women is only fair, voted to extend the ratification period until June 30, 1982.

If the Equal Rights Amendment is ratified in 1982, the effort will have taken fifty-nine years. Fifty-nine years! It is incredible that it should still be necessary, that it may not pass even with the extension. Half the population—my half—is not included in the Constitution of the United States. When I think about what that means, that I am not considered equal under the laws of this democratic country, that I am a second-class citizen, I get so angry I get tired.

An ever-increasing majority of the population, according to a 1980 Louis Harris poll, is for passage of the Equal Rights Amendment. But the majority of the people I talk to seem to be either bored, or bewildered, or both, by the issue. My attempts to explain what the Equal Rights Amendment is, why it is needed, and why it has not yet been ratified seem to be a sure way to start the people at any gathering looking for their coats and heading for the exit. This flight from knowledge is a pity. An informed electorate is always reassuring, but more than that, the ERA drama is a great story, full of passion and prejudice, politics and greed, betrayal and revelation. There are not too many jokes, but if your sense of humor is rather bleak, à la Woody Allen, you will probably be able to laugh at this story.

The Equal Rights Amendment reads:

> **Section 1:** Equality of rights under the law shall not be denied or abridged by the United States or by any State on account of sex.
> **Section 2:** The Congress shall have the power to enforce, by appropriate legislation, the provisions of this article.
> **Section 3:** This amendment shall take effect two years after the date of ratification.

The majority report of the Senate Judiciary Committee, issued after the hearings that preceded congressional passage of the Equal Rights Amendment, declares the intent and purpose of the amendment, and forms what is called the "legislative history" upon which subsequent legislation and court decisions depend.

The report begins: "The basic principle on which the Amendment rests may be stated shortly: sex should not be a factor in determining the legal rights of men or of women. The Amendment thus recognizes the fundamental dignity and individuality of each human being. The Amendment will affect only governmental action: the private actions and the private relationships of men and women are unaffected."

On the need for the Equal Rights Amendment: "While there has been some progress toward the goal of equal rights and responsibilities for men and women in recent years, there is overwhelming evidence that persistent patterns of sex discrimination permeate our social, cultural and economic life. . . . [S]ome legislative progress has been made toward equal rights, but not enough to wipe out all discrimination against women in State and Federal law. . . . Title VII of the Civil Rights Act of 1964, [and] the Equal Pay Act . . . fail to reach discrimination in many areas, allow for substantial exemptions in some cases, and have often been implemented too slowly."

On the Supreme Court: "The Supreme Court has been slow to move too. . . . The Court has consistently refused to apply the Fourteenth Amendment to discrimination based on sex with the same vigor it applies the Amendment to distinctions based on race. . . .

"On the whole, sex discrimination is still much more the rule than the exception. Much of this discrimination is directly attributable to governmental action both in maintaining archaic discriminatory laws and in perpetuating discriminatory practices in employment, education and other areas. The social and economic cost to our society, as well as the individual psychological impact of sex discrimination, are immeasurable. That a majority of our population should be subjected to the indignities and limitations of second class citizenship is a fundamental affront to human liberty."

After an extensive review of sex discrimination in Criminal Liability, Civil Responsibility, Education, Business and Labor, the report concludes: "Finally we cannot overlook the immense symbolic importance of the Equal Rights Amendment. The women of our country must have tangible evidence of our commitment to guarantee equal treatment under law. An amendment to the Constitution has great moral and persuasive value. Every citizen recognizes the importance of a constitutional amendment, for the Constitution declares the most basic policies of our Nation as well as the supreme law of the land.

"The Committee concludes that because of the pervasive legal sex discrimination which now exists, and because of the inadequacy of legislative and judical remedies, there is a clear and undeniable need for the Equal Rights Amendment."

"Proud" still wants to argue about toilets.

Perhaps "Proud" has never been on an airplane or a train, where the toilet arrangements are usually resolved to the satisfaction of both sexes. At any rate, passage of the Equal Rights Amendment would in no way threaten a citizen's already existing constitutional right to privacy, which guarantees sexually separate bathroom and sleeping facilities in public institutions and prisons.

"Proud" is also concerned about the loss of housewive's privileges, which she believes now exist and would disappear with passage of the ERA. She has emphasized her concern by heavy underlining and marginal notations on a pamphlet from an anti-ERA group called League of Housewives. The pamphlet asserts it is . . . "the right of a woman to be a full-time wife and mother, and to have this right recognized by laws that obligate her husband to provide the primary financial support and a home for her and their children, both during their marriage and when she is a widow."

Isn't that sweet?

If "Proud" were to get a divorce in Georgia, she would no doubt be surprised to discover that the house occupied by the family is the property of the husband even if the wife has earned the money and made the payments, unless she has kept her money and property entirely separate from his. If "Proud" and her husband should jointly run a business in Maine, the profits would be the property of the husband alone. These laws, and many others like them, are remnants of nineteenth-century common law, which viewed the wife as the property of the husband. But there are no laws, archaic or otherwise, which compel a husband to support his wife (still less his widow). Support is a matter of custom, not law. In current practice, the most a wife in an ongoing marriage can hope for legally is support for basic necessities, and she would, in most states, find no one (except creditors) very interested in enforcing that right until after the marriage has broken up.

If the League of Housewives really cared about the rights of homemakers, they would support the ERA, which will give constitutional sanction to the principle that the homemaker's role in marriage has economic value that entitles her to full partnership under the law. The ERA will also, just for an example, ensure that families of women workers receive the same pension, Social Security, and compensation benefits as the families of men workers.

People who believe a woman has a right to a husband who must support her even after he dies are obviously not going to find the notion of equality easy to grasp. But if the Equal Rights Amendment is not ratified, those people will find that husbands continue to be a personal matter and that equal pay was a viable alternative they denied all women, including themselves.

By this point in the argument, "Proud" has long since departed for the more invigorating atmosphere of a Stop-ERA vigil. Members of the majority, if they are still awake, can occasionally be encouraged to murmur "But isn't it true that we don't really know what the ERA would do?"

I'm so glad they asked that question. Sixteen states, most of them since 1971, have enacted provisions in their own state constitutions which directly prohibit discrimination based on sex. In none of those states has the law been interpreted according to the dire warnings of the opposition. There have been no homosexual marriages, no overturning of rape laws, no chaos in the courts. There have been advances in the position of women, particularly homemakers. All of the states report that implementation of the law has been neither costly nor unwieldy. Furthermore, a majority of the states, whether or not they have passed state equal-rights provisions, have tried to identify sex-based laws in anticipation of passage of the federal Equal Rights Amendment. So gradual (too gradual) has been the change and so in keeping with the general change in the role of women, that I would bet that most of the people in those states could not tell me whether or not their laws had been amended to prohibit sexual discrimination.

Someone always obliges me at this point by wondering: "But if there has already been so much change, why do we still need a federal Equal Rights Amendment?"

Because the laws designed to make women equal apply only to some parts of our lives, and in some parts of the country, and are subject to the whims of legislators and the interpretation of the courts. Without a federal Equal Rights Amendment we have no universal legal definition of equality of the sexes.

The majority thinks, rather vaguely, that equal rights for women would be a good thing. They do not understand why the amendment has not passed. One reason is the fact that the majority is not evenly distributed across the United States. Most of the holdout states are either in the South, where opinion is almost evenly divided on the issue and fundamentalist conservative religious groups are leaders of the opposition, or the far western states of Nevada, Arizona, and Utah, where the ferociously anti–women's rights Mormon Church dominates the state legislatures.

Ignorance has also been a factor. Even as thirty state legislatures hastened to vote for ratification in the mid-1970s, only half of American women polled in 1975 were aware of the Equal Rights Amendment, and of that half, three-fourths admitted they did not know enough about it to have an informed opinion. By 1978 women had changed. Realizing that no one was going to graciously grant us equal rights unless we fought for them, women's groups organized and won an extension of the ratification period.

Women were blamed for not properly explaining the Equal Rights Amendment. I would instead blame the press, which did not explain the issue to women. If the past six presidents, both political parties, all major trade unions, all principal church groups, and the American Bar Association support passage of the Equal Rights Amendment, it would seem to be a matter worth taking seriously. But the newspapers and television, instead of checking facts and clarifying issues, chose to "balance" coverage by extensive reporting on the opposition. Only as more women began to be in a position to do the reporting (and to do the arguing in editorial offices which precedes reporting) did the distinction between the opposition's view of the Equal Rights Amendment and reality begin to creep into the nation's information pipelines. But by then the ERA had begun to be a dull story, an endless series of small paragraphs noting yet another defeat in another state.

Small paragraphs rarely tell the whole story. Take, for example, the year 1977. If nine men in three states had voted differently that year, the Equal Rights Amendment would have become part of the Constitution of the United States.

In both Florida and North Carolina the ERA lost by two votes. In Nevada, if five men had voted for instead of against, the ERA would have passed. Of eleven men in Nevada who had supported the ERA in 1975 and 1976 but voted against it in 1977, nine had campaigned on a pro-ERA position, and some had accepted money and help from pro-ERA groups. Several of the men explained afterward that they were still personally in favor of the ERA. Some said they would vote for it if they thought it would pass.

Nevadans who worked for passage of the ERA believed it failed because James I. Gibson did not want it to pass. Gibson was majority leader of the Nevada senate. He also served as a regional representative, one of the two most powerful posts in the state, of the Mormon Church, which has made opposition to the ERA a national crusade.

In North Carolina two of the four men who switched their votes at the last minute had been committed, in writing, to supporting the ERA. They cited constituent pressure for their change of mind, and, indeed, busloads of women arriving with their ministers to kneel and pray at the State House are seldom easy for a politician to ignore.

James McDuffie, from Charlotte, one of the men who reneged on his promise, lost the next year's primary to a candidate backed by a coalition of national pro-ERA groups. He was defeated by the same pro-ERA campaign tactics that successfully ousted James Thomson in Virginia, the man who had seen to it that the amendment never got out of committee for a vote by the legislature. Thomson was replaced as majority leader by A. L. Philpott who also—rather pettishly—saw to it that the ERA never passed out for a vote.

North Carolina is the home of Senator Jesse Helms and former Senator Sam Ervin, both fierce opponents of the Equal Rights Amendment. In the state legislature pro-ERA people identified Lieutenant Governor Jimmy Greene as the chief stumbling block. He apparently feared the wrath of the state's fundamentalist groups more than he believed passage of the ERA would enhance the state's rather tarnished "new South" image.

In Florida, after the ERA was defeated, State Senator Ralph Poston was reported to have denied that his vote switch was connected with his hurried exoneration two days before by the Rules Committee of an influence-peddling charge. Instead, Poston explained: "I have trouble with women getting married and not taking their husbands' names."

Alan Trask, another Florida state senator, explained his switch by pointing out—as a recently reborn Christian—that the Bible abhors homosexuality, and anyway, he said: "I want to see women on a pedestal."

ERA supporters in Florida said the defeat had a less poetic explanation. They said Dempsey Barron, the grand old man of the Florida state legislature, and Lew Brantley, senate president, wanted to prove their own power. Insofar as they considered women's rights at all, it was as good ol' boys: women are so wonderful, they should stay in their place.

Illinois was the first state to vote for the federal suffrage amendment and has had a state equal-rights provision in effect since 1971. Why hasn't the federal ERA passed? Partly because although the amendment has received a simple majority in both the senate and house, Illinois requires a three-fifths majority for passage of a federal constitutional amendment. And three-fifths of the members have not yet been persuaded to take the issue seriously, in the sense that fairness, justice, and equality might be considered serious. In 1977 Republican Governor Jim Thompson was under attack from the right wing and his party was fighting for control of the legislature. One day, reaching for all the help he could get, he endorsed two anti-ERA candidates, and then publicly signed a roster of ERA supporters. In 1978 the black caucus of the state legislature torpedoed a potentially successful vote because they were mad about an entirely irrelevant matter—something about the Speaker failing to consult them on the choice of assistant majority leader. Two days after that two Republican men changed their minds and refused to vote yes because they were "tired" of voting on the issue.

Well, that's politics. The Equal Rights Amendment may be a constitutional issue, but it is not important in the way that conservative state legislatures gauge importance. In the smoke-filled rooms the ERA is only part of the tradeable agenda: I'll vote against the ERA if you vote for my dam. Or, if you vote for the ERA, I'll make sure you never again get a committee assignment you want.

Women haven't got much to trade. When we boycott conventions in states that have not ratified the ERA, or when we throw a few rascals out of office, or when we win extension of the ratification period, they say we are being unfair. They say we are trying to change the rules.

Yes, indeed, we certainly are.

It is possible—thousands of years of history make the suggestion—that the reason the Equal Rights Amendment has not passed is because too many people, both men and women, still fear, and despise women. I try not to dwell on that possibility. It is an unmanageable thought. Better to consider the problem in terms of fear of change. We are, after all, talking about change on the grand scale of revising those thousands of years of history.

I think about three objections to the Equal Rights Amendment I heard recently, in my own living room.

"This equal-rights stuff has gone too far," said a middle-aged husband. "My best friend is being sued for sexual harassment."

"I'm afraid women are losing their femininity," offered his wife.

"I think women are already too equal; they have all the power anyway," added a jolly lawyer who once went to court to desegregate the public-school system in his city and now regrets his civil-rights efforts because "we didn't know what would happen."

What were they all really saying? The husband had discovered that the sexual code, as he understood it, had changed—the behavior he and his best friend learned is no longer acceptable. He does not want to give up the power of his old code. Most of all, he is bewildered by his wife's changes. She owns three businesses. Her worries about "femininity" and her doubts about equal rights were reassurances to her husband, a smoke screen she uses to deny the fact that he no longer has all the power. The lawyer is more complicated, but I think he meant that he now knows that opening up a system to people who have previously been excluded means that some of those people may, in some minimal way, get some power—and he doesn't yet feel he has enough. He is not satisfied as things are. Who knows what losses he might suffer if things change?

None of those people would object to equal rights for women—not in principle. The majority of Americans could not bring themselves to answer a pollster with "I do not believe women should be equal." But their support falls short of the kind of fervor that sends people out to march in the streets, and their lingering ambivalence is yet another reason why the Equal Rights Amendment has not passed.

Which brings me to the last reason: the opposition. The woman who signs herself "Proud in Chicago" is part of that opposition, one of the few Americans who are willing, even eager, to say that women should not be. equal. When "Proud" writes: "America is already an immoral, socialistic state," she means (and her pamphlets repeat) that her fundamentalist acceptance of the Bible is affronted by public toleration of homosexuality and abortion. She means that she believes a wasteful government, and labor, and the poor, have somehow conspired to give away to less moral Americans something she believes is hers. She means that she sees the women's movement as proof that this great nation has at last knuckled under to Godless Communism.

In other words "Proud" is part of America's right wing. She shares the Right's peculiar, romantic yearning for a mythic golden past when life was less complex, and the certitudes of "natural law" and an established order applied. Her version of that order involved several simplifying assumptions: all blacks could be considered lazy, all foreigners ignorant, all women could be expected to stay home and care for their children, democracy was the divinely inspired route to world peace, and the world was a place in which children could be brought up to expect certain things.

If blacks and women and world peace did not prosper under those assumptions, if children have always grown up to live in an unexpected world, if the family and free enterprise never, ever existed in the blissful state of untrammeled self-sufficiency evoked by the Right—none of these realities matter to "Proud." The myth of a lost utopia—where everyone knew their place and whistled as they worked—is more comforting to her than the excruciating responsibilities of the society we have begun to achieve—where the choices of personal freedom must, every fragile minute, be tolerated and reconciled into a public good.

The Right understood that the notion of extending personal freedom to women—half our society—is truly revolutionary. The Right took feminism seriously (as the tepid majority did not) and used those issues that are most obviously women's—the Equal Rights Amendment and abortion—to organize itself into the "new" Right. Feminism, if presented in a certain way, could arouse people's most basic fears: fear of change, of freedom, of "the Other," of disorder. In this task they were ably assisted by Phyllis Schlafly.

Mrs. Schlafly was a woman of the old Far Right. She had for many years enjoyed a certain limited success objecting to sex education in the schools, the SALT talks, fluoride in public drinking water, etc.—the old Right's standard issues—which she vigorously denounced in her own apocalyptic newsletter, the *Eagle Forum*. In the mid-'70s a new theme began to share the pages of the *Eagle Forum*. Readers were advised of the urgent need to save the family by stopping the Equal Rights Amendment. Mrs. Schlafly had found a mission worthy of her ambitions. She would save American women from themselves.

She became a Star. Her opinion was sought, to the point that feminists began describing her as the only fully formed product of the Fairness Doctrine. She was not taken any more seriously than were the feminists—it was years before the press would bother to check her facts or assertions—but she filled up a lot of space, confused the issues, and was a very useful rabble-rouser. Thousands of anxious women entered the political process, rushing to join Schlafly spin-offs such as the League of Housewives and Stop-ERA. This fresh infusion of foot soldiers willing to run bake sales, stuff envelopes, and fill out contribution cards must have been very satisfying to the men who are the generals of the old and new Right. But now, as those men make new plans and pin their hopes for balanced budgets, school prayers, military might, and an end to "giveaways" on Ronald Reagan, they do not mention including Mrs. Schlafly. I wonder what will happen when she realizes that she is a woman too, and has been running a great crusade against herself?

In November of 1977 twenty thousand women (and a handful of men and children) attended the National Women's Conference in Houston, Texas. Thousands were delegates elected at prior state conferences to represent all American women. The purpose of the national conference was, by congressional mandate, "to identify the barriers that prevent women from participating fully and equally in all aspects of national life, and develop recommendations for means by which such barriers can be removed."

The Right saw the conference as a tremendous opportunity to dramatize the idea that the women's movement is the opening rumble of the final crack of doom. Mrs. Schlafly was much in evidence. She appeared on "Meet the Press," where she told the nation that the death of the women's movement was at hand because people would be able to see for themselves that "those" women were in favor of killing babies, for letting homosexuals teach and adopt children, for federally mandated child care, for women being drafted. She remained quite undaunted when her copanelists, four leaders of national women's groups, set the record straight.

The women reporters in Houston were especially eager to talk to Mrs. Schlafly. We had heard so much about her. Five of us went over to her press headquarters for a semiprivate chat one evening. She was handsome, with turquoise eyelids, nervous hands, and a very straight back. I wanted to ask her where she bought her Ultrasuede clothes and if she slept in the nude. My colleagues warned me about being serious.

They asked her about the question of Social Security for housewives. She said: "I think that is putting a tremendous financial penalty on your right to have a wife in the house." Since none of us had a wife in the house, we felt that her answer did not cover the full range of possibilities. Nor did her next answer reflect our experience.

She insisted that the ERA would say: "Boys, supporting your wives isn't your responsibility anymore, and then they would no longer see it as their duty." Then she added: "Most wives spend all their husbands' money. He's lucky if he has anything left over when she gets through spending their money."

I thought that was barroom talk. My colleagues went on politely and conscientiously asking about her solutions to problems such as battered wives, inequalities in education, discrimination in the job market. The next day she remarked to other reporters: "It is just simply beyond me how giving a wife who's been beaten an R and R rest tour or vacation at the taxpayer's expense is going to solve our problem." To us, she simply repeated over and over: "The ERA won't solve that."

Solutions to problems are not Phyllis's strong point. We turned to her personal life. Her greatest satisfactions, she said, have come from getting married and having her six wonderful children, and from working her way through college. Growing up was hard. "My mother had to go to work to support her family. When she first went to work, she, like displaced homemakers, I suppose, got the best job she could find, which was standing on her feet all day selling in a department store at twelve dollars a week. In 1932." Her father, she said, "often couldn't find a job."

Phyllis worked in a munitions plant to put herself through college. She was graduated from Washington University in St. Louis, and got a master's degree from Radcliffe in 1945. Before that, we learned later, she attended Maryville, a Sacred Heart College, and was a high-school graduate of City House, another Convent of the Sacred Heart in St. Louis.

How the memories rushed back when I learned of Phyllis's old schools. I, too, attended a Convent of the Sacred Heart in St. Louis, a sister school. It was thirteen years later than Phyllis, but tradition held firm in those days. I remember well the long anxious hours spent praying for the defeat of Italian Communists, the watch kept by the television set in the library as Senator McCarthy held up his lists. I remember being taught the horrors of sexuality and the subtle nuances of class. But above all, I remember being taught that the only solution to being a woman was to have a husband.

That is apparently the lesson that stayed with Phyllis, even through Radcliffe (where I seem to have gone a different route). Underneath all the ambition and achievements, she must really believe it would be as ashes if there were no husband to validate her as a person. What a lucky thing then, that there is a Mr. Schlafly. He—unlike Phyllis's father, unlike the millions of men she would bully into supporting their wives by denying their wives independence—has never failed in his duty to support his wife.

No society has ever had sexual equality, and the Equal Rights Amendment, if it succeeds, will be for that reason a leap into the unknown. But it will not be an immediate, revolutionary leap beyond the restraints of law and social custom. The ERA would cause change, but it is also an attempt to deal with the changes that have already taken place. The opposition wishes to reverse those changes, and the booklets that "Proud" has sent me, like all the anti-ERA propaganda, are an extremely clever method of aggravating her fear of the unknown.

It is propaganda that mixes up the legally impossible (unsegregated public toilets), and the hitherto unquestioned (Congress has always had the right to draft women if needed, and has the power to write legislation to implement *all* constitutional amendments) with threats that what has already happened without the ERA (federal power, fragmented families, working wives) will happen because of the ERA.

"Proud" is afraid of change. She may truly believe, for example, that allowing a married woman to keep her own name is an innovation that strikes at the heart of her definition of social order—an order that depends on inequality. But the people who exploit her fears so effectively are interested in protecting the free-enterprise system as they enjoy it, based on an enormous unpaid or low-paid labor force. Ninety percent of the people in America earning over $25,000 a year are white males. And 80 percent of the people in America earning over $15,000 are white males. Ask yourself, if the ERA passes, what group imagines it will lose? Equal opportunity for equal pay for comparable work would be, in fact, a massive redistribution of the wealth. It would also fulfill the theoretical principles of democracy.

If the Equal Rights Amendment does not pass, we will have admitted that sex discrimination is ultimately more basic to our social and economic structure than is equality.

Another correspondent, a man from Washington, has written to inform me that I can't fool him. His message is short and without elaboration. He says he knows that I am, as he puts it, "one of those lesbians, a female homosexual." He signs himself, "sincerely yours."

As it happens, I am not a lesbian. But what if I were? What would it mean?

The man from Washington seems to believe that the meaning is self-evident. It is enough to say the word, to point a finger, and the person accused will wither away. If the person accused has caught his attention in the first place by writing about problems he would prefer not to think about, why simply say the magic word— "lesbian"—and the problems will go away too.

He seems to be saying that my attempts to discuss inequality, economic disparities, and screwed-up social policies don't count, because he knows I am a lesbian. Because he knows I am lesbian, there are no such problems. And if there are, it is my fault, because I am a lesbian.

I am not a lesbian, and the fact that I feel I should say it again makes me realize what it would be like if I were. I would be very nervous. It is one thing to be dismissed as a thinking person because of sexual preference (or sex, for that matter). It doesn't exactly brighten the day, but it is something women, lesbian or not, are used to experiencing. It is quite another thing to be blamed for a society's ills.

Most of my friends would urge that gay rights are a good thing. If pressed, they might admit that they wish gays were a little more discreet. Not, actually, so discreet as to stay in the closet, but, on the other hand, not so loud that the children might notice. It is a troubling issue, my friends murmur, but to do them credit, they would never even imagine denying people their civil rights because they are gay.

It is probably time for people who are concerned about civil rights to stop murmuring and start defending. Homosexuals are the new scapegoats, and too many other people have decided that the country must be purged of the menace.

I thought Anita Bryant was a very bad joke until I went to Houston and met the folks who had assembled to protest the National Women's Conference. They held signs reading "God and Me and Anita B.," and "Follow Jesus Christ, your pastor and your husband." They were very worried about change and they had decided how to stop it.

I talked to a young woman who had ridden all night from

Chattanooga in a bus chartered by her church. She had come, she explained, to let people know that the women's libbers want things that are not God's way. The Equal Rights Amendment, she believed, will encourage homosexuals and give them opportunities to take children in our schools and teach them things that are not "God's way."

An elected official from a small city in Michigan, a member of H.O.W. Inc. (Happiness of Womanhood), explained to me why our children cannot read. "I speak to a lot of college students," she said, "and I am a person who listens. They tell me over and over again that the reason they can't read is because their teacher was a homosexual or a lesbian."

Those women were part of a very large crowd of people expressing the greatest enthusiasm for their sort of explanation. There was much talk of the dread example of the last days of the Roman Empire and of the necessity for driving out godlessness. People who can blame poor reading scores on homosexuals are just a step away from blaming inflation, pollution, Communism, and the divorce rate on homosexuals. So persuaded, how long can they avoid connecting a cure with a witch-hunt?

It definitely is time to stop murmuring if we believe in human rights for everyone. So somebody thinks I am a lesbian. So what?

———

The first thing I saw when I arrived in Houston, in November of 1977, for the women's conference was a newspaper ad that showed a little girl holding a bunch of daisies. The caption read: "Mommy, when I grow up can I be a lesbian?" It might just as well have read, "Mommy, when I grow up can I be a doctor?" A doctor is a figure of authority. Women who assume authority are unnatural. Unnatural women are lesbians. Therefore all the leaders of the women's movement were presumed to be lesbians. Some of them were, and we owe to their clearer understanding of discrimination a great deal of the strength of the early movement. We all understood discrimination—double discrimination—better as we arrived in Houston to find that the city was prepared for a seige of thousands of "militant" lesbians (presumably dressed in horned helmets) who would make the streets unsafe for decent women and their children.

The first thing I heard in Houston was an airlines clerk expressing the prevailing view by telling a woman who had inquired about the arrival of a chartered plane full of delegates: "I hope it crashes."

Not, really, a very heartwarming welcome.

The next thing I saw was about five thousand women sitting on their suitcases in the lobby of the Hyatt Regency Hotel waiting to check in. They were my sisters: all sizes, colors, ages, and classes. Some of them were state senators, some were welfare mothers, some were lesbians, some were Ph.D.'s. A few may have been all of above. Whatever they were, each one nursed a hidden agenda, a determination to see to it that her issue would not be lost in a general rush for unanimity. Such experience as they had had in trying to express those issues had been mostly bad. They had been overruled, overpowered, outtalked, and ignored all their female lives.

I thought I knew all about the issues. Well, maybe I admitted to being a little shaky on the problems of women and credit. Of the twenty-six resolutions on the agenda, "Women and Credit" was the only one to pass unanimously, which goes to show that I was just beginning to learn what women really cared about.

The Houston conference was the national Click! of the women's movement, the articulation of years of change. I am going to talk about my own private Click! It is not a story which does me much credit, but perhaps the point is worth the embarrassment. The point is that before Houston I really did not know, despite everything I had written, if women could work together, if there were certain issues that transcended all barriers and united all women, if there was such a thing as a national women's movement. I mean, everybody talked about it, but nobody had ever seen it, had they?

And then, when I saw it, I didn't recognize it.

The night before the conference opened, I heard that the minority caucuses were meeting. "Oh, yes, I know all about minorities," I thought. "Jobs, education, affirmative action." And I went off in pursuit of the majority, looking for the political nitty-gritty.

The next day I heard that the minorities were hammering out a new resolution of their own, having rejected, as completely inadequate, the one on the agenda. I assumed the minority women were applying the lessons of sixties: demanding that the people be allowed to speak, questioning the qualifications of those who did speak, shouting about priorities, and quibbling about adjectives. In other words, taking themselves seriously. They were, in fact, applying all those lessons. But I was not. I thought I already knew what they wanted. I think I even assumed that I knew best what they should want. So I was across town, learning about "God's way."

I spent the next day rushing around the convention floor tracking down the right-to-life delegates' plans to try to defeat the abortion resolution. Suddenly there was a great uproar. I saw one of the right-wing, white, male Mississippi delegates reach across the other men and take a black woman's hand. People were weeping and hugging. The delegates began to sing "We Shall Overcome." I began to suspect I might have missed something.

The minority resolution had passed. I had missed the anticipation and was being engulfed in jubilation as everyone—even, finally, me—realized that we had seen the women's movement, and it worked.

What had begun as a generalized minority discontent had turned into a demonstration of a process—the process of transforming the personal into the political. They had arrived in Houston to find their issues scattered through all the resolutions on the agenda. It was good to be included, but they felt it would be more useful if their problems and possible solutions were specifically identified. They began by identifying themselves: black women, American Indian and Alaskan native women, Asian/Pacific American women. Puerto Rican, Mexican-American, and Cuban-American agreed, with unprecedented amicability, that they were all Hispanic women.

Then they all fought and argued, as I had imagined, over the issues I had assumed, but also over things I had never considered: bilingual education, sex and race bias in insurance, tribal rights, the problems of wives of U.S. servicemen. And then they did something never expected of women, and never achieved by minority men: they worked together to transcend their differences and produce a common resolution.

The powerless—minorities, women, the poor—usually defeat themselves by fighting over slivers of the same small piece of pie. This tendency is encouraged by the powerful, who own the entire pie. In Houston, the minority women had refused to be so distracted, and thus their sum became greater than their parts, and they became part of the whole. "Now I can go back to my ladies and tell them there are white women who are with us," said a black housing-project manager from North Carolina. They had done it for themselves, without waiting to be told how, or if they could. It was a lesson joyously welcomed by the rest of the conference.

The resolutions supporting the right to choose abortion and an end to discrimination against homosexuals passed without further ado. Women who had come to worry about rural transportation found that they were considering wages for housework. Women who had come to discuss the effects of American foreign aid on Third World women found themselves, quite logically, exchanging business cards with women who wished to see more women in elective and appointive office. A woman who had come to protest equality for women said to me: "I learned a minority can stand up and make a statement. I want more of a role in government for the women of our side." (Something of a contradiction, that, for an antifeminist, but self-determination must begin somewhere.) A white, middle-class housewife from Illinois said: "If we can just do what the minorities did, learn to speak up and learn to listen and find the things we can agree on . . . we'll win!"

We. Not they.

We may not win for another hundred years, but no one, after Houston, could ever again ask, "What do women want?" and no one who was at the Houston conference would ever again say, "I'm not a feminist, but. . . ." We had made the connection. The personal had become political.

"My wife is different," American husbands told me. "She's liberated but she is not interested in feminism." They were speaking to me, but I wonder if they were listening to their wives.

"Women in other countries are different," insisted the same men. "Their cultures are different; they have different expectations; they are not interested in feminism.

Those men were surprised and disconcerted to discover that feminism is not simply a personal domestic inconvenience, but a worldwide movement. I would date the moment of the revelation as March 1979, when Iranian women demonstrated against the growing signs that they were to be excluded from the new society for which they, as well as men, had fought and died. Their jobs, their legal protections, their right to choose whether or not to withdraw beneath the anonymity of the *chador*, were being, almost reflexively, attacked by the new religious regime. Spontaneously they assembled shouting, "In the dawn of freedom, there is no freedom." Their protests were an international Click!

Time magazine sent me to Tehran to see what was going on. At last, I was a foreign correspondent. I acquired the necessaries— a passport and trench coat—and set off. A foreign correspondent's job, as I understood it, is to explain. But before I could begin to discover what it was I must explain, I had to explain myself. The desk clerk at the Intercontinental Hotel demanded a large cash deposit because, he said, I had arrived with a suspiciously small amount of luggage. He was not fooled by the trench coat.

The next day I met a journalist, Farzaneh Nouri, a feminist of incandescent kindness and intelligence. She asked: "Why are you here *now*? For years women fought and were tortured and the Western press did not pay attention. Why do you care *now*?" How could I explain even to myself, much less to her, that to most of the

Western press a protest demonstration is a media event, and routine torture by a vicious American-backed regime is not?

I went to see a group of professional women. Before they would speak to me, they demanded to know what I meant when I said I was a feminist. I sensed that a simple "Well, you know, feminism is feminism" would not be sufficient. I drew a deep breath and explained: women should not be considered inferior beings, women and all other oppressed people can no longer tolerate being excluded from the processes that control our lives, feminism is an impulse for justice and equality—and so on.

They began to ask me sharp questions about my view of the family and of femininity. After I explained, I asked what it was they had expected me to say. It turned out they had expected to hear what had been described to them: a bra-burner, a screeching man-hater, a woman who had abandoned her family in search of something unimaginable called self-fulfillment. A privileged middle-class woman who understood no problems but her own. That, to them, was American feminism. It was exactly like explaining myself to a group of neighborhood women in Chicago, or to housewives in Ohio, or to the minority groups in Houston. And the result of the conversation was the same: a long and detailed exchange on the issues women face all over the world; inadequate education, low wages, lack of political power, legal inequality, denial of control over our own bodies.

One night I went to welcome members of the International Committee for Women's Rights, who had flown from Paris as a gesture of support for their Iranian sisters. They did not recognize me as a sister. None of the Europeans, except my clear-headed friend Claude from Paris, would speak to me because I was neither Marxist, socialist, or Trotskyite. I was an American imperialist pig. Europeans traditionally organize their politics around ideology, and if they can work out equality for women while they split hairs, I wish them well in the task. But the American tradition is to organize ourselves around feelings, and I was hurt.

An Egyptian feminist of international reputation heatedly defended her turf by warning me that I could never understand women in the Islamic world. She alone *knew* what Iranian women suffered. Nor was she interested in what Farzaneh had to say on the subject. Finally Farzaneh waved her arm, pointed at the entire group, and said: "We do not need you to tell us what we want."

She was right. The world's women already know what they want. There are no cultural differences that make acceptable children dying of starvation, that make tolerable an illusory status that depends on the generosity of men who view women as inferior, that lessen the despair of absolute powerlessness.

Women possess only 1 percent of the world's wealth. We have no "secret" power, either matriarchal or economic. In most countries of the world a woman has at least equal rights in principle, but only *until* she marries. Half the population of the world, of which half is female, is rural and lives on less than $200 a year. Wherever female literacy rates rise, infant mortality rates drop, yet 75 percent of the world's 800 million illiterates are women, and our number is increasing. Women and children are 75 percent of the world's malnourished. Thirty million children die of starvation a year. In the United States it is estimated that at-home labor makes up 40 percent of the real gross national product, but "women's work" remains the unacknowledged, uncalculated, invisible economic base of our society. In less developed countries womens' contribution is much greater.

I have been told several times—sometimes by men whose work is economic development—that those facts cannot be true. I did not make them up. They came from the United Nations Division for Social and Economic Information.

A long time ago my friend Jane Kramer told me something she learned when she lived in Morocco and wrote one of her extraordinary books: *Honor to the Bride*. She said: "I was told, before I went to Morocco, that those women were different. But I lived in a village where I was the first Western woman they had ever really spoken to. And as I got to know them, I asked them to tell me their dreams. And always their dreams were like ours: of consideration and conversation, of peace and dignity."

I know now that she is right. Women share a common dream. But what of it? If They are We, that fact solves no problems. Recognition is only a beginning. If American women need not tell other women what they want, neither can we tell them how to get it. To try is to become lost in theory and suspicion, to dissolve the limiting particulars of time and place and possibility in the warm, impractical haze of general good. We can serve as an example that change is possible, but finally they, and we, must win equality for themselves. All I would ask, at the moment, is that American women try to change the things about our own system which make the lives of other women worse. And to do that, we will have to fulfill our own part of the dream.

Men say that women are different, that we have no sense of the larger issues, no understanding of *realpolitik*. They are really talking about power, about the kind of "differences" that have justified consigning Jews and blacks, Armenians and Vietnamese, Catholics, Protestants, Hindus—anyone who was different—to poverty, enslavement, and death. But the oldest justification of all, the one invoked and enjoyed even by powerless men, is the "difference" between men and women.

Women say that women are different. We are talking about the fact that we believe we understand that the world is populated by human beings. If we are so different, let us prove it.

Let us take very seriously the implications of our economic system, which is now run by men who view the world as a Market to be protected by any means not necessarily short of nuclear war. Take, for example, the result of marketing infant formula in Third World countries.

It must have seemed like such a good idea, back in the early seventies. The birth rate was dropping in the United States and rising in the underdeveloped countries. Logical to expand the market for infant formula into those underdeveloped countries. Might even be beneficial. Nutritional. Healthy.

It turned out to be tragic. Ironic. A classical example of the process known variously as cultural imperialism, capitalism, sexism, and multinational corporatism. In the underdeveloped world the infant-mortality rate for bottle-fed babies is now double that of breast-fed infants. The babies have been dying more, malnutrition has increased, since the manufacturers of infant-formula products began implying to Third World mothers that the bottle is better than the breast.

In fact, the bottle is almost never as good as the breast. If need be, formula can be an adequate substitute for mother's milk, if it is prepared with sterile water in sterile bottles, according to complicated directions, which only the literate can read, and kept refrigerated. In most of the Third World, it is impossible to fulfill those conditions. The bottle and the formula become contaminated disease transmitters.

Powdered baby formula can cost as much as one-third to one-half of a Third World family's income. Parents try to stretch the powder by diluting it too much. A 1975 study of the problem sponsored by the nonprofit organization Consumer's Union of the U. S., Inc., reported, "When the tin of formula is used up, if the women have no money and their breast milk has dried up they give the babies something else—usually tea or chocolate drink made with water."

Baby formula was originally sold through saturation mass-market advertising, especially radio advertising. For example, in 1973, Carleton University economist Steven Langdon made a study of multinational corporations' marketing practices in Kenya. During his study period, Nestlé's Lactogen accounted for 11.26 percent of total Swahili radio advertising. Nestlé's, a Swiss food company, depended more on mass marketing than the principal American manufacturers and distributors of infant formula at the time. The American companies often tended to rely more heavily on selling the idea of baby formula to health personnel.

Naturally, those companies denied any connection between their aggressive marketing practices and infant malnutrition and death. They did not deny the effectiveness of their marketing (as opponents do not deny the high quality of the products being marketed), but they contend that they were (and are) selling only to those groups that could afford and understand the product. They further insist that they have responded to the World Health Organization's recommendations designed to stop saturation advertising.

The International Boycott Committee formed to resist mass marketing of formula argue that Nestlé's has simply begun pushing the company more than the product and joined the other manufacturers in using health-care-service personnel as a promotion platform instead of mass-media advertising.

Infant formula is made appealing by the imposition of Western, middle-class values on women already made vulnerable by drastic social change. They are migrating into cities, into the labor market, away from the security of tradition. They confront such ideas as material about "mother-craft training" which suggests that the appropriate setting for breast-feeding includes privacy. They receive formula samples in clinics, and see "mother-craft personnel" and "milk nurses" who are paid by the formula companies.

It seems to me that the purpose is to create customers, not by filling a need, but by creating a need by implying to mothers that their own milk (and, by extension, their own selves) is inadequate. American mothers who go home from the hospital with a new baby and a huge package of free samples, including formula, have been subjected to the same kind of indoctrination. It worked in this country, and it works abroad.

According to Alan Berg, in his book *The Nutrition Factor* published by the Brookings Institution, to feed formula to one-fifth of the children born in underdeveloped, urban areas would cost $365 million per year. In 1970 the 84 percent reduction of breast-feeding in Chile alone took up the milk of thirty-two thousand cows. The money and protein would more usefully go to the mothers themselves. (In some African hospitals, nurses wisely feed free formula samples to the mothers, thus benefiting the babies too.)

Some women worry that the outcry is all a plot to push women back into traditional roles. But why should nursing mothers be required to abandon a vital and natural function in order to be included in society, especially in the economic systems? It is the society that must accommodate itself. There must be crèches at work, and maternity leave, and reeducation about breast-feeding. Those are World Health Organization recommendations, and they apply to the United States just as much as to the Third World. Perhaps we can still benefit from our mistakes, instead of dooming the rest of the world to repeat them.

———

Let us take very seriously the results of our foreign policy, which is now decided by men who seem to view the world as four-year-old boys might view a game of marbles—snatch and grab. I don't mean that we must sit around and talk very seriously about the fact that women are invisible, both in the world and in the game plans of our foreign-policy Establishment. I mean that more of us have to become unavoidably visible: speaking six languages, flourishing degrees in international affairs, demanding accountability for our constituents, hitchhiking around the world finding out for ourselves.

Take, for example, a few things I found out in 1977, when I visited Mali and Senegal with a group of Americans sponsored by the Overseas Development Council and the Charles F. Kettering Foundation. In Mali, one of the poorest nations on earth, we met Mme. Safiatou Diarra, who was then the organizing force behind the National Union of Malian Women. Her long blue dress was painted all over with the symbol of International Women's Year. "People, development, equality, those are our goals," she said, pointing to the symbol, adding, "which are, after all, men's goals too."

The translator at our meeting was a man who mysteriously lost his powers when Mme. Diarra spoke in French of her hopes for Malian women. It did not matter: the American women understood from the heart. "We want to raise women's political consciousness," she said, "to permit them to take part in the life of the country, to struggle against the prejudices which exclude them and are a threat to the development of the country."

How odd it seemed to me, that day, to remember that I once worried that housework might seem too trivial an issue. Instead, it is always everywhere, the one that women speak of first. So, too, did Mme. Diarra. "Women here are overwhelmed by housework," she said. "Our women's cooperatives try to find a way to make their job less arduous, to buy small mills for grain and ox carts for carrying firewood." We all dutifully wrote down in our notebooks that women tend the fields, grind the meal, care for the children, gather firewood and water. It sounded as though there should be enough time for literacy classes and cooperative work to grow a cash crop.

But then we visited the villages. We learned that it takes two to three hours to pound millet to make a meal, every day. The nearest well may be miles away from the village, and all the forests have been cut for great distances around each center. Women must carry the water and the wood on their heads. The bundles of firewood were too heavy for the Americans to lift.

One day, in Senegal, we saw a small procession of women and girls. They were celebrating a clitoridectomy ceremony, the ritual removal or mutilation of the clitoris. The men in our group warned us not to ask questions, not to intrude on the cultural differences of another society. It is odd, the way differences are described as political when they apply to men, but as cultural when they apply to women. If the people of any culture ritually removed the sexual nerve endings of the men, would it be seen, tolerantly, as a cultural habit, or would it be recognized as a political act of oppression, a physical denial of the full human experience of a class designated inferior? (Is that instinct for oppression so different in the West, where Freud won a place in history with such opinions as "The elimination of clitoral sexuality is a necessary precondition for the development of femininity"?)

We asked questions anyway, and no one could give us any coherent explanation at all of why female genital mutilation seemed, to some African groups, to be a natural thing to do. The most chilling answer, from men, was: "It makes women better workers." During planting season in Mali women work fifteen

hours a day. All of this work—the carrying, pounding, and till-
ing—is done with babies tied to their backs. In many groups the
men have no responsibility to feed their wives and children.
Women must support themselves and their families, and achieve
any status and ease only when their sons marry and daughters-in-
law take over some of the burden.

In Africa women do 75 percent of the labor of producing, sup-
plying, and distributing the food. They perform all the most basic
functions, not only of the economy, but of the society. And yet in
Senegal the Minister of Development, when asked about women's
inclusion in development plans, said, "Women do not play a very
large role in the economy."

America has contributed a great deal to this dismissal of
women's work. We have exported our patriarchal, postindustrial
assumptions that only men need be trained to earn wages and learn
new skills. Our foreign-aid programs pay men to learn agricultural
skills, but women continue to do the work.

The effect is to make women more dependent because, for
example, only men know how to fix the tractor. As a country devel-
ops, women fall further and further behind. Most of the women
are not trained in new technologies, or educated for the new jobs.
They enter the labor force as the cheapest labor pool, and they
continue to perform all the household tasks. The power of the elite,
the educated and trained men, increases—and thus increases, and
sometimes their Swiss bank accounts also increase. Consciously or
unconsciously, Americans help to perpetuate injustice.

Actually, according to our stated public policies, we Americans had hoped it would work out differently. The Percy Amendment to the Foreign Assistance Act of 1973 says ". . . we are dealing
with a very serious issue, for improving the status of women is not
only a matter of social justice, it is also a significant means of
achieving economic and social development." The amendment
required that our AID programs pay attention to women. But until
very recently our own AID material on individual countries listed
only male occupations. Very recently a few women began to be
slightly visible inside the State Department. Before that nobody

remembered to include the realities of women's work and women's lives because nobody remembered that women exist.

The simple act of recognition, of remembering, will change the system. Think, for example, what might have happened if enough Americans had recognized, and taken seriously, the reports that the men of Afghanistan—whom our children were being asked to register for the draft to support—were fighting the Russians not because they hated and feared communism, but because they resented the fact that the Russians were beginning to educate Afghan women. We might have asked questions. We might have disagreed on the meaning of the larger issues. We might have doubted that discussions of the viability of chemical warfare and limited nuking could provide real solutions to the problems of Afghans, men or women. We might have added new dimension to the phrase "complexities of foreign policy." The establishment would be very irritated. Their power depends on over-simplification.

In the meantime the Establishment will continue to tell us— having seen no astonishing evidence to the contrary as yet—that we couldn't possibly be so naive as to really believe that women will make a difference.

Yes, we will. One women won't, but many women helping each other—feminists—will. If our half of the population of the world determines to take control of our own lives, it will eventually make a difference. The Establishment is not so naive as to believe it won't.

Our dream, our vision of our own dignity, is not new. It is the old, old dream of self-determination. But it is new for women to dream it for ourselves. I would not claim that women are more virtuous than men. I only know that we are presently demonstrating that human nature is not immutable, that change is possible. On such change depends the future, not just of women, but of the world.

IX.

The Girl
I Left Behind

Twenty-one years ago I was a bride. In another twenty-one years I will be sixty-five.

Which makes me forty-four. I like being forty-four. The actresses in television ads who play young housewives scrubbing their floors are younger than I am, and I don't care. Good luck, young housewives. There is a sweet pleasure all its own in being told, "Gee, you don't look forty-four," although, as Gloria Steinem says, this is the way forty-four looks. Gloria, being two years older, is my leader in inspirational aging.

I had always hoped to wither gracefully, like a prune, or like Georgia O'Keeffe. Alas, I appear to be settling, but until it turns into sagging, I am not going to worry. By the time I have jowls I intend to be wise, and I consider that a fair trade. For the moment, I will settle for the completely unexpected benefit of middle age: I know my own mind. I know who I am and what I can do. I know what I want to do and what I won't do. I will learn to tap dance, I will not learn to ski. I might still be angry, but I will not be depressed.

By the time I am sixty-five I won't be so sure of myself. Life, I have observed, has a way of undoing yesterday's certainties. I have an extremely good chance—if I last and the world lasts—of ending up my life alone and poor. That is the final destiny of more than half of American women over sixty-five today and I would like to change it—for them and for me.

216

Perhaps my son will help me out. Perhaps his future wife, a rich lawyer, will help him help me out. Maybe they will have a baby. I hope it's a girl. Or a boy. I guess I won't get to choose, and I certainly hope they don't. The prospect of a world filled with deliberately anointed first-born sons is more than I can contemplate. Maybe they will want to choose a girl, and be able to give her a nice start in life by having her grown in an artificial womb. In theory this technological advance would mean a great saving of physical stress for the rich lawyer, but in practice I am afraid that twenty-five years also will not be a long enough time for the idea of feminism to safeguard us against the possibilities of parthenogenesis. If men don't need us to have babies, there is always the chance that they will decide they don't need us at all. What will we do then? Wage the ultimate war between the sexes?

Well, as I was saying, if I last and the world lasts, maybe I will have a grandchild. I don't really feel it is important if my son and the grandchild's mother are married, but I hope they stay together. I would wish for them the kind of family that is a "still point of the turning world." They will promise each other love, courtesy, and equality. But, when the baby comes, it will all fall apart.

Until the first midnight nursing my grandchild's mother will have been unfailingly, prematurely certain. She will have been kind to the old dingbat (me) but she will have been secretly positive that the problems I worried about are, for her, solved. Maybe she will be right. Maybe she will live in a world of excellent day care, where maternity leave is paired with paternity leave and neither parent will lose seniority. Maybe her law firm will see her need to go home at three o'clock in the afternoon as a positive plus in her efforts to achieve partnership. But I doubt it.

I think she will be another in a long generation of sorrowful young women who think they have changed the system by becoming part of it, until they discover that caring for a baby is not considered part of the system. She will discover that mothers cannot, after all, have it all, *not even* if they change the system. Neither can fathers, if they want to raise their children too. I will be interested to see how the mother of my grandchild works it out. I will be absolutely fascinated to see how my son works it out. I'm sure he doesn't expect to have to take care of anyone, but I'm not absolutely certain he doesn't expect to be taken care of, either.

While they are working it out, I will get to see a lot of my granddaughter. Okay, I did care. I had a son. Now I want a girl. I know, I know, she's not mine. But, still, I plan to give her chicken soup and Junket with chocolate bits in the bottom and I will read her *Mary Poppins* on the couch under the window with the blooming narcissus. Just like my mother, and my grandmother, did for me.

I know, I know. My son and his family will actually be living in Alaska, and they will never remember to write. Just like me. But the only way I can imagine getting to sixty-five is to plan a perfect day twenty-one years from now, and the plan requires a granddaughter and narcissus.

A few more details: I will be living in Vermont in a house with a porch, fifteen bib-front aprons, and three rocking chairs. And a typewriter. The first peas will be ripe, and the pond almost warm enough for swimming. My granddaughter will have come to visit because she wanted to. She will be small and quick, with snapping black eyes and a ferocious curiosity. She will, as yet, suspect neither her possibilities nor her limitations. Obviously she takes after her mother's side of the family, although when she smiles there is a trace of her father, and when she scowls there is a trace of me. We will sit on the porch, shelling peas and rocking, and we will talk about history.

She will begin, as we all do, with the personal. "There is a boy I like," she will say, "but he doesn't like me. How can I make him like me?"

"Why should you make him like you?" I will answer. "You are a wonderful person. Wouldn't it be more sensible to like a boy who knows that?"

She will ignore me. "Why do I feel so funny when I am around him? I don't feel like myself. I feel . . . *little*."

I will put down the peas, and gaze across the meadow, and say: "I know. It is like a disease we pass on, from mother to daughter. It's called being a woman in a man's world."

She will be irritated (being, after all, only fifteen.) "What do you know about it?" she will demand. "Nobody loves you." And then she will add, with painful contrition, "Except me, of course. And your friends. And Daddy. And Mom."

After twenty-one years, this point will still pain me. "I tried," I will explain, more to myself then to her. "I tried very hard. But there was some fatal lack of coincidence between men and women of my generation. The men seemed to suffer some dreadful lack of imagination, a tragic failure of generosity. And meanwhile, the women learned things that could never be unlearned. We knew, when we lost our innocence, that we risked the loss of love. But our certainty that enlightenment is always worth the pain was cold comfort when we discovered, more often than not, that we could not apply what we had learned to our private lives without destroying love."

"But," I will then say briskly, "your generation will be different. It is possible, you will see, for love to be defined as an attachment between equals instead of as a power struggle."

Naturally, she will be more interested in the drama than in my unproven optimism. "But then what happened? Weren't you very sad? What did you *do?*"

"Oh, yes," I will remember, "many of us were very sad. And angry. And frightened. One part of our society seemed to be learning to get in touch with their feelings while the women had to learn to control ours. We had to practice self-confidence the way you practice French."

"What was the hardest thing?" she will ask.

"Not giving up," I will answer at once. "I was not especially brave myself. I could hide behind words. I did not have to stay with a mean husband or face every day an office or a factory where I was not wanted." She will nod at this, remembering her third-grade year, when she was very unpopular.

"For me, and most of my friends, the hardest thing was to keep going. When we were about your mother's age, in our forties, many of us had managed to change our lives. We had become people we never expected to be. Doctors, politicians, foreign correspondents. And then we found that we had become only ordinary extraordinary women. We were not so special after all, but only doing what men had done all along. We had changed ourselves, but we had not yet changed anything else, except perhaps the expectations of our children. And we no longer had the time to do the things we had done so well—to comfort and nurse and make Junket. It was awful. We felt like failures and we blamed ourselves and denied that our successes were worth having." I will hesitate here, remembering a summer when every woman I knew went limp, declared her job boring or insupportable, decided she did not *feel* like a doctor or a politician or whatever. That was the summer—one of many—when we no longer knew who we were.

"Then what?" my granddaughter will ask, her attention wandering.

I am not sure I will be able to answer: "We kept going, and we changed things. We learned how to combine the responsibilities of masculinity with the tenderness of femininity. We invented a new way to live, and we taught men."

She will jump up, scattering peas, and run down to the pond, saying: "Anyway, everything's solved now." But talking is not a solution. It isn't now, and it won't be in twenty-one years. Talking is only a start.

That night at dinner the girl I will leave behind me, the girl we have given a start, will look at me and say: "But, Granny, were you happy being a feminist?"

Of course I was happy being a feminist. After all, consider the alternatives.